Mike Wittmer wisely navigates through the rough waters of Christian extremism, showing that robust theological confession (belief) and Christlike practical compassion (behavior) are always meant to go hand in hand.

— Tullian Tchividjian
Pastor of New City Church, Coconut Creek, Florida,
and Author of *Do I Know God?*

On all sides Christians are being pressed to make false choices: doctrine or life, orthodoxy or orthopraxy, conviction or humility, faith or works. In *Don't Stop Believing,* Mike Wittmer challenges this type of thinking and injects a whole lot of sanity into contemporary church life and discipleship. No one who has adopted one side or other of these false choices will be happy with this book, and we will all be challenged, but nobody will be bored. It treats some of the most serious problems and wonderful opportunities in the church today with great wisdom, simplicity, and refreshing clarity.

— Dr. Michael Horton
J. Gresham Machen Professor of Systematic Theology
and Apologetics
Westminster Seminary California

As a raving fan of *living* like Jesus, I am delighted that Michael Wittmer has so effectively reminded us that you can run to Jesus but you can't hide from the important belief structure that undergirds the way Jesus lived. This is an important read for all of us — especially for those of us who want to impact our world with the power of Jesus' presence through us.

— Dr. Joseph M. Stowell
President, Cornerstone University

DON'T STOP BELIEVING

DON'T STOP BELIEVING

Why Living Like Jesus Is Not Enough

MICHAEL E. WITTMER

ZONDERVAN®

ZONDERVAN.com/
AUTHORTRACKER
follow your favorite authors

ZONDERVAN®

Don't Stop Believing
Copyright © 2008 by Michael E. Wittmer

Requests for information should be addressed to:
Zondervan, *Grand Rapids, Michigan 49530*

Library of Congress Cataloging-in-Publication Data

Wittmer, Michael Eugene.
    Don't stop believing : why living like Jesus is not enough / Michael E. Wittmer.
      p. cm.
    Includes bibliographical references and index.
    ISBN 978-0-310-28116-0 (softcover)
    1. Evangelicalism. 2. Theology, Doctrinal. 3. Postmodern theology. I. Title.
BR1640.W59 2008
230'.04624—dc22
                                        2008021321

Published in association with the literary agency of Credo Communications, LLC, Grand Rapids, MI 49525.

Interior design by Ben Fetterley

Printed in the United States of America

---

08 09 10 11 12 13 14 • 22 21 20 19 18 17 16 15 14 13 12 11 10 9 8 7 6 5 4 3

For Laverne and Mary Wittmer,
who love their children more than anyone could.
You gave us the discipline of hard work,
the delight of play, and the desire to follow Jesus.

CONTENTS

List of Illustrations   11

Acknowledgments   12

Introduction: A Friendly Warning   13

1. A New Kind of Christian   21
2. Must You Believe Something to Be Saved?   32
3. Do Right Beliefs Get in the Way of Good Works?   45
4. Are People Generally Good or Basically Bad?   59
5. Which Is Worse: Homosexuals or the Bigots Who Persecute Them?   73
6. Is the Cross Divine Child Abuse?   84
7. Can You Belong before You Believe?   98
8. Does the Kingdom of God Include Non-Christians?   109
9. Is Hell for Real and Forever?   122
10. Is It Possible to Know Anything?   134
11. Is the Bible God's True Word?   147
12. The Future Runs through the Past   161

Epilogue   178

Notes   180

Discussion Questions   222

Case Studies   226

LIST OF ILLUSTRATIONS

0.1	Contemporary Perspectives on Doctrine and Ethics	19
1.1	Challenges of Culture	30
2.1	The Pendulum of Belief and Ethics	37
2.2	Why We Must Believe Something to Be Saved	40
2.3	What Christians Believe	43
3.1	A Postmodern Objection to Doctrinal Statements	49
3.2	Right Belief Produces Right Practice	57
4.1	Are People Good or Bad?	64
4.2	Natural Goodness	65
4.3	Supernatural Goodness	67
5.1	Public and Private Morality	81
6.1	Who Is the Target of the Cross?	86
6.2	Two Paths to Two Destinies	91
6.3	Evangelical Perspectives on the Atonement	94
7.1	How Do People Join the Church?	100
7.2	Why Different People Do Church Differently	103
7.3	Combining Modern and Postmodern Views of Church	106
8.1	How and How Many Are Saved?	113
8.2	Where Is the Kingdom of God?	119
9.1	Which Life Matters?	123
10.1	The Modern Structure of Knowledge	137
10.2	How Do You Know?	140
10.3	The Christian Structure of Knowledge	145
11.1	The Battle for the Bible	158
12.1	How We Got Where We Are	167
12.2	A Third Way Forward	173

ACKNOWLEDGMENTS

Many friends diligently read and gave constructive feedback to significant portions of this book. I am indebted to the insights of Zach Bartels, Brian McLaughlin, Paul Engle, Ben Irwin, Jim Ruark, Jonathan Shelley, Sean Ryan, Kay Wood, Chris Brewer, John Duff, Gary Meadors, Dave Conrads, Tom Lowe, Byard Bennett, Matt Laidlaw, and Steve Dye. Thank you for sharpening my ideas and suggesting better ways to communicate them.

I am most thankful for my wife, who not only encouraged me throughout the writing process and read the entire manuscript, but continues to create a loving home in which following Jesus makes perfect sense to our three children. Thank you, Julie, for bringing so much joy to our journey.

A FRIENDLY WARNING

I am caught in the middle. On my right are some conservative Christians who demand lockstep allegiance to their narrow doctrinal statements. Even though I agree with many of their conclusions, they are not satisfied unless I hold all of their beliefs with tenacity and certainty. They interpret doubts, questions, or even appreciation for the other side as the first signs of a long slide toward liberalism.

On my left are some postmodern Christians who attempt to pry open the minds of conservatives by questioning many of their traditional assumptions. But the way they often go about it — offering new and unusual interpretations of key biblical texts, poking holes in conservative views while only vaguely hinting at their own positions, and brushing aside difficult questions as unworthy of their attention — discredits their arguments.

It's not surprising that dialogue between these two camps tends to drive them further apart. Each suspects that the other may not be sufficiently Christian: conservatives fear that postmoderns don't care enough about doctrine, and postmoderns think that conservatives don't care enough about people. Conservatives say that we must believe in Jesus, while postmoderns say it matters most that we live like him. This book attempts to bring both sides together, eliminating the extreme views of each party and uniting them around a biblical center.

Before I address the issues that divide us, some readers may want to know what I mean by "postmodern" and "conservative." For their benefit, here are the top ten signs that you might be either.

You Might Be a Conservative Christian If . . .

10. You have heard ten sermons on the text "Preach the Word" from men who didn't.

9. You cheer for the Cleveland Cavaliers because they are led by King James.
8. Your church supports more than two hundred missionaries at less than twenty-five dollars per month.
7. You have ever scheduled a business meeting after the evening service on Super Bowl Sunday.
6. You sweat when you preach.
5. Other people sweat when you preach.
4. You think that "Just as I Am" has twenty-seven verses.
3. Your Memorial Day patriotic service fell on Pentecost Sunday — and no one knew.
2. You have the plan of salvation on your answering machine.
1. You think Aunt Maude and Uncle Clem are unequally yoked because she's a Baptist and he's a Nazarene.

You Might Be a Postmodern Christian If . . .

10. You have never read Left Behind, never said the prayer of Jabez, and never led the Forty Days of Purpose.
9. You think you saw a megachurch on VH1's *I Love the 80's.*
8. You wouldn't be surprised to see Gandhi in heaven, but you would be floored to find Jerry Falwell.
7. In a debate with Jack Van Impe, you'd likely argue that the bear is America and the antichrist is Pat Robertson.
6. Your preacher just swore, and it seemed appropriate.
5. You honored your pastor with a box of fine cigars and beers on the house.
4. Your cool hair resembles a Midwestern version of Ryan Seacrest.
3. You use the word *groove* as a verb — and don't sound like a dork.
2. You purchase church supplies from the Buddhist Bookstore.
1. Your favorite Carson is Johnny.[1]

These lists may not have helped much, so to better explain where I am coming from and how I am using "postmodern" and "conservative," I will define two sets of key terms: *modernity* and *postmodernity* — which address variations in culture, and *liberalism* and *conservatism* — which speak to differences in theology. This discussion will be a bit technical. If it does not interest you, please skip ahead to chapter 1.

CULTURAL DIFFERENCE: MODERN AND POSTMODERN

Modernity, synonymous with the Enlightenment or the Age of Reason, began in the seventeenth century with Francis Bacon and René Descartes and climaxed in the eighteenth century with Isaac Newton and John Locke. It emphasized the ability of each individual to dispassionately study nature to discover objective, universal, and absolute truth. Freed from centuries of religious superstition and certain that the scientific method would unlock the secrets of the universe, modern society promised unending progress on all fronts, especially in technology and ethics. Humanity would build its own utopia, creating a little heaven on earth.[2]

Postmodernity arrived in the twentieth century with the thought of philosophers Michael Foucault, Jacques Derrida, and Richard Rorty and the tragedy of colonialism, two world wars, and the Holocaust.[3] Postmodernity retains modernity's emphasis on human reason, but it is much humbler about what our minds can discover. Postmoderns recognize that while modernity made great strides in technology — shuttling astronauts to outer space, deciphering our genetic code, and creating the iPod — it utterly failed in ethics. The same technology that improved our mastery over the world enabled us to master others — colonizing and sometimes killing those who were not up to our standards.

Postmoderns react by turning the modern paradigm on its head. Modernity wrongly believed that objective knowledge would produce right actions; postmoderns now think that good behavior requires that we admit our inability to access universal, absolute knowledge. They have learned from the horrors of the twentieth century that those who think they possess the unvarnished truth will likely use it to hurt others.

Their solution is to resist violence with compassion, which they demonstrate by humbly tolerating other points of view. Rather than shout down different perspectives, they embrace diversity and permit everyone to have their say. The good life does not demand that everyone agree, but only that they get along. Ethics, or living well, is now more important than epistemology, or knowing right.[4]

THEOLOGICAL DIFFERENCE: LIBERAL AND CONSERVATIVE

Liberal and *conservative* are loaded, elusive terms that are often used to describe our politics (Are you a Democrat or Republican?), morals (Is your motto "Try it you might like it" or "It's a rule for a reason"?) and religious views (Is your faith open to new interpretations, or do you embrace conformity to the past?). Here I am using these terms in a more limited way to explain how we understand and practice theology.

This distinction is important. Many theological conservatives, myself included, are frequently embarrassed by the Religious Right and do not think that God would necessarily vote Republican, demonize homosexuals, or try very hard to turn America into a "Christian" nation. We wish that God would stop talking to Pat Robertson and that Anne Coulter would just stop talking.

So I realize that the terms *liberal* and *conservative* come cluttered with much cultural baggage. Yet there are no better words to explain the theological battles of the last century or one's theological orientation today. For all our longing for some third way, everyone puts the world and the Word together either by leaning toward the side of reason (liberalism) or revelation (conservatism).[5]

Theological *liberalism* began in the nineteenth century with Friedrich Schleiermacher, who argued that religious beliefs are merely an expression of our "feeling of absolute dependence." He meant that our beliefs about God, rather than beginning with a transcendent revelation, are generated from below, arising from our own minds, cultural perspective, or religious experience.

This self-centered theological method led Schleiermacher and his successors to reinterpret many of the traditional beliefs of the Christian faith. Since modern culture could no longer believe in the supernatural, committed liberals denied the deity of Jesus, his virgin birth, numerous miracles, substitutionary death, bodily resurrection, and imminent return. Some even found it impossible to believe that God was a distinct being, separate from his creation.

Unable to reconcile traditional Christian beliefs with modern culture, liberals reduced the Christian faith to ethics. They did not believe that the Christian faith is literally true (e.g., Jesus' tomb is not empty), but that it still teaches us the best way to live. Jesus may not be the divine Son who bore our sins, but his death on the cross does teach us how to love others. If we follow his example and sacrificially serve others, then we too will be children of God, points of light in a dark world.[6]

Theological *conservatives* opposed this liberal reductionism and sought to reclaim the traditional beliefs of the church. Led by Princton theologians — Charles Hodge in the nineteenth century, B. B. Warfield at the turn of the century, and J. Gresham Machen in the 1920s — conservatives defended what they called "the fundamentals of the faith." They insisted that loving your neighbor was not enough, but that Christians must also believe in the truthfulness of Scripture, the virgin birth and deity of Christ, his substitutionary atonement, and his literal, physical resurrection and return. These "fundamentalists" would continue to believe "the old, old story" of the gospel, regardless of how untenable it seemed in a modern, naturalistic world. Unlike their liberal counterparts, they refused to accommodate the gospel to contemporary culture.[7]

MY FOCUS: POSTMODERN AND LIBERAL

Since modern/postmodern and liberal/conservative address different issues, it is possible to mix and match these categories (see fig. 0.1). A modern Christian may be either a theological liberal, such as Schleiermacher, or a conservative, such as Hodge and Warfield. Likewise, a postmodern Christian may be theologically conservative. I put myself in this category, for while I am conservative when it comes to traditional Christian beliefs, I am postmodern to the extent that I emphasize the importance of presuppositions (initial perspectives on the truth), the Bible as narrative, and the need for the church to be a missional community that humbly serves others with compassion.

So not all postmoderns are theological liberals. Not by a long shot. But there is something in postmodernity that tilts toward liberalism. Both postmodernity and liberalism tend to favor good behavior more than right belief — postmodernity because the modern quest for "right" belief led to violence and oppression, and liberalism because scientifically informed moderns could no longer believe what they read in Scripture. Postmoderns emphasize good behavior as an antidote to modern aggression; liberals emphasize good behavior because, after eliminating belief in the supernatural, it is all they have left.

This postmodern turn toward liberalism is penetrating the evangelical church. As I will explain in this book, an increasing number of postmodern Christians are practicing a liberal method: accommodating the gospel to contemporary culture and expressing greater concern for Christian ethics than its traditional doctrines.

These postmodern Christians call themselves "younger evangelicals," "postconservatives," and the "emerging church." I will avoid using these terms in this book, for these big tent names include more than the focused group I have in mind. For example, Kevin Vanhoozer describes himself as postconservative, and Dan Kimball, Mark Driscoll, and John Burke belong to the emerging church, yet to my knowledge none of these lean in a liberal direction.

I would prefer to avoid names altogether, for my goal is not to define a certain segment of Christianity but merely to examine the specific questions that many postmodern Christians are asking. I am interested in their concerns, not in how to label the people who raise them. Still, since it seems prudent to call this group something, I will distinguish them from other postmodern Christians with the neutral term *postmodern innovators*. This name seems appropriate, for they say that they want to create "a new kind of Christian" who will transcend traditional church and theological boundaries. In short, I am using *postmodern innovators* to represent what I perceive to be the left wing of the emerging, postconservative, or younger evangelical church.[8]

Despite the similarities between postmodern innovators and liberalism, there is also an important difference. As hinted above, the reason why these postmoderns value ethics more than doctrine differs significantly from classical liberalism. Postmodern innovators counter modernity's violence with compassionate inclusivism — and since nothing divides people quicker than disputes about doctrine, they desire to downplay the church's traditional beliefs in the name of Christian love.[9] This is a much better reason than that given by modern liberals, who, besides their agreement that "Doctrine divides; love unites," primarily discard conventional doctrines because they deny the supernatural.

Most important, although postmodern innovators are trending liberal, most have not yet reached liberalism's conclusions. They still believe in the Trinity, the deity of Christ, his resurrection and return, and many other Christian beliefs that liberals have historically denied.

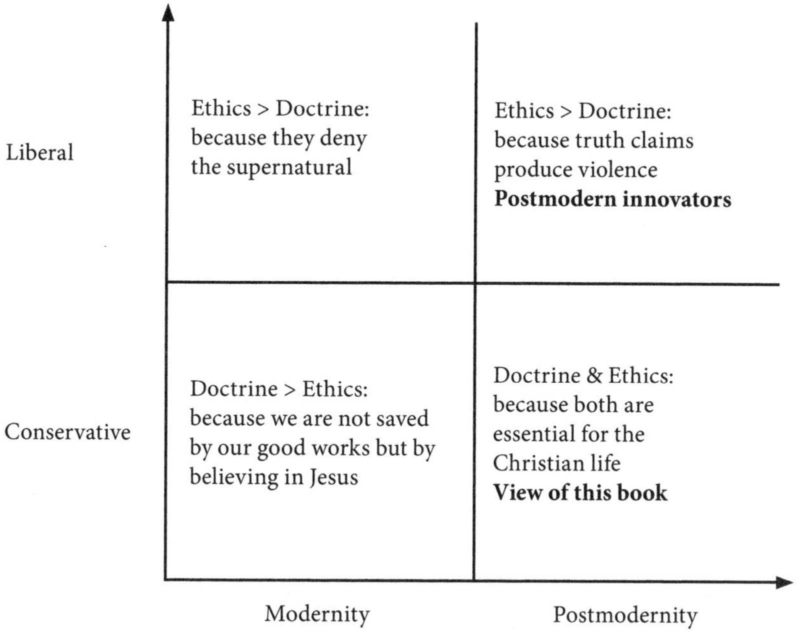

Liberal	Ethics > Doctrine: because they deny the supernatural	Ethics > Doctrine: because truth claims produce violence **Postmodern innovators**
Conservative	Doctrine > Ethics: because we are not saved by our good works but by believing in Jesus	Doctrine & Ethics: because both are essential for the Christian life **View of this book**
	Modernity	Postmodernity

Fig. 0.1. Contemporary Perspectives on Doctrine and Ethics

So I intend this book as a friendly warning. Many of the leaders whom I quote in this book are friends whom I love and respect. This is why I only cite by name what they have put in print, choosing to keep anonymous any controversial comments heard in less formal settings, such as lectures and sermons. I am thankful for their emphasis on authentic Christian living. Their vision for what the church can become is both exhilarating and challenging.

My only concern, and the point I will press in this book, is that their quest to correct the abuses of previous generations must not lead them to err on the opposite extreme. Perhaps our parents emphasized right belief more than good behavior, but that must not become an excuse to teach good behavior at the expense of right belief. If we continue down this road, it may not be long until our liberal method leads to liberal conclusions.

Authentic Christianity demands our head, heart, and hands. Our labor for Christ flows from our love for him, which can arise only when we know and think rightly about him. Genuine Christians never stop serving, because they never stop loving, and they never stop loving, because they never stop believing.

CHAPTER 1

A NEW KIND OF CHRISTIAN

It comes down to this: What kind of faith are we passing on to our children?" My friend was explaining why his family had left their conventional church to start a house church, and I completely understood. We had been raised in traditional families who attended church three times per week and believed that those who attended less were barely saved and those who did not come at all probably were going to hell.

But something has changed since we were children. Going to church is still important, but it no longer seems enough. We do not want our children to equate the Christian life with sitting through sermons. We want our families to practice our Christianity, to feed the poor, bring justice to the oppressed, and share our lives with a community of fellow travelers who embrace us just as we are. We value the Christian life as much as the Christian faith.

But not more than. The history of the church is a series of pendulum swings, and right now the momentum seems headed toward Christian practice and away from Christian belief. This book is an argument for both.[1]

A former teacher often reminded me that Christianity is a living faith, and all living things must grow. Like a child who reaches adolescence and then matures into an adult, so our understanding of God develops across time. As there is both continuity and change as a boy grows into a man, so our present proclamation of the gospel must be rooted in church tradition even as it surpasses what came before.

My teacher warned that if we stop growing — if we merely repeat what we have said in the past — then we will eventually lose the gospel. I did not understand what he meant, for I was young enough to have known only one kind of world. The faith that I had learned from my parents still seemed plenty relevant. Why must I change?

I must be getting older, for I am now experiencing the first widespread cultural change of my life. My students are asking new and interesting questions. Beliefs that used to be assumed are now open for discussion. Classroom conversations are passionate and important. Being a professor has never been more exciting.

But it is also a bit scary. While I enjoy our dialogues and admire my students' enthusiasm, I am concerned about where their quest might lead. They rightly reject the narrow fundamentalism of their parents' generation — in which beliefs about baptism, social drinking, and the premillennial, pretribulational return of Christ often seemed as important as the doctrines of the Trinity and the deity of Christ.

But sometimes their generous spirit seems to stretch too far. It is one thing to jettison a former generation's additions to the Christian tradition; it is quite another to question foundational elements of that tradition. We must do the former to own and embody the gospel for our day. We must avoid the latter, or we will lose the very gospel we are attempting to apply.

THE MORE THINGS CHANGE, THE MORE THEY STAY THE SAME

In my students' defense, most are merely applying my mentor's theological rule: to remain faithful to the gospel we must regularly update our understanding of it. We can't merely repeat the old, old story in the same old way. To say the same thing we have always said is not being faithful to the gospel; it is to fossilize it.[2]

One way we update our understanding of the gospel is to incorporate important insights from culture. The more we learn about God's world, the more accurately we can interpret God's Word. Consider how the following cultural developments have enhanced our perspective on the Christian faith.

Science. Copernicus's discovery that the earth revolves around the sun enables us to properly interpret Psalm 93:1: "The world is firmly established; it cannot be moved." In Copernicus's day, most Christians took this verse as proof that the earth is the stationary center of the universe. Even Martin Luther criticized Copernicus for allowing his newfangled view of the world to contradict Scripture.[3] While a few such dinosaurs still exist, most Christians today rightly read Psalm 93:1 not as a scientific description of the earth's immovability but as a poetic promise of God's provision for his creation (full disclosure: my seventh-grade science fair project argued for geocentricity on the basis of Scripture and a few allegations from the fundamentalist fringe of science — an embarrassing bunch of quackery that somehow received a red ribbon!).

Politics. Many nineteenth-century Americans used Paul's commands that slaves should obey their masters as biblical support for slavery.[4] But now, in part due to our country's emphasis on democracy and human rights, no one outside of an occasional white supremacist uses the Bible to condone slavery.

History. Until recently most theologians believed that God is impassible, meaning that he does not experience emotions (a sign of weakness for an omnipotent and extremely rational God). Typical is Anselm, who, in an eleventh-century prayer to God, wrote that we may "feel the effect of Your mercy, but You do not experience the feeling.... You do not experience any feeling of compassion for misery."[5] Try preaching that! In part because we have just passed through the bloodiest century in history — from the Holocaust to Hiroshima to *Hotel Rwanda* — Christians are rediscovering the first (because it was smallest) verse they ever memorized: "Jesus wept."[6] We have learned from painful experience that we not only need a God who is strong, but also a God who weeps and suffers with us.

Society. Not that long ago and still every now and again, various conservatives cite Genesis 1:28 in the King James Version to justify their right to "dominate" the rest of creation. Thankfully, society's increasing concern for the environment leads most Christians to interpret God's command to "have dominion" as his call to responsible stewardship rather than wasteful abuse of his world.[7]

COMMUNICATE WITHOUT COMPROMISE

So we must read Scripture in one hand with a newspaper, textbook, or telescope in the other. The more we learn about God's world, the better we can understand God's Word, and the more easily we can bring the two together. This is something we must do.

But it is a dangerous job. Every culture is fallen, and every aspect of our world is flawed (including our interpretation of Scripture). The same culture that delivers fresh insights into the gospel may also blind us to key aspects of it. The very attempt to communicate the gospel to our culture may lead to compromise. It has always been this way.

1. Early Church

The early church benefited from its integration with Greek culture. The first Christians not only wrote their New Testament in Greek, but also they used Greek terms such as *logos*, *ousia*, and *hypostasis* to better understand the nature of Jesus and the Trinity. Since these helpful words made it into our ecumenical creeds, they remain an essential part of orthodoxy today.[8] The early church also relied heavily on Greek philosophy — especially versions of Plato — to lead many Greeks to Christ (Jesus is the fulfillment of your Platonic thought), read difficult passages of Scripture (allegorize the hard parts), and write powerful prose ("you have made us for yourself, and our heart is restless until it rests in you").[9]

But this immersion in Greek thought came at a steep price — sometimes the early church sounded more Platonic than Christian. They often misconstrued God as a merely transcendent being — an immutable, impassible force who is unable to enjoy genuine relationships with his creatures.[10] They misunderstood what it means to be human, often implying that we are essentially souls trapped inside bodies until death liberates us from this decaying world and our spirits fly to our true home beyond the sky.

This low view of the physical world cheapened creation and shortchanged salvation from God's cosmic redemption to the evacuation of righteous souls from planet Earth — in the end producing an anemic, truncated gospel that still afflicts the church.[11] It also supplied a rationale for persecuting heretics, for killing the body to save the soul was actually doing them a favor.[12] And don't get me started on the early church's allegorical interpretation of Scripture, by which any passage of Scripture could be contorted to mean just about anything, so long as it seemed orthodox.

2. Medieval Church

The church's promising and perilous dance with culture continued in the Middle Ages. The first half of this period is often called the Dark Ages, for between AD 500 and 1000, most Europeans were serfs simply struggling to stay alive. In the latter half, when most basic necessities were met and these Christians turned their attention to developing culture, they soon realized that they were outclassed by the advanced Muslim societies in Spain and North Africa, who had developed their culture on the wisdom of Aristotle. By the middle of the thirteenth century, Europe's greatest theologians realized that they would need to master Aristotle if they wished to remain relevant.[13]

They were led by Thomas Aquinas, whose *Summa Contra Gentiles* and *Summa Theologica* not only restored Christianity to intellectual respectability, but in the process used Aristotelian categories to enlarge our understanding of the existence and attributes of God. To this day every informed discussion of God's nature runs through Thomas (tipping the scales at nearly three hundred pounds, few discussions have the energy to go around him). Theologians may disagree with some of his conclusions, but Aquinas remains too important to ignore.

Yet the saying that "he who marries the present culture becomes a widow in the next" was never truer than in the case of Thomas Aquinas. His reliance on Aristotle, an immense strength when Aristotle was the rage, became an insurmountable weakness when the modern world moved beyond this philosophy. Copernicus's discovery that the sun is the stationary center of the universe and Kepler's insight that heavenly bodies move elliptically and change speeds challenged Aristotle's view that the earth is the focal point, surrounded by a series of concentric, perfectly circular spheres controlled by a hypothetical Unmoved Mover (Aristotle's term for God). Aristotle was finished off by William of Ockham, who asserted that Aristotle's cherished forms did not exist; Descartes, who said that there are no individuals to actualize these forms; and Galileo, who argued that inertia rather than things seeking to embody their forms better explains the cause of motion. Thus, the brilliant work of Thomas Aquinas, so essential to the church's survival in his day, had become largely irrelevant by the next.[14]

3. Modern Church

The trend of benefiting from and getting burned by culture continued into the modern world. The sixteenth century witnessed the rise of the individual. Politically, German princes challenged the authority of the foreign Roman Church; theologically, individual

Christians followed their lead and began to question some of the church's beliefs. The printing press dispersed their ideas throughout Europe, infusing more individuals with the courage to stand up for themselves.

This new attitude empowered a trembling monk to announce before the emperor, "My conscience is captive to the Word of God. Thus I cannot and will not recant, for going against my conscience is neither safe nor salutary. I can do no other, here I stand, God help me. Amen."[15] Martin Luther's bold stand launched the Reformation, a long overdue movement that preserved the integrity of the gospel from its medieval abuses.

Still, Luther's principle of individual soul liberty is often carried far beyond what he intended. Evangelical Christians tend to turn Luther's cherished *sola scriptura* (Scripture alone) into *nuda scriptura* (naked Scripture), so that Scripture becomes our *only* rather than *final* authority.[16] Rather than read Scripture through the lens of church tradition, we throw out tradition and claim that we learn all of our doctrine from Scripture alone. "My faith has found a resting place," we sing, "not in device nor creed." (Why not change this great hymn to "My faith has found a resting place, it's in the Apostle's Creed"?)

Discarding our tradition is the quickest way to heresy.[17] Have you ever sat in a Bible study where eight people offered ten different interpretations of a passage, and no one could say which were right and which were wrong? We all read Scripture through some lens. Better to interpret it through the best of our heritage than by ourselves. As a wise professor once taught me, "Little ships should stay close to shore."[18]

Another, more sinister form of modern individualism surfaced in philosophy. Led by Descartes, modern thinkers attempted to throw off centuries of superstition by choosing to hold only those beliefs that they could indubitably prove. They would discard any belief that they could possibly doubt. This method may lead them to believe less, but what they did believe they would know for sure.

The big word for this new approach to knowledge is *autonomy*, a Greek term that comes from *nomos*, which means law, and *auto*, which means car. Actually, *auto* means self, but that is where the term for car comes from, for an *automobile* is a car that you drive by yourself (whoever came up with this name probably was not married).

So autonomy means "self-law." Autonomous philosophers used their own minds to determine what is true and false rather than take another's word for it — especially if that other was the church or Scripture. This need to prove everything helped produce the scientific method, which, though enormously beneficial to our world, was lethal when turned on the Christian faith.

Autonomous readers of Scripture scoffed at its supernatural parts. It was easier to believe that Jesus was simply a good man whose followers beatified him after his death than to think he was actually God who walked on water, fed thousands from a boy's lunch, and rose from the dead. The result was liberal Christianity, a neutered faith that followed Scripture's moral lessons even as it dismissed its miracle stories.

Conservatives smelled heresy and insisted on the complete truthfulness of Scripture, but often in a way that also capitulated to the modern mind. We treated God as if he were an object of science, reducing him to a set of facts, our worship services to an information dump where we learn these facts, and the gospel to four spiritual laws (meant to correspond to the natural laws of science). We had the answers and weren't much interested in wrestling with the questions. If modern science could be certain of its facts, then we must also be sure of what we believed. Many of us grew up in churches where "beyond the shadow of a doubt" was spoken as one word, as in "I know I'm saved, beyond-the-shadow-of-a-doubt!"

Not only were we sure of what we believed, but also we thought we could prove the faith to others. We had arguments — evidence that demands a verdict — that easily established the existence of God, that Jesus was his Son, and that the Bible was his revelation. Give us a few minutes, and we could prove to anyone that Jesus rose from the grave. Segue to the four spiritual laws, and our overmatched friend would soon recite the sinner's prayer to invite Jesus into her heart, another convert to our modern form of Christianity. But like Aquinas with Aristotle, just when we got really good at our modern faith, the world changed.

4. Postmodern Church

We are now entering a new age, an age so young that we don't even know yet what to call it, so we just say it is postmodern — the age that comes after and is somewhat critical of the modern period.

We now realize that the modern attempt to dispassionately discover objective facts that everyone would accept was a bit naive. Every search for knowledge is colored by the perspective of the person making the inquiry. Is acupuncture good medicine? Should Iran have nuclear weapons? How should I lower my cholesterol? While most of us may quickly and easily answer each question (No, No way! and Lipitor), we are also aware that others, say Chinese immigrants living in Iran, may answer differently (Yes, Yes, and red yeast rice). Our take on the truth is influenced by, among other things, our personality, where and how we were raised, and to which community we belong.

But the modern world was not only naive; it was also naughty. Many modern people believed that they had found the truth and that they could demonstrate it to others. Those who refused to be educated and see things the right way had to be punished. After all, you can't allow a few foot-dragging dimwits to hold everyone else back, can you? So white people used their supposed superiority to oppress blacks, men dominated women, and the wealthy Western world colonized and plundered the resources from the (perceived to be) uncultured natives of the developing world.

Embarrassed by this history of abuse, postmodern youth strive to embrace everyone, especially those who are different or disenfranchised. If their parents' claim to knowledge gave them power to hurt others, then the surest way to stop the abuse is to question anyone's access to objective, universal facts. Rather than claim an inside track on right and wrong, truth and falsehood, we should accept and even celebrate our differences. Let a thousand flowers bloom! Every voice must have its say, the more diverse the better, for as we listen to various perspectives, we will appreciate where they are coming from and learn not to criticize. The one Bible verse that everyone today seems to quote (and misquote) is Matthew 7:1 — "Do not judge, or you too will be judged."

As with previous eras, so our postmodern age presents great opportunity and grave peril for the church (see fig. 1.1). On the plus side, we agree with our culture that personal perspectives largely determine how we interpret reality. This is why we need the Holy Spirit, for only he can transform our biases until they conform to God's Word and so properly interpret God's world. Until others receive this work of God, we cannot expect them to see things entirely our way.

And who can argue with the postmodern critique that those "in the know" have often used their position to oppress the weak? Christians should be leading the charge against this abuse of power, for we claim to follow a Savior who humbly befriended those on the outside looking in, whether women, lepers, or tax collectors. The Trinity itself supplies the model for inclusive love — three persons who sacrifice their own desires so the others might flourish (see chap. 3).[19] And it's hard to read much of the writing of the Old Testament prophets without hearing God's repeated warning to watch out for those who can't watch out for themselves. So far so good.

But our culture's priority on tolerance can go too far. If we are going to love and embrace people who are different, so the thinking goes, then we should also learn to tolerate their beliefs. How can I say I accept you if I reject those things, such as religion, that lie at the core of who you are? Who am I to say that you must believe what I believe to be accepted by God?

And why must we think that beliefs matter that much anyway? Postmoderns argue that if the modern world (and 9/11) taught us anything, it's that those who claim to know the truth are typically a threat to others. Better to focus on how we live rather than what we believe. After all, it's not as if on judgment day God is going to open our brains to check whether we can verbalize the right facts about him.[20] But he will judge us according to our actions — did we love our neighbor as ourselves? As long as we are doing that, does it really matter how we got there — whether by following Jesus, Mohammed, or the Dalai Lama?

HOW MUCH TOLERANCE?

Not that I am against tolerance. It is a necessary virtue found in every facet of life. For instance, the wheels on a car have a grease tolerance. When mechanics tighten the nut on a wheel bearing, they back off the nut a quarter turn to allow grease to lubricate the bearing.[21] The mechanic who forgets to back off the nut and allow for a grease tolerance is like some conservative Christians. They insist that every belief is important and do not give others room to breathe, to differ even on minor issues. Lacking sufficient grace to lubricate their lives, metal grinds on metal until their wheels over-heat and eventually seize up, crippling their faith.

	Early Church	Medieval Church	Modern Church	Postmodern Church
Communication	Used Greek language and philosophy for New Testament, Trinity, and evangelism	Used Aristotelian philosophy to compete with Islam	Used rising individualism to challenge authority and ignite the Reformation	Humbly admit our dependence on the Holy Spirit to know truth and love those who are different and disenfranchised
Compromise	Produced a Platonic view of the Bible, God, humanity, the world, and salvation	Discredited when Aristotle's worldview was disproved by Copernicus, Kepler, William of Ockham, Descartes, and Galileo	Led liberals to deny the super-natural and conservatives to ignore tradition and reduce the gospel to a set of facts	Too much of the wrong kind of tolerance elimi-nates all claims to truth

Fig. 1.1. Challenges of Culture

Recently I exited an interstate behind a Buick that sported a bumper sticker with a cross and the words "Truth, not tolerance." As we turned onto the East Beltline, we passed a young man dressed in Goth attire with spiked hair, kneeling on the sidewalk to light his cigarette against the wind. I watched as the plump driver looked in her rearview mirror and made what appeared to be a sarcastic comment to her fellow passengers, who turned and laughed at the poor "degenerate" outside. In that moment I caught a glimpse of the ugly underbelly of conservative Christianity, the air of intolerant superiority that makes me wonder if Jesus feels closer to the fellow outside than to his supposed followers inside the car.

If conservative Christians sometimes lack enough tolerance, some postmodern Christians seem like the mechanic who backs off the wheel nut too far. These postmodern innovators seem so tolerant that what they are driving no longer resembles historic Christianity. They permit so much play that their wheels wobble from the beginning and, when they hit a pothole, may quickly fall off and disable their faith.

This book seeks to avoid the most extreme forms of both conservative and postmodern Christianity and hit the sweet spot of appropriate tolerance. Against some conservatives, not every belief is equally essential, and just because someone disagrees with you does not mean that he or she has stopped believing the Bible. Remember, many of our younger evangelicals are reacting against you. They have been raised in your churches, and they are not impressed with the experience. You have oversold some of your beliefs, and you can learn from their perspective.

Against some postmodern innovators, being a child of God involves more than merely being a good person. You rightly note that loving actions are essential, but what about the specific, historic doctrines of the Christian faith? Don't you also have to believe something to enter the kingdom of God?

This book examines the disputed issues between conservative Christians and postmodern innovators: What does it mean to be a Christian, and how do you become one? What are we able to know? In what sense is the Bible true? Are people good or bad? What are the chief sins of our day? How does the atonement work? Can people belong to the church before they believe? Do other religions participate in the kingdom of God? and What should we think about hell?

Each chapter presents a common conservative extreme and a postmodern overcorrection, then closes with what I believe is the correct, biblical view. I will find common ground whenever possible, for often what we agree on is more important than what we do not. If my perspective could fit on a bumper sticker (not a good omen for anyone's view), it would not read, "Truth, *not* tolerance," but "Truth *and* tolerance." Or, as the classic Christian motto puts it: "In essentials, unity; in nonessentials, liberty; in all things, charity."

CHAPTER 2

MUST YOU BELIEVE SOMETHING TO BE SAVED?

Last week my sons, Avery and Landon, prayed to repent of their sins and receive the gift of Christ. This momentous occasion came on the heels of vacation Bible school, a weeklong warning about sin, the coming judgment, and their need for Jesus to save them. Landon seemed a bit less concerned, for, after watching his older brother bow in prayer, he said that he wanted to do the same — as soon as he finished with his Legos.

I am a bit ambivalent about my sons' prayer. I am pleased, because their act represents another step along the path of belief. Already they have sat for Bible stories, recited Bible verses, prayed before bed, and shared toys. The fact that they asked God to forgive their sins through the work of Christ means that they are continuing to receive rather than reject God's grace. What more could a parent want?

Nevertheless, I do not want to make too much of it. I prayed to receive Christ hundreds of times during my childhood, especially whenever Jack Van Impe and his prophecies of impending doom came to town. I remember walking home from school in the second grade, clutching invitations to a Van Impe crusade, and panicking when I didn't immediately find my mother. I frantically ran to our Christian neighbors, not for protection, but for assurance that if they were still here, then I hadn't missed the rapture. Likewise, if my sons are half as neurotic as me, they will repent of their sins and receive the gift of Christ many more times before they escape childhood.

I have also seen the sinner's prayer abused. Some conservative churches treat the prayer like a magical incantation that guarantees an individual's salvation. I was told by pulpit-pounding preachers to write the date of my conversion in the flyleaf of my Bible (which one — the first time I prayed or the forty-second time I nearly missed the rapture?) so that should I ever wonder whether I was saved, all I had to do was open my Bible, read the date, and know beyond-a-shadow-of-a-doubt that I was going to heaven.

This possession of certainty often produced carnality. It didn't take long to figure out that if saying the prayer saves us no matter what we do, then it doesn't ultimately matter what we do. We accepted Jesus as Savior by saying the prayer; whether we then followed him as Lord was up to us. Even the easily doable act of baptism was reduced to an optional "step of obedience," something we should consider but not vital to our salvation (would any of our Christian ancestors know what to make of our unbaptized believers?).

Preachers responded to the mess they had made by delivering long diatribes against carnal Christians — which to my young mind sounded deliciously close to "caramel" and only made me fidgety and unable to concentrate on the sermon. Carnal Christians had said the prayer, and that was pretty much it. Their nonchalant Christianity raised questions about their spiritual health. Were they merely backsliding, or were they imposters bound for hell? One mother spoke for many when she asked, "My oldest son isn't living for the Lord, but he did pray to receive Christ as a child. Do you think he is a Christian?"

Postmodern innovators are properly appalled by this blind reliance on the sinner's prayer. They complain that modern conservative churches often imply that coming to Christ is merely a matter of believing the right things. Get your facts straight, know what you would say when God asks why he should "let you into heaven," and accept God's forgiveness for what you have or haven't done. But what if this focus on *believing* the right things obscures our need to also *do* the right things?

Postmodern innovators also charge that the sinner's prayer method contributes to a fair amount of condescension. Those who have said the prayer often feel smugly superior to the "heathens," "pagans," or "worldly unbelievers" who have not. Again, they have a point. It is strange to think that the everlasting difference between me and the fellow in the next cubicle is a twenty-second prayer that I said and he did not. Is becoming a Christian merely a matter of reciting the right words, and is evangelism simply an attempt to put these words into other people's heads? Shouldn't how we live count as much or more than what we believe? Is it plausible to assume that the ax murderer who gave his heart to Christ goes to heaven while his non-Christian victim does not?

The prayer method often values knowing the right *facts* more than doing the right *acts*. Conservative Christians may not concede this (who knowingly champions bad behavior?), but their bottom line — believe in Jesus and everything is forgiven — often communicates as much. Some postmodern innovators have overreacted to this imbalance by embracing the opposite extreme, implying that the Christian life is all about *doing* and not much, if at all, about *believing* the specific, historic doctrines of the Christian faith.

THE CURE CAN BE WORSE THAN THE DISEASE

Brian McLaren is a leading postmodern innovator.[1] He tells of his encounter with Sam, a Jewish neighbor who had offered to water some young trees at Brian's church. When Brian walked over to thank him, Sam volunteered that he wasn't interested in Christianity because he had heard a television preacher say that God would have forgiven Hitler and taken him straight to heaven if only he had asked Jesus into his heart. Sam then told Brian about his son, an Israeli soldier who had been arrested for bravely preventing other soldiers from humiliating a Palestinian at a border checkpoint. Sam wanted to know, "Would your God send my boy to hell because he never said, 'Jesus save me,' but he'd let Hitler go to heaven for saying the magic words? Is that what you believe, like that TV preacher?"

Brian — one of the kindest persons you'll ever meet — said that he did not answer Sam's question because he "didn't know how." He merely assured Sam that his son "acted a lot like Jesus would have acted," that he could "see why you're so proud of him," and that "God must be proud of your son too. Anyway, thanks so much for watering our trees."[2]

While Brian's sensitivity is commendable, why didn't he know how to answer Sam? "Saying the magic words" does not save, but isn't it necessary to believe something? In *The Last Word and the Word after That*, McLaren has his fictional pastor Dan summarize Jesus' take on the gospel: "It wasn't 'hold the right beliefs,' 'affirm the right doctrines,' or anything like that. Instead, Jesus was clearly interested in action, in what we do, in how we treat others especially, and in whether we trust him enough to follow his teaching even if it means difficulty and persecution."[3] Markus, the wisest character in the book, states that some conservatives wrongly believe that "on judgment day, all God will care about is opening up our skulls and checking our brains ... to see if we had the right notion of salvation by grace through faith in there somewhere."[4]

McLaren counters this extreme view by claiming that God judges people on the quality of their works rather than on what they believe.[5] So pastor Dan exclaims: "How am I supposed to believe that after all Shirley's father suffered (during the Holocaust), he's going to burn in hell forever, eternally tortured, because he didn't believe in Jesus? What kind of God would add his own eternal torture to the obscenity of human torture her father suffered? ... If people's lives end in eternal torture, if every good thing they ever did is swept away into insignificance because they weren't one of the chosen or they weren't lucky enough to believe the right things, how can I be calm?"[6]

These ideas are more explicitly spelled out in Spencer Burke's *A Heretic's Guide to Eternity.*[7] Burke confidently declares that right beliefs are unnecessary for salvation: "For most of my Christian life, I have heard people say that it is not enough to do good works or care for the world. There has to be faith in Jesus — which usually means assent to a set of propositions. But actually, the apostle Paul said it is good works without love — not good works without a belief system — that are empty and worthless."[8]

Burke says that we do not need to believe in Jesus, because everyone begins life accepted by God, and we stay in his grace unless we opt out.

> Religion declares that we are separated from God, that we are "outsiders." Grace tells us the opposite; we are already in unless we want to be out. This is the real scandal of Jesus. His message eradicated the need for religion. It may come as a surprise, but Jesus has never been in the religion business. He's in the business of grace, and grace tells us there is nothing we need to do to find relationship with the divine. The relationship is already there; we only need to nurture it.[9]

Burke believes that we start out with God because we are actually a part of God. He professes to be a panentheist (everything is in

God), which "is like saying God is the ocean and we are the fish in it."[10] Since we are already in God, we do not need "to convert to any particular religion to find God. As I see it, God finds us, and it has nothing to do with subscribing to any particular religious view."[11]

But what about Jesus' statement that "I am the way and the truth and the life. No one comes to the Father except through me"?[12] McLaren warns that we must not read this statement in an exclusive way. Jesus did not mean that "'I am in the way of people seeking truth and life. I won't let anyone get to God unless he comes through me.' The name of Jesus, whose life and message resonated with acceptance, welcome, and inclusion, has too often become a symbol of elitism, exclusion, and aggression."[13] McLaren fears that "for some people, it seems that Jesus is not the way to God, but rather he is *in* the way to God, as if he is saying, 'No you don't! You can't come to God unless you get by me first!'"[14]

Burke adds that rather than command people to believe in him, Jesus simply meant that others should follow his way. They should live like him, striving to be spiritual rather than conform to any religion or belief system. Burke writes: "When Jesus described himself as 'the way,' he seemed to be telling his followers that violence or conformity to other systems and structures is not the way to God. Instead, the way is found in the path he laid out." This path "is not about competing with other faith traditions. It's about living out a way of grace, love, forgiveness, and peace."[15]

These writers are influential leaders, and their view is shared by many in the evangelical church. I heard one prominent pastor tell a national conference that we must update our theology to remain relevant to our culture, which he said meant that we must be willing to reconsider and potentially relinquish every Christian belief. When asked if that included such staples as the Creator-creature distinction and the deity of Christ, he replied that, yes, everything is up for review. Another popular pastor agreed: "Our faith is in God, not what we say about God. I have heard people say that the absolutes aren't up for discussion. But the only real absolute is God, and everything is up for discussion, isn't it?"

Two pastor friends of mine wondered aloud whether God would accept the faith of Mormons and Jehovah's Witnesses. While these groups deny that Jesus is fully God and fully human, they still follow Jesus in their own way, and that has to count for something, right? Concerned about this doctrinal slide, on separate occasions I asked a parachurch leader and a dean of the faculty at an evangelical seminary whether people had to believe anything to be saved. Both replied that they did not know. While I appreciate their candor, their answer reveals how unimportant beliefs have become in certain segments of postmodern Christianity.[16]

BE A BELIEVER OF THE WORD AND NOT A DOER ONLY

So conservatives sometimes give the impression that only beliefs matter, and some postmodern innovators overreact and claim that it does not matter what you believe as long as you are living well (see fig. 2.1). But why must we choose? Doesn't God demand both right beliefs and right actions? The apostle John writes that God commands us both "to *believe* in the name of his Son, Jesus Christ, and to *love* one another as he commands us."[17] The next chapter will examine how sound doctrine and good behavior combine for a flourishing Christian life. For now I want to explore why John says that it is not enough to love others, but it is also necessary to believe.

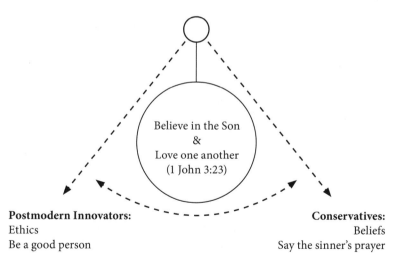

Fig. 2.1. The Pendulum of Belief and Ethics

John's gospel describes Jesus' encounter with Nicodemus, an extremely religious, just, and powerful man who used his influence for good. John says that Nicodemus later used his seat on the Jewish ruling council to defend Jesus and, after the crucifixion, helped bury his body.[18] Nicodemus was the prototype of the good Jewish man, the man who, like Shirley's Jewish father in McLaren's story, should not "burn in hell forever, eternally tortured, because he didn't believe in Jesus."

And yet, contrary to the expectations of many postmodern innovators, Jesus told Nicodemus that his good life was not good enough. Nicodemus was a sinner like everyone else, and so, like everyone else, he must receive the gift of regeneration. "I tell you the truth," Jesus said, "no one can see the kingdom of God unless he is born again."[19]

Startled, Nicodemus asked how a new birth is even possible. Jesus replied that the spiritual regeneration he was talking about occurs only through the cleansing grace of the Holy Spirit: "I tell you the truth, no one can enter the kingdom of God unless he is born of water and the Spirit."[20]

" 'How can this be?' Nicodemus asked."[21] How does the Holy Spirit wash away our sin and regenerate us?

Jesus answered with the most famous verse of Scripture (you have seen its reference — John 3:16 — enthusiastically raised behind the goal post during televised field goal attempts): "For God so loved the world that he gave his one and only Son, that whoever *believes in him* shall not perish but have eternal life." Jesus added that belief in Christ is the sole difference between those who live forever and those who are condemned to destruction: "Whoever *believes in him* is not condemned, but whoever *does not believe* stands condemned already because he *has not believed* in the name of God's one and only Son." Again, "Whoever *believes in the Son* has eternal life, but whoever *rejects the Son* will not see life, for God's wrath remains on him."[22]

Do not miss Jesus' point: we cannot enter the kingdom of God unless we are born again, and we are born again only by a supernatural work of the Holy Spirit, a work that is accomplished through believing in the truth about Jesus. Paul concurs: we are "saved through the sanctifying *work of the Spirit* and through *belief in the truth*."[23] We must believe in truth to be saved, for it is truth that the Spirit uses to regenerate and bring us into the kingdom of God.

This is why, immediately after announcing that "everyone who calls on the name of the Lord will be saved," Paul emphasizes the need for people to know something about this Lord in order to call on him. He writes: "How, then, can they call on the one they have not believed in? And how can they believe in the one of whom they have not heard? And how can they hear without someone preaching to them? And how can they preach unless they are sent? As it is written, 'How beautiful are the feet of those who bring good news!' "[24] We cannot call on someone we have not believed, we cannot believe what we have not heard, and we cannot hear unless a preacher tells us the good news. The act of regeneration starts with truth.

Martin Luther understood this biblical emphasis on truth and taught that the Holy Spirit does not save people without it (see fig. 2.2). The Holy Spirit is not some unmediated bolt from the blue that randomly zaps unsuspecting sinners. Rather, the Spirit operates within a person as God's Word is outwardly proclaimed to that person. Luther said:

> Outwardly [God] deals with us through the oral Word, or the Gospel and through visible signs, as Baptism and the Lord's Supper. Inwardly He deals with us through the Holy Spirit and faith ... but always in such a way and in this order that the outward means must precede the inward means, which come afterwards through the outward means. So, then, God has willed that He will not give to anyone the inward gifts (of the Spirit and faith) except through the outward means.[25]

Likewise, John Calvin argued that the Spirit and the truth of the Word are inextricably united. He wrote: "For by a kind of mutual bond the Lord has joined together the certainty of his Word and of his Spirit so that the perfect religion of the Word may abide in our minds when the Spirit, who causes us to contemplate God's face, shines; and that we in turn may embrace the Spirit with no fear of being deceived when we recognize him in his own image, namely, in the Word."[26] Again, "Therefore the Spirit ... has not the task of inventing new and unheard-of revelations, or of forging a new kind of doctrine ... but of sealing our minds with that very doctrine which is commended by the gospel."[27]

Thus, the apostle John, the apostle Paul, Martin Luther, John Calvin, and most important, Jesus, agree that the Holy Spirit uses truth to regenerate his children, and that without truth it is impossible to be saved.[28] But what is this truth that we must believe?

Fig. 2.2. Why We Must Believe Something to Be Saved

WHAT BELIEVERS MUST BELIEVE

In one of history's spectacular conversions, a trembling Philippian jailer cried out to Paul and Silas: "'Sirs, what must I *do* to be saved?' They replied, '*Believe* in the Lord Jesus, and you will be saved....'"[29]

The New Testament uses the term "believe" in two different ways. Sometimes "believe" can mean mental assent, as in James's assertion that even the demons believe in God, but their intellectual acceptance of his existence is not enough to save them.[30] Paul and Silas were using "believe" in a second, higher sense. Beyond mere mental assent, they called the Philippian jailer to act on his knowledge — "believe" is their response to what he must *do*.

The gospel of John tells a story that illustrates both meanings of "believe." John says that once a group of people saw the miracles that Jesus did "and believed in his name." But knowing what was in their hearts, Jesus "did not believe," or "entrust himself to them."[31] The crowd possessed superficial knowledge of Jesus, but they lacked the commitment that would turn their knowledge into genuine faith. And so Jesus refused to commit himself to, or have faith in them.[32]

Faith requires knowledge, for we cannot believe in what we do not know. But it also requires commitment: we must place our entire weight on what we claim to know. For example, I understand that skydiving is a fairly safe activity. With a backup parachute, a partner, and a helmet (how much will that help?), the statistical chance of being injured by jumping from an airplane is surprisingly slim. And yet my fear of heights prevents me from possessing genuine faith in parachuting. I have sufficient knowledge, but I lack the commitment to act on that knowledge — to step into blue sky, entirely dependent on my parachute. When it comes to skydiving, only those in free fall have faith.

So Paul and Silas urged the jailer to believe, to know about, and to fully commit to the Lord Jesus. But what is it about Jesus that we must rely on?

In one of history's pivotal conversions, Peter told the Gentile Cornelius that "everyone who believes in him [Jesus] receives forgiveness of sins."[33] This echoed Jesus' preaching, which linked turning from sin with receiving new life in the kingdom: "The kingdom of God is near. Repent and believe the good news!"[34] Paul also saw the connection between repentance and regeneration, telling the Ephesian elders that "I have declared to both Jews and Greeks that they must turn to God in repentance and have faith in our Lord Jesus."[35]

Thus, being committed to Jesus means turning from sin in order to receive his forgiveness. This turning requires, at minimum, that we believe that we are sinners and that Jesus saves us from our sin. This knowledge lies at the center of the gospel, without which it is impossible to be saved — for how can we turn from sin we do not know we have to a Savior we do not know exists?

While repentance from sin and reliance on Christ is the heart of the gospel, these actions point to, and are only properly understood within, the larger story of God (see fig. 2.3). The revelation of Christ tells us something about God — that he is transcendent and triune, a God who rules over all as Father, Son, and Spirit. From Christ we learn that God is perfect — both loving and free — kind enough to care for our plight and strong enough to do something about it.

Christ also reveals something about ourselves. As our Creator, we learn from Jesus what it means to be in the image of God — noble creatures responsible for stewarding creation on his behalf. As our Redeemer, we learn from Jesus that something has gone terribly wrong with our world. We are rebels whose opposition to God has dehumanized ourselves and destroyed the rest of creation.[36]

But Jesus has acted in grace, saving us who are not merely undeserving but are sworn enemies of his reign. He redeemed us by becoming one of us — fully God and fully human — and then he died on the cross in our place, rose again to conquer sin and death, ascended to the right hand of the Father to be enthroned as King, sent his Spirit to build his church and extend his kingdom in the world, and will soon return to finish the job — overthrowing sin, restoring creation, and living forever with his people on the new earth.

How much of this larger story must we believe to be saved? Only God knows for sure, and I am glad that the final call is left to him. It seems possible to be saved and get large chunks of the story wrong — or at least it better be — for Christians regularly misunderstand the goodness of creation, the primacy and function of the corporate church, and our final destiny on a restored earth. While their confusion distorts God's story and obscures its beauty and power, few would argue that missing on these doctrines puts their salvation at risk.

Not so with other parts of the story. An important confession from the early centuries of the church, the Athanasian Creed, claims that rightly understanding the doctrine of the Trinity and the person of Christ are essential for salvation. It opens with these words: "Whoever wishes to be saved must, above all else, hold the true Christian faith. Whoever does not keep it whole and undefiled will without doubt perish for eternity." Then, after explaining what Christians believe about the Trinity and the two natures of Christ, the creed ends with this solemn warning: "This is the true Christian faith. Unless a man believe this firmly and faithfully, he cannot be saved."[37]

The creed's warning may be taken in two ways: that only those with a developed doctrine of the Trinity and Christology can be saved, or that only those will be saved who, upon hearing what Christians believe, embrace rather than reject it. I prefer the latter, less severe reading; otherwise children, new Christians, and the apostles themselves would not be saved. (The doctrine of the Trinity and the two natures of Christ, while grounded in the New Testament, were not officially clarified until the fourth and fifth centuries.)

Either way the Athanasian Creed warns that rejecting the early church's understanding of the Trinity (that God is one essence and three persons) or its view of Jesus (that he is fully divine and fully human) is heresy that dooms one to hell. Perhaps the reason why the creed considers these doctrines indispensable is that it is impossible to tell the story of salvation without them. Without a Trinity, we cannot explain what happened on the cross (that the Son offered his life to the Father) or in the resurrection (that the Father vindicated his Son by raising him from the dead through the power of the Spirit). And without a robust view of Jesus' two natures, we cannot explain how he became our substitute (that Jesus must be human, because we owed the debt, and he must be God, because only an infinite, sinless person could pay it).

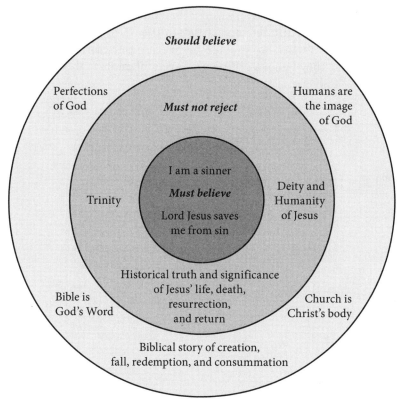

Fig. 2.3. What Christians Believe

Thus, the essential beliefs of the Christian faith are clustered around the story of salvation: the triune God, a fallen humanity, the God-man who died in our place, and our need to repent of the sin that is killing us and claim the forgiveness and new life offered in Christ. These are the truths the Holy Spirit uses to regenerate us and bring us into the kingdom of God. Some of these we must know — that we are sinners forgiven in Christ; and some we at least must not reject — that God is triune and Jesus is the God-man.

Contrary to what some postmodern innovators believe, those who reject these foundational doctrines of the Christian faith cannot be saved, no matter how swell they are and how well they behave. Being good is not good enough. We must know and believe something — the basic facts about salvation — to be saved.

Nevertheless, even if they concede that right beliefs are important, postmodern innovators worry that too much attention to doctrinal detail may hinder our Christian life. How can we say that we love others when we exclude them from our community simply because they believe differently? We will address this question next.

CHAPTER 3

DO RIGHT BELIEFS GET IN THE WAY OF GOOD WORKS?

I grew up in conservative churches that asked little from me: sitting through a sermon was all it took to be considered a faithful follower of Christ. If I did it three times per week — twice on Sunday and once on Wednesday night — I might become a youth group leader. If I missed the midweek service, I was a double-minded Christian who cared about God but was also entangled in the cares of this world. My friends who skipped both Wednesday and Sunday nights were backsliding souls who were allowed to play softball — if they could help the team — but they could forget about teaching Sunday school or doing anything on the platform.

Pastors used both carrot and stick to encourage us to attend as many services as possible. "Come back tonight for a treat," they would say before Sunday morning's benediction. "You won't want to miss the special service we have planned for you." When the coming service was somewhat less scintillating, they sometimes used Scripture to prod us with guilt. "'Let us not give up meeting together, as some are in the habit of doing,'" they said, "but let us begin and end our day in the house of the Lord."[1]

But despite this emphasis on church attendance, we were not expected to do much once we arrived. The centerpiece of each worship service was the sermon — delivered by a lone individual to us who passively sat and stared at the backs of other people's heads. On Sunday mornings we sang hymns for twenty minutes, shook someone's hand and said hello for thirty seconds, and then sat back and soaked in a sermon for the final forty minutes. Sunday evenings were the same, just slightly less formal. Even Wednesday evenings, though touted as prayer meeting, usually had no more than ten minutes of prayer to make room for another Bible message.

I appreciate my church's emphasis on the Word of God. I know the Bible much better than friends who grew up in other traditions. But my heritage also subtly reduced the Christian life to little more than an information dump. Outside our parties and potlucks and the occasional service project or mission trip, the purpose of every gathering was to learn more information. Even our special meetings — weeklong evangelistic, mission, or prophecy conferences — were opportunities to hear more sermons. Although I know better, I still tend to evaluate my spiritual condition — and that of my friends — by services attended and sermons heard.

This is one area where I have learned much, and continue to learn, from postmodern innovators. They rightly remind us that authentic Christianity must involve more than accumulating information. The church is not a building or a worship service but a community of God's people sharing life together. Not content to greet each other in the ten-minute window before and after a worship service, many postmodern Christians intentionally seek creative ways to open their lives to one another. For some this means replacing a worship service with a small group — a fellowship of friends meeting in homes to study the Word and serve each other. Others have taken the more radical step of creating a "new monasticism," where Christian families and singles live, eat, and struggle together to extend the kingdom of Christ in their neighborhood.

These believers are passionate about righting the wrongs of society. To paraphrase Marx, the goal of their Christianity is not merely to learn facts about the world, but to change it. What good is it to learn information about Jesus and salvation if it does not prompt us to share his love in real, tangible ways? So postmodern innovators may spend less time in church and more time volunteering in soup kitchens, distributing medicine to the poor, or demonstrating to save the environment or stop genocide.

The result is an attractive faith that works. As Brian McLaren wisely observes, "Our faith has too often become for us just another rigid belief system instead of a unique, joyful way of living, loving, and serving."[2] The solution, according to McLaren, is to "*turn from doctrines to practices,*" where "unity is built less around a list of things one professes to believe and more around how one pursues truth and puts beliefs into action through practices. In this way, churches ... see themselves as communities of practice."[3]

EXCLUSIVELY INCLUSIVE

I appreciate this renewed turn *to* practice, but wonder why we must turn *from* doctrine to get there. If modern, conservative churches replaced concern for right living with right doctrine, shouldn't postmoderns be wary of falling off the other edge — replacing concern for right doctrine with right living? Perhaps the pendulum swings so quickly because these younger evangelicals believe there is something about doctrine that hinders the Christian life.

They correctly note that the Christian life is about loving God and loving neighbor, but as is typical of postmodernism, they often define love in exclusively inclusive terms. McLaren speaks for many when he says, "The thrust of Jesus' message is about inclusion — shocking, scandalous inclusion."[4] Rather than "create an in-group which would banish others to an out-group; Jesus wanted to create a *come-on-in group*, one that sought and welcomed everyone."[5]

Indeed, since the kingdom of God amounts to "*purposeful inclusion,*" it turns out that the only people excluded from the kingdom are those who exclude others.[6] McLaren writes, "To be truly inclusive, *the kingdom must exclude exclusive people*; to be truly reconciling, the kingdom must not reconcile with those who refuse reconciliation; to achieve its purpose of gathering people, it must not gather those who scatter."[7]

And nothing excludes faster than belief. Beliefs are better at building walls than breaking them down. People believe so many different things about God, religion, and the way of salvation, that claiming that your view is the only right one will surely prevent others from joining with you (see fig. 3.1). This is why McLaren warns that "Jesus did *not* come to create another exclusive religion — Judaism having been exclusive based on genetics and Christianity being exclusive based on belief (which can be a tougher requirement than genetics!)."[8]

Tony Jones agrees. The national coordinator of Emergent (a leading voice among postmodern innovators), Jones declares that his organization "is an amorphous collection of friends who've decided to live life together regardless of our ecclesial affiliations, regardless of our theological commitments." He compares statements of faith to "drawing borders, which means you must load your weapons and place soldiers at those borders. It becomes an obsession to guard the borders. That is simply not the ministry of Jesus."[9]

To support this view, Emergent emailed a statement to its members from LeRon Shults, a significant theologian who gave three reasons why their group should not write a doctrinal statement. Besides being unnecessary and inappropriate, because "Jesus did not have a 'statement of faith,'" and "the struggle to capture God in our finite propositional structures is nothing short of linguistic idolatry," Shults argues that standardizing our beliefs would be a disaster. He worries that "a 'statement of faith' tends to stop conversation. Such statements can also easily become tools for manipulating or excluding people from the community. Too often they create an environment in which real conversation is avoided out of fear that critical reflection on one or more of the sacred propositions will lead to excommunication from the community."[10]

The result of this "loving" refusal to commit to a statement of faith is illustrated in Ikon, an emergent gathering led by Peter Rollins. Rollins claims that God so transcends the limits of our finite minds that he is unable to reveal himself to us. Because God is incomprehensible, he is also unknowable.[11] Our inability to know God eliminates the possibility of drawing doctrinal conclusions, which leads Rollins to concede that Ikon has a hole in its center. He explains, "Just as a doughnut has no interior, but is made up entirely of an exterior, so Ikon has no substantial doctrinal centre."[12]

Since there is nothing to know, Rollins turns his attention to the only part of the Christian faith left — how we live. He replaces "right belief" with "believing in the right way," which means "believing in a loving, sacrificial, and Christlike manner."[13] He suggests that while our Christian beliefs never describe "the Real or reality," yet somehow they are able to transform us into lovers who follow the way of Jesus by embracing others.[14] Rollins explains that "in Ikon we are unified, not on the level of some specific set of doctrines, but rather in our desire that our beliefs, whatever they are, help to enable us to be more open to the divine and more open to one another, exhibiting a loving, caring and Christlike way of being in the world."[15]

While I appreciate this concern for charitable conversation and our need to embrace others — and the last thing I want is to unnecessarily and arrogantly divide people into in- and out-groups — the idea that we should include others regardless of what they believe raises several questions.

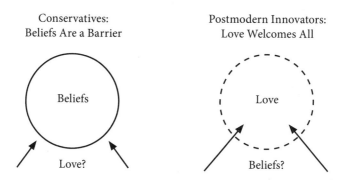

Fig. 3.1. A Postmodern Objection to Doctrinal Statements

Must love always include? Love means to care for, be committed to, and seek the best for the other, and while this usually involves accepting rather than judging, sometimes love must be tough. Parents who love their boomerang children eventually kick them and their Star Trek collection out of their basement. Coaches who want their star player to train harder sometimes demote him to second string. And churches that learn that one of their own is unrepentantly sinning sadly remove that person from membership.[16] In each case love temporarily excludes the other in hope that they will see the error of their ways and rejoin the community as a contributing member.

So there are times when love excludes those who are behaving badly. But does love ever exclude others because of what they believe? Not that long ago this was the motivation behind evangelism. We believed that our friends were excluded from the kingdom because of their wrong views about God, sin, and salvation. Love compelled us to warn them about their looming destiny in hell and urge them to repent and believe the gospel.

But now questions about hell and other religions are causing many to reconsider the meaning of evangelism. Many postmodern innovators believe that we should dialogue with other faiths, seeking to learn as much or more from them as we want them to learn from us. One leader comments on his interaction with other religions: "Evangelism or mission for me is no longer about persuading people to believe what I believe.... It is more about shared experiences and encounters. It is about walking the journey of life and faith together, each distinct to his or her own tradition and culture but with the possibility of encountering God and truth from one another."[17]

Peter Rollins claims that evangelism is a two-way street. Rather than bring the knowledge of God to "unreached" peoples in "unreached" places, he says that Ikon members "seek to be evangelized" as they learn from other religions.[18] He explains: "We deemphasize the idea that Christians have God and all others don't by attempting to engage in open two-way conversations. This does not mean we have lapsed into relativism, as we still believe in the uniqueness of our tradition, but we believe that it teaches us to be open to all. We are also genuinely open to being wrong about parts and perhaps all our beliefs — while at the same time being fully committed to them."[19] Rollins summarizes Ikon's contribution to the conversation: "When it comes to God, we have nothing to say to others and we must not be ashamed of saying it."[20]

Recently a leader of a Christian organization announced that his group would not break fellowship with a friend who had published some unorthodox views on the Christian faith. "Our community is about relationships," he said. "And even though we disagree with some of his beliefs, there will always be a place for him at our table." When asked if he could think of any unorthodox belief that might justify removing someone from his organization, this leader paused, and after five seconds of awkward silence, replied, "I don't know."

How long can those committed to such inclusivism remain authentically Christian? If, as we learned in chapter 2, Christians are defined both by how they live and what they believe, then those communities that downplay the specific, historic doctrines of the Christian faith in order to "share experiences and encounter God in other traditions" will soon become a baptized version of a Rotary or Kiwanis Club. They may be a gathering of good people, but they will no longer be distinctively Christian.

CHRISTIANS MAKE THE BEST LOVERS

If love cashes out as inclusion and nothing excludes faster and more arbitrarily than beliefs, then it is understandable why this new generation believes that it must rise above the divisive doctrines of the Christian faith. But what if love is broader than inclusion? What if it means to seek the best for the other, to sacrificially give of yourself so that the other might flourish, and what if the unique items of the Christian faith supply both the *model* and the *motive* for doing this? In that case our distinctive beliefs would help rather than hinder a life of love. Here's why.

Christians believe that the true God is not one person, as Jews and Muslims suppose, but that he is Father, Son, and Holy Spirit — three persons who share a single essence. These monotheistic religions agree that God is one, and so he is to be feared and praised above all gods. But only the Christian faith, which adds that God is also three, best explains why God is love.

The New Testament portrays the triune God as a fellowship of friends, a community of self-giving lovers.[21] The Father proudly announces at his Son's baptism: "This is my Son, whom I love; with him I am well pleased."[22] The Son loves him back, telling his disciples "that I love the Father and that I do exactly what my Father has commanded me."[23]

Their love remains strong even when it hurts. In Gethsemane the Son set aside his own desires when he prayed, "Father, if you are willing, take this cup from me; yet not my will, but yours be done."[24] Although he preferred any other way, the Son honored his Father by agreeing to be crucified. This moment must have been even more excruciating for the Father. What father can stomach the suffering of his child? Even worse, what father can wield the knife? God the Father did both. He allowed his Son to go to the cross, and turned his back on him there, so that the Son might be glorified as the exalted Redeemer of the world. So both Father and Son set aside their own interests to serve the other. The Spirit does likewise, obeying whatever task the Father and Son send him to do.[25]

Can you imagine any of these persons wanting out? What if the Son complained, "Why do I always get the hard jobs? Let someone else be crucified." Or can you hear the Spirit retorting, "At least you're noticed. Thank God for the Pentecostals. Without them I'd get no attention." This would never happen, for from eternity past each person of the Godhead has been committed to the others' flourishing. The Father glorifies the Son, the Son glorifies the Father, the Spirit honors both and they watch his back.[26] Jesus said that those who sin against the Son may be forgiven, "but anyone who speaks against the Holy Spirit will not be forgiven, either in this age or in the age to come."[27]

When the Son prayed "Not my will, but yours be done," he wasn't saying anything new, but was merely repeating what he has always told the Father. This pattern of self-giving love, of setting aside one's own interests to serve the other, supplies the model for our relationships.

An early Christian hymn says that we should adopt this attitude of Christ:

> *Who, being in very nature God,*
> *did not consider equality with God something*
> *to be grasped,*
> *but made himself nothing,*
> *taking the very nature of a servant,*
> *being made in human likeness.*
> *And being found in appearance as a man,*
> *he humbled himself*
> *and became obedient to death —*
> *even death on a cross!*
> *Therefore God exalted him to the highest place*
> *and gave him the name that is above every name,*
> *that at the name of Jesus every knee should bow,*
> *in heaven and on earth and under the earth,*
> *and every tongue confess that Jesus Christ is Lord,*
> *to the glory of God the Father.*[28]

The second word of this hymn, the rather bland term "being," is better translated "because." Precisely *because* Jesus is God — and God is a community of self-giving lovers — it was the most natural thing in the world for him to humbly serve others by becoming a man and dying on the cross.[29]

Why does God love us? Not because we're worth it. God has enough business sense to run a cost-benefit analysis and realize that the life of an infinite Creator easily trumps the lives of his finite creatures. No number of people — even six billion and counting — could justify taking the life of the infinitely valuable Creator.

Back up one step. Why did God make us in the first place? Philosophers have long pondered why there is something rather than

nothing. Why did God create the world? Augustine said that someone responded to a similar question, "What was God doing before
he made the world?" by replying that he was making hell for those
who ask such questions.[30]

We can't say precisely why God made the world, because he
certainly did not have to. But we can say that creating the world is
a Godlike thing to do. If God is a community of self-giving lovers,
then it follows that a God who has always loved the others within
the Trinity might also create new others to love. Furthermore, when
these others rebelled and got themselves in trouble, this God would
do anything necessary to love them back to wholeness. God loves
us because that is just the way he is wired. He can't help it. He is
love.[31]

Besides informing us that humble, self-giving love is the nature
of God, the hymn also promises that such sacrifice is rewarded.
Those who give themselves away so that others might flourish
find that their very sacrifice also causes them to flourish. "Therefore" — because Jesus obeyed all the way to the cross — the Father
has highly exalted him as the Lord of the universe.

What is true about God is also true about we who are made in
his image. "Whoever wants to save his life will lose it," Jesus said,
"but whoever loses his life for me will find it." In the preceding verse
Jesus said something which is frequently misunderstood. "If anyone
would come after me, he must deny himself and take up his cross
and follow me."[32]

For most of my life I thought Jesus here was offering the "big
trade." Those who want rewards in the next life must give up all
happiness in this one. Every missions conference ended the same
way: would I lay my all on the altar, giving up the good life in America to travel to the furthest, most forsaken place on the planet if
that is what God wanted? I associated serving God with suffering.
I tried not to enjoy anything too much, for I knew the moment I
did, God would ask me to give it up. I believed that the higher my
misery index — the more I disliked my calling, country, and general
circumstances — the more God was pleased with me.

I was wrong. Jesus wasn't telling us that we must be miserable
now to enjoy the good stuff in the next life. He was actually telling us how to thrive now. He was saying, "Do you want to enjoy
the fullest life possible? Then do what I and the other members of

the Trinity do. Deny yourself. Live for someone else. Take up your cross — because your selfish nature must die — and follow me. If you want to prosper like God, then you must do what God does. Lose your life and you will find it."

Jesus' advice seems counterintuitive, but experience teaches that it is true. Think of your happiest days, when you were most thrilled to be alive. Weren't they the days you lived for someone else? You surprised a friend with a home-cooked meal, shingled a family's roof, or drove five hundred miles to wish a loved one a happy birthday. You were genuinely happy because, on these days, you were moving with the grain of the universe. You were living like the triune God, who wired you to be like himself. You only find your life when you give it away.

GRACE AND GRATITUDE

Besides offering the model of love, the Christian story also supplies the motivation for good behavior. Just as no other religion has a Trinity — a God who is a community of self-giving lovers — so no other religion teaches salvation entirely by grace. For example, despite the Koran's claim that Allah is "most gracious" and "most merciful," Islam encourages its members to do the best they can and hope it is enough to earn Allah's approval.

Christianity believes that good works are best done, not in an effort to merit salvation, but in response to acceptance already granted. The apostle Paul writes that "the grace of God ... teaches us to say 'No' to ungodliness and worldly passions, and to live self-controlled, upright[33] and godly lives ... eager to do what is good."[34] How exactly does grace teach us to be good?

Luke tells the story of a prostitute who so desperately wanted to see Jesus that she interrupted his dinner in a Pharisee's house. Moved by his love for people like her, she began to sob, wetting his feet with her tears. Now embarrassed, she began to dry them with her hair, and then, overcome with emotion, began kissing and pouring perfume on them. This scene made everyone uncomfortable, and the host harrumphed to himself and said, "If this man were a prophet, he would know who is touching him and what kind of woman she is — that she is a sinner."

Jesus turned to him and posed this question: "Two men owed money to a certain moneylender. One owed him five hundred denarii, and the other fifty. Neither of them had the money to pay him back, so he canceled the debts of both. Now which of them will love him more?"

"I suppose the one who had the bigger debt canceled," the host replied.

Jesus told him that the same was true with this prostitute. She loved Jesus more than he did because she had been forgiven more. "But he who has been forgiven little loves little."[35]

Those who have received love naturally want to pass it on. Those who have received grace desire to extend grace to others. This is a chief insight of the Reformation.

Martin Luther became a monk in a futile attempt to save his soul. He went far beyond what his monastery required — fasting totally for three days or sleeping through frigid nights without a blanket (my wife does this too, but she says it is my fault for hogging the covers). Luther later admitted that his austerity had permanently damaged his health. Looking back on his experience, he said that "I was a good monk, and I kept the rule of my order so strictly that I may say that if ever a monk got to heaven by his monkery, it was I."[36]

But Luther realized that his best was never good enough to please a holy God. How could anyone do enough to satisfy his infinite standards? Luther said: "Yet my conscience would never give me assurance, but I was always doubting and said, 'You did not perform that correctly. You were not contrite enough. You left that out of your confession.' "[37] He conceded, "I was myself more than once driven to the very abyss of despair so that I wished I had never been created. Love God? I hated him!"[38]

After years of torment and driving his confessor crazy, Luther finally discovered that the righteousness he needed was not his own but that of Christ. He read Paul's admonition that "the righteous will live by faith" not as a command to become righteous but as a promise of being covered with Christ's righteousness: "he who through faith is righteous shall live."[39]

Rather than strive to satisfy God's holy demands, Luther realized that he could rest in what Jesus had achieved for him. He said that "I felt myself to be reborn and to have gone through open doors into paradise. The whole of Scripture took on a new meaning, and whereas before the 'justice of God' had filled me with hate, now it became to me inexpressibly sweet in greater love. This passage of Paul became to me a gate to heaven."[40]

Shortly thereafter Luther wrote *The Freedom of a Christian*, a little book that in his mind "contain[ed] the whole of Christian life in a brief form."[41] Luther said that before his Reformation breakthrough, he spent all of his resources trying to save his own soul. But now that he realized his soul was safe in Christ, he had a lot of time on his hands. No longer worried about securing his own salvation, he could use his time and money to serve others.

And so a Christian is free, not to live as he pleases, but to become a little Christ to his neighbor. Luther explained:

> Although I am an unworthy and condemned man, my God has given me in Christ all the riches of righteousness and salvation without any merit on my part, out of pure, free mercy, so that from now on I need nothing except faith which believes that it is true. Why should I not therefore freely, joyfully, with all my heart, and with an eager will do all things which I know are pleasing and acceptable to such a Father who has overwhelmed me with his inestimable riches? *I will therefore give myself as a Christ to my neighbor, just as Christ offered himself to me*; I will do nothing in this life except what I see is necessary, profitable, and salutary to my neighbor, since through faith I have an abundance of all good things in Christ.[42]

Here is Luther's Christian calculus: sin → grace → gratitude → love. Only when we understand the depths of our depravity can we appreciate the amazing grace "that saved a wretch like me." And once we understand grace, our immediate reflexive response is gratitude (in the original New Testament, the Greek word for gratitude, *eucharistia*, is built on the word for grace, *charis*). If grace does not generate gratitude, it can only mean that we don't yet get it.

According to question two of the Heidelberg Catechism, when we understand "how great my sin and misery are," only then can we appreciate "how I am set free from all my sins and misery," which then automatically leads us to wonder "how I am to thank God for such deliverance." And thankful Christians devote themselves to good works, seeking to please God by loving their neighbor.

BELIEVE IN LOVE

Thus, against the postmodern view that beliefs get in the way of good behavior, the specific, historic doctrines of the Christian faith supply the best — dare I say only — rationale for a life of love. We need a model and a motive to love others, and the Christian view of the triune God and salvation by grace supplies both. If we downplay these historic doctrines, striving to rise above them in an attempt to include people with more diverse beliefs, we will undercut the ground for good works. The result will be less love, not more (see fig. 3.2).

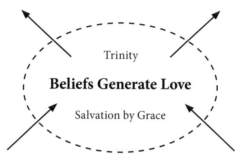

Fig. 3.2. Right Belief Produces Right Practice

But can't non-Christians also love others? Yes, but they do so despite rather than because of their beliefs. For example, social scientists committed to philosophical naturalism (there is no God, just nature) believe that each person seeks his or her own interest in a cosmic survival of the fittest. Why do some people sacrificially love others? According to these scientists, altruistic people suffer from "docility" (they do what others tell them) and "bounded rationality" (they are dumb). Should these scientists themselves ever genuinely love — and God help their families if they do not — they have by their own standard become stupid wimps.[43]

What about other theists? Muslims often show kindness to others. But Islam is a performance-based religion grounded in fear: do the best you can and hope that it will be enough for Allah to accept you. While this religious system may encourage Muslims to do many good deeds, it cannot turn them into lovers. Frightened people are too focused on themselves to put others first. When Muslims genuinely love others, they are acting inconsistently with their religious beliefs.

Not so with Christians. We believe that we are made in the image of the triune God, whose nature is love, and that our God has loved us twice — in creating and then redeeming us. As John writes, "We love because he first loved us."[44]

Perhaps you are wondering why, if the Christian faith supplies the only rationale for love, so many professing Christians can be so unloving. Part of the answer lies in the conservative tendency to emphasize right beliefs over right action. Right beliefs do not guarantee right behavior, for we still must act on what we know. Conservatives need to heed James's warning that "faith without deeds is dead" and Paul's admonition that knowledge without love is nothing.[45]

But perhaps our lack of love arises from a deeper crisis in belief. Follow Luther's chain backward: love → gratitude → grace → sin. If we are not loving others, it is because we are not thankful. If we are not thankful, it is because we do not appreciate grace. And if we do not appreciate grace, it is because we do not understand the extent of our sin. We who easily spot greed, selfishness, and hypocrisy in others often don't really believe that we are that bad off.

Thus, loving others begins with a right view of ourselves. Are we generally good or basically bad? This foundational question is disputed in our day, and to it we now turn.

CHAPTER 4

ARE PEOPLE GENERALLY GOOD OR BASICALLY BAD?

My conservative upbringing taught me to fear the world, the flesh, and the Devil — and pretty much in that order. The world was full of public school teenagers who swore, had sex, and listened to rock and roll. I was taught to fear them because their sins might become mine, but in truth I feared them because they seemed bigger and better at everything my Christian school tried.

Their teams were taller (the star of our varsity basketball team was an eighth grader), their concerts were cleaner (our clarinets squawked their way through the "Twelve Days of Christmas") — even their buses were bigger (we rode to school in conversion vans).

Yet despite the fact that they were better — or perhaps because of it — we took comfort in knowing that we were "in." We belonged to the family of God and were bound for heaven, while most of those talented brutes were headed for hell. They were already suffering the effects of removing God from their schools — rising drug use and violence — and unless they repented, their problems would only get worse.

Sometimes we took our comfort a bit too far. There is a denomination in my part of the country that was founded on the idea that God hates the nonelect (those sinners he did not choose to save). Our hearts may break for the Jewish father who grimly stood with his son before a German firing squad, but God feels no pity. Inasmuch as Jews are not Christians, they are loathed by a holy God who sheds no tear for their demise. Who said Calvinists weren't lovable?

Although these extreme friends managed to make even Jesus seem mean, we did agree with them that we were different. To quote a more generous Calvinist, a turn-of-the-twentieth-century Dutch leader named Abraham Kuyper, there is an antithesis between Christians and those who have not been born again. In his words, "there are two kinds of people" doing "two kinds of science."[1] Kuyper meant that while Christians and others — say secular humanists — may agree on many things, their different foundational beliefs will produce dramatically different views of the world.

For example, both groups may cooperate on clinical trials for a new vaccine. Both know how to separate control from experimental groups, administer a placebo to one and a live virus to the other, and add up the results to determine whether the vaccine should be available to the public. But when we step back and ask what it all means, the Christian scientist will praise God for creating a stable world in which experiments are possible and for empowering his children with the intellectual ability to join his work of redemption. The nontheist, on the other hand, will likely suppose that our apparently predictable world is grounded in random chance and that his work on the new vaccine is merely another step in the survival of the fittest — one man's lonely attempt to stave off the extinction of the human race, which is doomed anyway because our rapidly expanding universe will continue to pull apart until it inevitably disintegrates into countless cold, dark pieces of antimatter.

Kuyper's antithesis, and my childhood memory that we Christians were different from the world, is grounded in an awareness of our own depravity. We believed that *we were different because we were very much the same.* As Paul reminds the church in Corinth, some of us were "sexually immoral ... idolaters ... adulterers ... male prostitutes ... homosexual offenders ... thieves ... greedy ... drunkards ... slanderers ... [and] swindlers." The only difference between us and them is that we "were washed ... sanctified ... justified in the name of the Lord Jesus Christ and by the Spirit of our God."[2]

We had a low view of the world because we had a low view of ourselves. We often hung our heads and mournfully sang during the Lord's Supper: "Alas! and did my Savior bleed? And did my Sovereign die? Would He devote that sacred head for *such a worm as I?*"[3] One pastor began his sermon by asking his congregation what it meant to be human. "What are you?" he asked. "Sinners!" they shouted back. Of course, they were Calvinists.

UP WITH PEOPLE

The preacher told his people that they were wrong. He told them that they should find their identity in Creation, which informs them that they were made in the image of God. God's work always trumps ours, and so his bellowing "Yes!" of Creation blows away our squeaky "no" of the Fall.[4] Just as we cannot obliterate the goodness of God's creation in the world around us, so we cannot eliminate the goodness he has placed within us.

We will always bear the image of God, which is why our sin is a tragedy. *Girls Gone Wild* is sadder than *When Animals Attack*, for, spring break evidence to the contrary, the girls in these videos — and the guys who watch — are corrupting a higher good. Nobody ever lectured a worm for wriggling off its hook: "Bad worm! Your disobedience deeply disappoints me!" It's a worm, and so its misdeeds don't count for much.

Not so with us. A broken image of God is infinitely worse than a broken anything else. And contrary to Matthias Flacius, a sixteenth-century Lutheran who argued that our sin turns us into the *imago satani* (image of Satan), we remain, even in our brokenness, the *imago Dei* (image of God).[5] We never have been — nor will we ever be — worms.

Abraham Kuyper noted the staying power of Creation in his doctrine of common grace. Despite the antithesis between Christians and those who do not follow Jesus, we share a basic human goodness and many of the same dreams. We all want healthy children, meaningful work, a vibrant economy, and world peace. Quite often we find ourselves on the same team, pulling together to right the wrongs and boost the goods in our world. We cooperate in our efforts to stop global warming, the bird flu, and child abuse as we jump-start schools, hospitals, and just governments for those who too long have done without.

And yet, if conservatives sometimes stretch the difference between Christians and the world to unhealthy extremes, postmodern innovators tend to pick up what we have in common and pull in the opposite direction. As we learned in chapter 3, they are reluctant to divide people into in- and out-groups, where one group is excluded because of what they believe, but rather emphasize that we are all in this together.

Recently I happened upon a radio interview in which a leading postmodern innovator was asked whether Protestant Christians believe that salvation is by grace through faith alone. He answered yes, for we believe that salvation is a gift. There is no quota of works that we must meet, but we simply *accept our acceptance by our Creator*.

This is a provocatively incomplete answer. True as far as it goes (God is our Creator), it is sufficiently incomplete to mislead (don't we also need God the Redeemer?). This may be the first time a Christian has affirmed salvation by grace through faith without mentioning Jesus Christ, his death and resurrection, and our need to repent and believe this good news. Shorn of their context in Jesus Christ, the notions of grace and faith are reduced to empty caricatures. Salvation is no longer turning from sin and trusting Christ's sacrifice on our behalf, but is now merely believing that God has accepted us all along.

Spencer Burke elaborates on this new view of grace, writing that it is *"not conditional on recognizing or renouncing sin,"* but "it comes to us whether or not we ask for it. We don't have to do something to receive it, nor do we even have to respond to it in some way. It simply comes." In this way "grace is offered to all people, everywhere, regardless of religious affiliation."[6]

Burke believes that we must move beyond traditional notions of sin. He explains:

> Although the link between grace and sin has driven Christianity for centuries, it just doesn't resonate in our culture anymore. It repulses rather than attracts. People are becoming much less inclined to acknowledge themselves as "sinners in need of a Savior." It's not that people view themselves as perfect; it's that the language they use to describe themselves has changed. "Broken," "fragmented," and "lacking wholeness"—these are some of the new ways people describe their spiritual need. What resonates is a sense of disconnection.[7]

Tony Jones agrees that gospel presentations have focused too much on sin. He writes:

> A generation or two ago, defenses of Christianity that focused on human sinfulness were potent; a common metaphor showed God on one side of a diagram and a stick figure (you) on the other; the chasm between was labeled "Sin," and the only bridge across was in the shape of Jesus' cross. But emergents ask, "What kind of God can't reach across a chasm? Chasms can't stop God!"[8]

I am not sure what Jones is objecting to here, for the metaphor's point is that while the chasm prevents us from coming to

God, it does not stop God from reaching across. Perhaps he means that God should be able to reach us in some other way besides the cross? Or perhaps that our sin does not separate us from God? Jones acknowledges that "many emergent Christians will concur that we live in a sinful world, a world of wars and famines and pogroms. But they will be inclined to attribute this sin not to the distance between human beings and God but to the broken relationships that clutter our lives and our world."[9]

I agree that we suffer from broken relationships and many varieties of social evil, but are these the main source of sin? Didn't Jesus say that sin comes from the heart — from the inside out rather than from the outside in?[10] If sin is external, then the cross need only be, in Jones's words, "an act of divine solidarity with the suffering and broken world."[11] But if the root cause of sin lies within every human heart, then the cross must be powerful enough to cleanse us from the inside (see chap. 6).

This low view of sin may explain why some postmodern innovators are reconsidering the perspective of the fifth-century heretic Pelagius. Doug Pagitt suggests that Pelagius should not have been excommunicated by the church, for his belief in the inherent goodness of human nature supplies a welcome counterbalance to Augustine's emphasis on our depravity. Pagitt argues that Augustine's belief that "people were born separate from God" fit the Greek understanding of God popular in the Roman Empire. This allowed him to defeat Pelagius's alien, Druid notion that "people were born with the Light of God aflame within them, if even dimly lit." But since neither view is better than the other, Pagitt says that we should seek to learn from both, remembering that "different cultures will have different expressions" of the Christian faith.[12]

Now we can see why our view of ourselves matters. We learned in chapters 2 and 3 that we need to know and believe the gospel because truth is what the Holy Spirit uses to birth sinners into the family of God. But if we are already good enough, we do not need to be born again. And if we do not need to be born again, then neither do we need to believe the truth that gives new birth.

Thus, the popular view that God would not send someone to hell simply because he or she believed the wrong things rests on a prior assumption that people are already good (or at least not bad enough to deserve damnation). But what if—as Augustine believed—we are born sinners, polluted and guilty for Adam's sin? And what if the Holy Spirit uses truth to solve our problem of original sin? Then it matters a lot what we believe.

The history of theology is a story of pendulum swings. The church pursues one line of thought until it reaches an extreme, and then, like the pendulum on a grandfather clock, swiftly swings to the other side. Sometimes we can see the correction coming and yet are powerless to stop it. This is one of those times.

Some modern, conservative Christians reflected on human depravity until they concluded that we were worms and the non-Christian world was worse. Now postmodern innovators, many of whom grew up in conservative churches and saw firsthand the consequences of a worm-affirming, world-hating theology, have swung to the other side where they emphasize the natural goodness of both ourselves and the world. This new extreme is exciting—it holds out hope for the world and the possibility of progress—but it is still an extreme. Is there a better, more biblically balanced way to keep the goodness of Creation while doing justice to the devastation of the Fall? Like Abraham Kuyper, can we believe in both the antithesis and common grace? (see fig. 4.1).

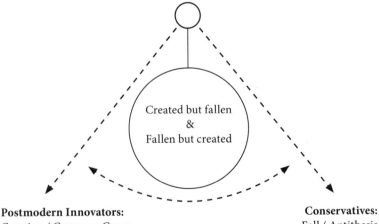

Postmodern Innovators:
Creation / Common Grace
Everyone is good

Conservatives:
Fall / Antithesis
Everyone is depraved

Fig. 4.1. Are People Good or Bad?

IT'S ALL GOOD

Are people good or bad? This is a complex question that requires a nuanced answer. Like "Have you stopped beating your wife?" or "Do you support our troops by supporting the war?" this question confounds a simple yes or no.

Yesterday my six-year-old pounded out his first recognizable tune on the piano, and I made quite a fuss about it. "Landon, that is 'Mary Had a Little Lamb'! You are playing the piano! Good job!" And it was — especially good for a beginner and far better than anything I can play. But compared to my wife or a concert pianist, it was not very good at all. Goodness is a relative term. It depends on what we are talking about.

Thanks to God's gift of common grace, there are at least three distinct kinds of goodness that all people — saint and sinner alike — may and even should possess (see fig. 4.2). The most basic is what Lewis Smedes calls "mere morality."[13] Not everyone can be a Mother Teresa, but everyone is expected at least not to hurt others. People who take what does not belong to them, whether that is another's life, property, or sexual integrity, land in jail. No one has ever won an award for being merely moral, but many have ruined lives for not meeting this fundamental requirement (e.g., Hitler, Saddam Hussein, and the cheating leaders of Enron).

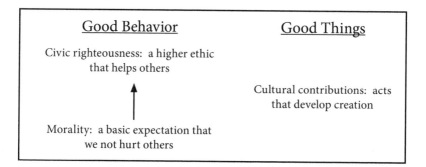

Fig. 4.2. Natural Goodness

But we do give awards for those who go beyond not hurting others and lend a helping hand. We applaud the generosity of Warren Buffett and Bill and Melinda Gates, who together have pledged more than $67 billion[14] to cure and educate the poorest of the poor.

We honor the sacrifice of the firefighters who on 9/11 raced up the stairs while everyone else was fleeing down. And we thank God for the garden-variety courtesies of shared umbrellas, held doors, and simple thank-yous that abound in our world.

When I visited Japan, I was surprised to find a barrel of umbrellas by the front door of a subway station. When I asked my host why they were there, she told me that the Japanese take one when it is raining and then put it back when they are done. I marveled at this picture of civic virtue. Though the Japanese have other sins (their sex tours into Thailand are legendary), yet through common grace this predominantly non-Christian nation is able to do something my Dutch city of churches is unable to pull off (we pinch pennies from the change cup by the cash register).

Besides this ethical goodness, common grace also empowers everyone to produce cultural goods. John Calvin said that we should thank God for the cultural contributions of non-Christians, for their efforts are inspired by the general grace of the Holy Spirit.

> If we regard the Spirit of God as the sole fountain of truth, we shall neither reject the truth itself, nor despise it wherever it shall appear, unless we wish to dishonor the Spirit of God.... But if the Lord has willed that we be helped in physics, dialectic, mathematics, and other like disciplines, by the work and ministry of the ungodly, let us use this assistance. For if we neglect God's gift freely offered in these arts, we ought to suffer just punishment for our sloths.[15]

The first cultural connoisseurs came from the cursed line of Cain: Jabal, "the father of those who live in tents and raise livestock"; Jubal, "the father of all who play the harp and flute"; and Tubal-Cain, "who forged all kinds of tools out of bronze and iron."[16] And these Cain-raisers have been blessing us with their innovations ever since. Non-Christians gave us algebra, computers, and the automobile. They gave us longer, healthier, and happier lives: discovering cures that extend our years and then filling our days with food, shows, and hobbies they helped create. Imagine your favorite sports team without its non-Christian players, and you will realize how dependent we are on the contributions of every corner of the human race. Most of our pleasures are made, at least in part, by those who do not follow Christ.

WHEN IT'S BAD, IT'S VERY BAD

So everyone possesses a relative goodness that enables us to help others. But when we lift our eyes above our natural level and compare our goodness with God, we confront a double problem: God's higher standard and our sinful brokenness (see fig. 4.3).[17]

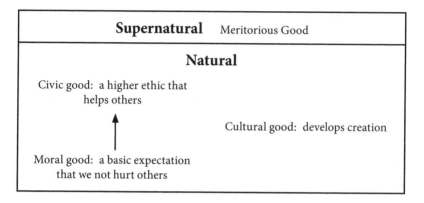

Fig. 4.3. Supernatural Goodness

Imagine trying to win an Olympic medal in figure skating without skating lessons. Even worse, imagine that your shaky presence somehow threatened Tanya Harding, who ordered her goons to take an iron bar and whack you in the knee. What are the odds that you will finish your free skate standing up, let alone impress the judges enough to medal?

Augustine said that our sinful wills are like broken legs that cripple any chance of doing good on our own before God.[18] He argued that we are born with original sin — corrupted and guilty for our connection to Adam's sin.

Original sin is held by nearly every Christian tradition, whether the Orthodox, Roman Catholic, or any of the hundreds of Protestant denominations.[19] And it seems to be the one doctrine that can be empirically proved. Observe any nursery. No one taught little Johnny to grab the ball from his playmate's hands, punch her in the nose when she would not let go, and then throw a tantrum when an adult intervened. He figured it out on his own.

We are born sinners, and left to ourselves we will sin whenever we can and as much as we can.[20] We desperately need grace:

common grace to do natural good for others, and special grace to perform supernatural good that merits praise from God.

Augustine said that our "wounded, injured, beaten," and "ruined" natures need the grace of God to heal and empower us to do the good that God requires.[21] Citing Philippians 2:13, "it is God who works in you to will and to act," Augustine declared that without grace we can "do nothing good whether in thinking, in willing and loving, or in acting," but we must rely on the Holy Spirit to "unfailingly and invincibly" cure and compel us to do good.[22] Because grace is the ultimate cause of our good, when God rewards our merits, he crowns nothing but "his own gifts."[23]

The Reformers saw Augustine's emphasis on our depravity and raised it. They taught that meritorious works are not only impossible without grace, but they are impossible period.[24] Our sinful wills corrupt everything we do, so even our best efforts require the forgiveness of Christ. Lutherans declared that "even though they are still impure and imperfect," yet "the good works of believers are pleasing and acceptable to God ... for the sake of the Lord Christ through faith, because the person is acceptable to God."[25]

John Calvin called this our "double acceptance ... before God," by which God accepts both our *person* and our *works* through the blood of his Son.[26] Just as God forgives our sinful person by covering us with the righteousness of Christ, so he forgives our sinful works in the same way. Calvin explained in a sermon:

> Although the good which the faithful do is not worthy to be received by God, yet he accepts it in good worth. And wherefore? For he of his own goodness wipes away all the faults that are in them. So then when we labor to do well, though we are not able to attain to perfection because of the frailty of our nature, yet God will receive our service as acceptable, *as though* he had nothing to say against it.... And how? We have not fulfilled all, it is true, but yet God passes it in his accounts, *as if* all were performed, inasmuch as we are made clean by the blood of Jesus Christ. And as we are cleansed, so are our works also, and when they come before God, he accepts them *as though* they were thoroughly good, righteous, and perfect.[27]

This is a severe sense of human depravity. We never do an entirely good act, for even our best efforts are not accepted on their own merits, but only *as if* they were good. Not everyone will agree with the

Reformers on this point. Some, like John Wesley, believe that sinful humans who are filled with the Holy Spirit can do genuinely good deeds and even become perfect.[28] So it is possible to acknowledge our depravity and yet not follow the Lutherans and Reformed this far. Still, their belief seems to agree with Scripture, which declares that no one can achieve righteousness through good works because before God "all our righteous acts are like filthy rags."[29]

Their view also resonates with my experience. My best moments are marred by impure motives. I anonymously give money to a needy friend and secretly hope to be discovered. Or congratulate myself that I do not care. Then my conscience kicks in, and I realize that my act of giving is contaminated by pride. So I repent of my arrogance, but even as I am confessing, I think, "Great catch, Mike! You must be close to God, for you are sensitive to a sin that less pious people would barely notice." Realizing that this thought itself is conceited, I confess the pride in my confession, pat myself on the back for catching it, and on it goes. "The heart is deceitful above all things and beyond cure," wrote Jeremiah. "Who can understand it?"[30]

I also appreciate how this strong sense of sin enlarges the size of grace. If my need is so big that everything I do must be forgiven, then God's salvation must be larger still. This is the point of John Newton's powerful hymn "Amazing Grace." Troubled by the twenty thousand people he sold into slavery, Newton wrote in his memoir: "Although my memory is fading, I remember two things very clearly: I'm a great sinner, and Christ is a great Savior."[31]

But perhaps this deep view of depravity actually denigrates grace. Doesn't it insult God's power for us to pessimistically say that we will always continue to sin? Is the omnipotent God powerless to change us?[32]

I reply that it is no knock on God that our every act is sinful. We are like pianos that are out of tune. So even when the Holy Spirit strikes all the right notes, our song never sounds quite right. The Spirit may empower us to do the right thing, but the impure motives from our broken wills make our work sound flat. Not until the next life, when our wills have been overhauled and confirmed in righteousness, will we be able to do an entirely good deed.[33]

For now we continue to make progress. When our Father says, "Well done, good and faithful servant!"[34] he does not mean "Great job! You lived exactly as I wanted." But neither does he mean "You were horrible, you stunk up the place, but I forgive you." I think his meaning is somewhere in the middle: "You are not perfect, but you are making progress. You are less sinful today than you were yesterday, and any remaining flaws are forgiven on account of my Son."

This is something like what I mean when I tell my son he is playing well on the piano. "Mary Had a Little Lamb" is not a terribly impressive song, and if he is still playing it next year, we will discuss whether he is cut out for the piano. But it is a song — his first one — and so I applaud his progress.

Our heavenly Father is similarly patient with us. He has "compassion on those who fear him; for he knows how we are formed, he remembers that we are dust." He does not hold us to an impossibly high standard, but "as far as the east is from the west, so far has he removed our transgressions from us."[35]

FALLEN CREATURES

We are now prepared to answer our question: are people good or bad? Scripture's opening act of Creation informs us that, on a natural level and through common grace, everyone is able to do much moral, civic, and cultural good. This general goodness unites us with all people. It is why we grieve with Muslim families blown up by suicide bombers, Buddhist villages washed away by tsunamis, and Hindu homes shaken by earthquakes. Our natural, human goodness reminds us that we are all image bearers of God, pulling together to make our world a better, more peaceful, and prosperous place. We would not want, and cannot even imagine, living in a world without our non-Christian friends.

But the biblical story of the Fall tells us that, despite our appreciation for each other, when we drill down beneath our natural goodness, we discover that we are sinners. "All have sinned," writes the apostle Paul, "and fall short of the glory of God."[36]

We may often be good to each other, but none of us is good to God. Adam and Eve bit the fruit in a futile bid to "be like God," and their children have not stopped chasing the dream.[37] We all want to play God, running our lives as we see fit and doing whatever we perceive to be in our best interest. Thanks to common grace, this normally involves being kind to others, for it is hard to get ahead by making fresh enemies who will root against us. But when necessary and when we think we can get away with it, who is not tempted to cut corners, break promises, and stretch the truth to get our way? We must succeed, and no one — not even God — may block our rise to the top.

Our sin is why we need saving. Paul said that we are saved when we confess that Jesus — not us or anyone else — is Lord.[38] This quickly became a test for the early church. Would they succumb to pressure from the government to burn a pinch of incense and say, "Caesar is Lord," or would they boldly declare that no one is Lord but Jesus? Those who suffered for their faith realized that they were different from those who pledged allegiance to Caesar, and the antithesis between Christians and those who did not follow Christ was born.

But against conservatives, this antithesis is no cause for pride. We believe that we all are sinners, and that the only difference between us and non-Christians is that we have received the Holy Spirit, who alone enables us to say, "Jesus is Lord."[39] Grace must humble. Few things are uglier than a cocky Christian who looks down on others for not understanding what he knows. The Christian faith is all about grace, and if that does not humble, then we just do not get it.

Against postmodern innovators, our sinful condition requires regeneration, which in turn requires a knowledge of the gospel. We need to know the truth about Jesus because we need to be saved, and we need to be saved because we are sinners. People do possess large amounts of natural goodness, but none of it offsets the brokenness of original sin. We are born with a burning need to play God, and we remain his enemy until we lay down our weapons and proclaim with the church, "Jesus is Lord."

Shortly after college I spent two years in China, where I became especially close to two best friends, whom I will call Sun Yi and Li Xei Ping. They knew I was a Christian and I knew they were atheists, but we still had a blast together — boiling handmade dumplings with their families on New Year's Eve, rowing boats at the Summer Palace, and playing badminton until they finally conspired to let me win.

Our heart-to-heart talks taught me that for all our religious, cultural, and linguistic differences, we were pretty much the same. We loved our families, cared for our countries, and even laughed at many of the same jokes. We would always be friends — and that is how we saw each other: friends first, and then American or Chinese.

The year after I returned home, Sun Yi wrote that she had become a Christian. When I called to rejoice with her, we could tell that we were connecting at a deeper level — that we really understood each other now. I felt as if a burden had been lifted from my shoulders, my prayers had been answered, and if not in this life, we would meet again.

And yet I did not suddenly care more for her than Li Xei Ping. The Christian view of sin and salvation does not necessarily bottom-line everything, so that lives without Jesus are completely and in every way wasted. I still miss Li Xei Ping and pray that she repents of her sin and follows Jesus as her Lord. But even if not — though the consequences are too dreadful to contemplate — I will always remain her friend, thankful for the good that is there, while hoping for so much more.

People are created, and so we may unreservedly love them. People are fallen, and so there is a difference between those who are running their own lives and those who are striving to follow Jesus. Our common creation enables Christians and non-Christians to cooperate, and our response to the Fall explains why we often compete.

Sometimes it is hard to keep this straight — to know which side we are on — and never more than in the present controversy surrounding homosexuality. Should Christians side with a plain reading of Scripture that homosexuality is wrong, or should we defend homosexuals against religiously induced discrimination? This question is a symptom of a deeper issue, which we will examine next.

CHAPTER 5

WHICH IS WORSE: HOMOSEXUALS OR THE BIGOTS WHO PERSECUTE THEM?

Today I witnessed a clash of Christian civilizations. Soulforce, a group of mostly Christian young people who are protesting discrimination against homosexuals, bisexuals, and transgender people, visited my conservative Christian university. My school was founded by fundamentalists who opposed premarital, extramarital, and enthusiastically marital sex, so the sinfulness of homosexual acts was an easy call.

Not for Soulforce. They believe that homosexuality is a civil rights issue, and that religious people like us are committing "spiritual violence" against others by saying that any sex outside of heterosexual marriage is sin. They argue that homosexuals are a new minority. Just as we regret oppressing women and blacks, some day we will be embarrassed that we ever opposed gay marriage or refused to hire pastors or professors because of their sexual preference. Why can't we love and accept everyone?[1]

As it turned out, Soulforce's peaceful protest was productive for both sides. My school used their visit as an opportunity to stand on principle. We declined their request to visit campus, and when they showed up anyway, reminded them that they were not welcome — a point we reinforced by arresting two of them. This in turn delivered the photo op they were after, which, combined with pictures of their candlelight vigil, raised awareness of their issue in our community.

Beyond the public relations tactics, what interests me is how both sides use Scripture to declare that they are on God's side and that the other view is immoral. Soulforce claims that they are merely following God's command to love their neighbors, which trumps the few — and inconclusive — biblical statements on homosexuality. Conservatives respond that Scripture clearly condemns deviant sexual acts, and that they love their neighbors by warning them to stop their self-destructive behavior.

While I believe that conservatives have the better argument, we can still learn much from conversations with groups like Soulforce. We may never agree on the rightness or wrongness of homosexuality, but we can find some common ground on how we respond to those who consider it part of their identity. I will explore this common ground right after I briefly present a defensibly biblical view on homosexuality.

NOT THAT THERE'S ANYTHING WRONG WITH THAT

It is hard to ignore Scripture's statements against homosexuality. Despite numerous attempts to explain away the biblical evidence, it seems obvious to most readers that the Bible says that homosexual acts are sin.[2]

1. *Genesis 1–2*. Creation reveals that God prefers heterosexual marriage. Although I detest the derisive spirit in which it is often said, it seems significant that the first couple was "Adam and Eve" rather than "Adam and Steve." Only men and women are physically able to comply with God's plan to unite and "become one flesh."[3]

Even those who do not believe the Bible must still confront biology. It is surprising when a cultural leader such as Jon Stewart says — in a serious interview — that gay marriage is "the natural progression of the human condition."[4] If two men or two women having sex is natural, wouldn't nature have given them complementary sexual equipment?

The natural pairing of male with female is why hardware stores sell pipes with male and female ends. You would not want to live in a house where a plumber mixed and matched pipes on the theory that every linkage was as natural as any other. At least I'd recommend not turning on the water! As with plumbing so with sex — the burden of proof lies with those who claim that homosexuality is natural. They must provide an argument — merely repeating their claim that it is natural doesn't make it so.

2. *Leviticus 18:22; 20:13.* If homosexuality does not appear in Scripture's story of Creation, then we would expect it to be part of the Fall. And that is what we find. Leviticus 18 lays out a long list of unlawful sexual acts. God told the Israelites not to have sex with their mother, sister, aunt, daughter-in-law, sister-in-law, animal, close relative, or person of the same gender ("Do not lie with a man as one lies with a woman; that is detestable").[5] Defenders of homosexuality claim that these sexual rules belong to the Old Testament's holiness code, which though relevant to ancient Israel, no longer applies to Christians who today live under grace. Just because Israel was told to abstain from homosexual acts does not mean that we should.[6]

This is a good point. Leviticus by itself does not make a slam-dunk case against homosexual practice. Yet it seems suspiciously selective to argue that it is morally acceptable today for men to have sex with men but not with the other sexual partners listed. While some locales allegedly tolerate having sex with one's cousin, most people think it is still morally wrong to have sex with one's mother, sister, aunt, or close relative. If these sexual partners are still impermissible, why should we think that homosexuality alone has changed?[7]

At the very least, even defenders of homosexuality must admit that this act appears in a bad neighborhood, in a list of deviant sexual partners that God calls detestable. God closes this list with a warning: "Do not defile yourselves in any of these ways, because this is how the nations that I am going to drive out before you became defiled. Even the land was defiled; so I punished it for its sin, and the land vomited out its inhabitants."[8] God does not seem fond of homosexual behavior.

3. *First Corinthians 6:9.* Paul includes "male prostitutes" and "homosexual offenders" in a list of wicked people who will not "inherit the kingdom of God." He seems to base his claim on Leviticus 18:22 and 20:13, for his Greek term for "homosexual offenders" comes from a word found in the Septuagint translation of these passages. Paul's term is *arsenokoitai*, which translated as "perverts" in 1 Timothy 1:10, literally means "male bedder" or "men lying with males." The word for "male prostitutes" is *malakoi*, which means

soft or effeminate men. Taken together, these two terms denote both the male aggressor (*arsenokos*) and the passive, effeminate partner (*malakos*) in the homosexual relationship.[9]

While most readers believe that Paul is condemning all homosexual activity, defenders of homosexuality say that Paul's words must be understood in their historical context. Most homosexual behavior in Paul's world occurred in pagan temples where adult men had sex with underage, soft-skinned boys who played the role of women. So when Paul writes against homosexuality, he is actually opposing pedophilia. We cannot say for sure what Paul would say about homosexual behavior among consenting — and especially committed — adults, for this type of homosexuality did not exist in his day.[10]

This theory raises several questions: Is it likely that Paul was unaware of homosexual activity among consenting adults?[11] Given his allusion to Leviticus 18 and 20, isn't it probable that he opposed both the pedophilia and homosexual elements of temple prostitution? And most important, doesn't Paul clearly condemn adult homosexual behavior in Romans 1?

4. *Romans 1:26 – 27.* This is the clearest denunciation of homosexual practice in Scripture, for not only does it appear in the New Testament, but also it plainly involves sexual activity among adults. Paul declares that God reveals his wrath against sinners who "suppress the truth by their wickedness" and have "exchanged the truth of God for a lie."[12] God's wrath here is passive, as it amounts to allowing sinners to sink more deeply into their sin. First God "gave them over ... to sexual impurity," and then he "gave them over to shameful lusts. Even their women exchanged natural relations for unnatural ones. In the same way the men also abandoned natural relations with women and were inflamed with lust for one another. Men committed indecent acts with other men, and received in themselves the due penalty for their perversion."[13]

Despite Paul's powerfully direct language, defenders of homosexuality offer two arguments to reconcile these words with a gay lifestyle. Some suggest that the unnatural sexual relations may not have anything to do with homosexuality. Perhaps women were assuming the dominant position during intercourse or engaging in nonprocreative oral or anal sex with their male partners.[14]

Recognizing that this is unlikely, defenders move on to their main argument that homosexuality today differs from what Paul knew. Paul says that people fell into sin when they abandoned God and pursued their undisciplined sexual urges. But this differs from today's Christian homosexual, who has not abandoned God and seeks to express his sexuality in committed, monogamous marriage. Paul says that the homosexuals he knows have changed their sexual preference, choosing to exchange "natural relations [heterosexual] for unnatural ones [homosexual]." But this differs from today's homosexual, who often is born with a homosexual orientation. He did not choose to and cannot stop being this way, and so he does not fall under God's condemnation.[15] Perhaps if Paul had known more about sexual orientation, how one's genetic, social, and psychological makeup form homosexual tendencies, he would have written more graciously about them here.[16]

This new interpretation of Romans 1:26 – 27, while hypothetically possible, seems to reflect the homosexual sympathies of the reader more than the text. The traditional view would respond that if homosexual acts are sin, then anyone who practices them has by definition and to that extent abandoned God. Paul does not say that the homosexuals he knows have changed *their* sexual preference, but that their homosexual acts go against God's natural order.[17] Thus, those born with a homosexual orientation are not off the hook.

Perhaps Paul does not distinguish between ways one becomes a homosexual (whether through birth or later choice) or between homosexual acts (whether between consenting adults or men with boys), not because he was unaware of such distinctions, but because he did not think they mattered.[18] He simply denounces all forms of homosexual practice as an element of the wrath of God.

Proponents of homosexuality are good at raising questions — Could this verse mean this or that passage mean that? — but ultimately a view must do more than suggest provocative new readings. Especially when a position seeks to overturn two thousand years of church tradition, it needs more proof and less "anything is possible." Since we lack compelling arguments to the contrary, it seems prudent to side with the normal, historical way the church has read these biblical texts. Heterosexual marriage is God's design. Sex with anyone else is sin.[19]

POLITICALLY INCORRECT

This traditional interpretation of the Bible seems laughably absurd to contemporary culture, where Scripture's opposition to homosexual practice is often taken as seriously as its old covenant rules about diet and disobedience. If we no longer avoid shellfish or stone adulterers, then why should we follow its prohibition against homosexual acts? Wake up and join the modern world.

Even Christians who believe that homosexual practice is a consequence of the Fall are tempted to find reasons to tolerate it. Lewis Smedes writes that "homosexuality is a burden that some of God's children are called on to bear, an anomaly, nature gone awry." Rather than oppose all homosexual acts, Smedes argues that we must "improvise on nature's lapses," permitting homosexuals to marry and remain in the church, for in their brokenness they "are fulfilling their God-given human need in the only way available to them, not what the Creator originally intended for his children, but the only way they have."[20]

I agree with Smedes that homosexuality is part of the brokenness of the Fall and no worse than many other sins.[21] But rather than act out our brokenness, declaring that we must be true to ourselves, which cannot change, why not offer our brokenness to God?

Supporters of gay marriage seem to accept the modern idea that self-fulfillment is our natural right. Every modern romance, like *Romeo and Juliet* and *West Side Story*, rests on the premise that individuals have the right to reject any outside authority, such as family or cultural norms, that stifles their romantic destiny. America was founded on the idea that all people have the "inalienable rights" to "life, liberty, and the pursuit of happiness." If we find happiness in homosexual relationships, who can say we are wrong?

But what if our highest allegiance is to God rather than ourselves? Then we will choose to live out our broken condition within the confines of God's will. We will choose to be celibate. This sounds harsh, especially given society's expectation that everyone except the chess club will lose their virginity in high school, but it is not impossible. And it is right. Scripture does not deny homosexuals the opportunity to enjoy intimate friendships, only the right to engage in homosexual acts.

Brian McLaren compassionately questions whether this perspective is helpful in exceptionally difficult cases. His fictional story includes Pat, an intersexual who was born with male and female sexual organs. She felt ostracized and condemned by Christians, many of whom thought her sexual confusion was caused by either disease or disobedience. She said that the Christian mantra to "love the sinner but hate the sin" struck her "as ghastly and cruel — as if what we are is a sin."[22] What would our traditional view say to her?

First, I would ask Pat's forgiveness for the ignorant bigotry she endured from the church, and I would weep with her for her sexual brokenness. But I would remember that her case is the exception, not the rule.[23] Her situation calls for humility and prayer, but it does not change God's ideal. We follow God's revealed will in normal situations and humbly pray for guidance and forgiveness for those few cases that are less clear.

Second, I would add that Pat must stop finding her identity in the Fall. Practicing homosexuals are one of the few groups who take their sin personally. Bill Clinton and Newt Gingrich do not object when someone says adultery is sin; shoplifters do not cry, "You hate me!" when police stop them from stealing; but homosexuals often argue that those who oppose their sexual activity are rejecting them.[24]

Third, I would remind Pat that her identity is defined by Creation rather than the Fall. She is primarily and essentially the image of God. She is only secondarily and accidentally a (potential) sexual transgressor. I would tell Pat that Jesus loves her exactly as she is, and that he loves her too much to let her stay this way.[25]

This concludes my brief case for the traditional view on homosexual practice. Given that I believe homosexual acts are always sin, what common ground is possible with its defenders? A surprisingly high amount.

PERSONAL VS. PUBLIC SIN

Jerry Falwell died in May 2007. By all accounts a gracious and generous man, he was unfortunately remembered by the media as an outspoken critic of homosexuals. Falwell belonged to a generation of conservative Christians who preached that AIDS was God's judgment on homosexuals. He blamed them for the terrorist attacks on 9/11 and outed a children's character named Tinky Winky, the purse-toting purple Teletubby who turned out not to be gay, just British.

Falwell established the Moral Majority, a political organization that emphasized private morality by supporting laws that discouraged such personal sins as homosexuality, pornography, abortion, euthanasia, and not praying in school. But Falwell's conservative generation was strangely silent on some of the larger issues of public compassion, such as racism, poverty, and caring for those with AIDS. I have heard thousands of sermons in theologically conservative churches, and not one has addressed any of these topics.

These issues are discussed frequently in liberal churches. In his classic 1917 lectures, *A Theology for the Social Gospel*, the liberal theologian Walter Rauschenbusch argued that social ethics, such as how to act virtuously in a greedy, materialistic economy, is more important than the conservative fixation on avoiding "drinking, dancing, card playing, and going to the movies."[26] Such petty peccadilloes pale before our larger obligation to love our neighbor as ourselves.

While the distinction between private and public morality must not be pressed too far — for example, abortion is both private because it occurs within a woman's body and also public because it destroys another human — yet the distinction does explain a significant difference between liberal and conservative Christians. Tell me what sins you confess, and I will tell you where you fall on the Christian spectrum. If you ask forgiveness for skipping daily Bible reading and prayer, you are probably a conservative. If you repent of your silent complicity with the systemic racism and regressive tax code of your community — or even know what this means! — you are likely a liberal.

As we have already seen, liberals and conservatives tend to push each other to opposite extremes (see fig. 5.1). Liberals avoid issues of private morality in part because they do not want to seem conservative. So they emphasize personal freedom, declaring that individuals may do whatever they want with whomever they want so long as they do not hurt others. When things go wrong, they blame the larger structures of society, such as failing schools, blighted neighborhoods, and unaffordable health care.

Conservatives avoid issues of public compassion in part because they fear being associated with the "social gospel" of liberalism. They emphasize personal responsibility, declaring that undisciplined freedom is the root of all evil. When things go wrong, they blame personal vices, such as sexual promiscuity, drug addiction, and absentee parenting.

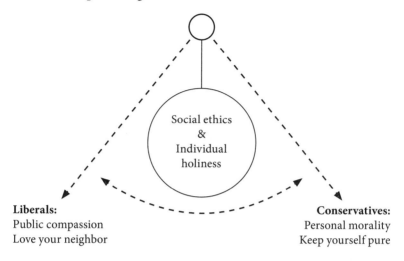

Liberals:
Public compassion
Love your neighbor

Conservatives:
Personal morality
Keep yourself pure

Fig. 5.1. Public and Private Morality

But why must we choose between the liberal and conservative agenda? God cares about both personal morality and public compassion. His prophet Isaiah castigates Judah for their social injustice. They will be carried into captivity for "grinding the faces of the poor" and choosing to "make unjust laws ... issue oppressive decrees ... deprive the poor of their rights and withhold justice from the oppressed ... making widows their prey and robbing the fatherless."[27] Yet when Isaiah received a vision of God in his holy temple, the sin he felt was both personal and corporate. "I am ruined!" Isaiah cried, "For I am a man of unclean lips, and I live among a people of unclean lips."[28]

Likewise, Jesus taught the importance of personal holiness, warning his followers to stamp out unrighteous anger and lust and to pray and fast in secret.[29] Yet he said that our destiny is determined by our acts of public compassion. Everlasting life is taken from the Pharisees for oppressing their followers and given to those who, like the Good Samaritan and the sheep on Jesus' right, do good to their neighbor in need.[30]

The apostle Paul also argued for both public compassion and private morality. He challenged the church in Rome to love their neighbors, for "love is the fulfillment of the law." Then he turned to what many today would leave to personal freedom, ordering the Roman Christians not to participate in "orgies and drunkenness ... sexual immorality and debauchery ... dissension and jealousy."[31]

Applied to homosexuality, these Scriptures suggest that Christians should be as vocal about the human rights of homosexuals as we are about their sin. We may never concede the morality of homosexual marriage, but we should adamantly defend their right to live, work, and prosper among us. We should speak up when homosexuals are denied health insurance and weep when they are the target of hate crimes. Being gay is not an excuse for abuse.

One of Jerry Falwell's close associates left Lynchburg in 1987 to pastor a church in Grand Rapids. Ed Dobson decided that his church would balance their conviction that homosexual acts are wrong with compassion for those suffering from its effects. So he called an AIDS hotline, which put him in contact with the pastor of a pro-homosexual church in his community. Dobson told the pastor that while they never would agree on the morality of homosexual practice, they could agree to work together to help those who were struggling with AIDS.

Dobson's compassion soon earned the respect of the homosexual community. One gay radio talk show host introduced him by saying, "Our guest does not believe what we believe on issues of sexuality. But I've invited him to appear because there are many people suffering with AIDS who attend his Saturday night services. While his congregation disagrees with us on sexuality issues, they love people and stand with us on the AIDS issue."

Dobson's greatest criticism came from his congregation, many of whom feared that their church would be overrun with homosexuals. Dobson replied that "that will be terrific. They can take their place in the pews right next to the liars, gossips, materialists, and all the rest of us who entertain sin in our lives." He added, "When I die, if someone stands up and says, 'Ed Dobson loved homosexuals,' then I will have accomplished something with my life."[32]

Dobson's ministry is evidence that we need not compromise our moral code to reach out to those who have violated it. Homosexuals are guilty of illicit sex. We often are guilty of not caring about them or their plight. Our sin is greater, and it isn't even close.

Whatever our sin, both conservative Christians and postmodern innovators agree that it is taken care of by the cross of Christ. But they disagree how. Is the conservative interpretation of the cross a beautiful expression of love, or is it a despicable case of divine child abuse? This important question is the subject of our next chapter.

CHAPTER 6

IS THE CROSS
DIVINE CHILD ABUSE?

I grew up with a simple, straightforward understanding of the gospel. I believed that I was a sinner who could never do enough good to compensate for my disobedience and satisfy the wrath of a holy God. Fortunately, I didn't have to. God sent his perfect Son to die on the cross for my sin. Jesus bore my penalty and was punished in my place. If I merely accepted his gift, God would mark my account "paid in full" and grant me everlasting life.

Nearly all conservative Christians agree that this is precisely how sinners are saved. Our favorite illustrations — two cliffs bridged by a cross, or a judge who passes sentence upon himself — explain that the Son of God suffered the consequences of our sin so that we can be reconciled to God. Our favorite songs make the same point: "What can wash away my sin? Nothing but the blood of Jesus.... For my pardon this I see, nothing but the blood of Jesus."[1] Or "Because the sinless Savior died, my sinful soul is counted free; for God the just is satisfied to look on Him and pardon me."[2]

What most Christians don't realize is that this view is only one of several perspectives on the gospel. Theologians call this the "penal substitution" view of the atonement, because it explains that Christ reconciles us to God (atonement) by bearing our penalty (penal) in our place (substitution).

This way of understanding the cross enjoys broad biblical support, from the Old Testament sacrificial system, where spotless lambs were killed instead of sinners, to Paul's repeated statements that Jesus bore our penalty when he died in our place.[3] Paul wrote that "God presented [Christ] as a sacrifice of atonement, through faith in his blood," that "Christ redeemed us from the curse of the law by becoming a curse for us," and that "God made him who had no sin to be sin for us, so that in him we might become the righteousness of God."[4]

Despite being rooted in Scripture, the notion that Jesus died as our substitute to satisfy God did not become the dominant view of the atonement until the eleventh century. Let that sink in. What many Christians think is the only way to interpret the cross did not become popular until the Middle Ages. Then Anselm declared that the Son of God became human to repay the honor that our disobedience had stolen from God. Since humans must pay but only God could, the only person who could make the sacrifice was the God-man, Jesus Christ.[5]

When Anselm's idea of satisfaction entered the modern world, his feudal concept of stolen honor morphed into the legal penalty of our criminal justice system. Calvin said that Jesus' trial before Pilate mirrored the courtroom of heaven. Just as the frenzied mob yelled that Jesus was guilty and deserved to die on the cross, so the Father transferred our guilt to Jesus and condemned him to die in our place.[6]

This penal substitution view so dominates today that most Christians think that anyone who questions it is denying the gospel. Yet many postmodern innovators are doing just that. Some of their criticisms are helpful, while others are not. Let's start with what we can learn from them before moving on to where we must push back.[7]

PROBLEMS WITH PENAL SUBSTITUTION

1. Too Limited

Critics of penal substitution rightly observe that it alone is unable to capture the multifaceted power of the cross.[8] Jesus' life, death, and resurrection not only appease God but also bear immediate consequences for Satan and ourselves. For these we must turn to other theories of the atonement (see fig. 6.1).

The early church emphasized the effects of the cross on Satan. Their "Christus Victor" view taught that Jesus came to defeat the Devil, who had become the ruler of humanity and their world when he led Adam and Eve to switch their allegiance to him. When Satan discovered that he could not tempt Jesus into changing alliances, he derisively killed him as he had destroyed every other person under his power. But Satan's victory became his defeat. Too late he learned that he had played into God's hands. By killing Jesus he had unwittingly brought life to the world.[9]

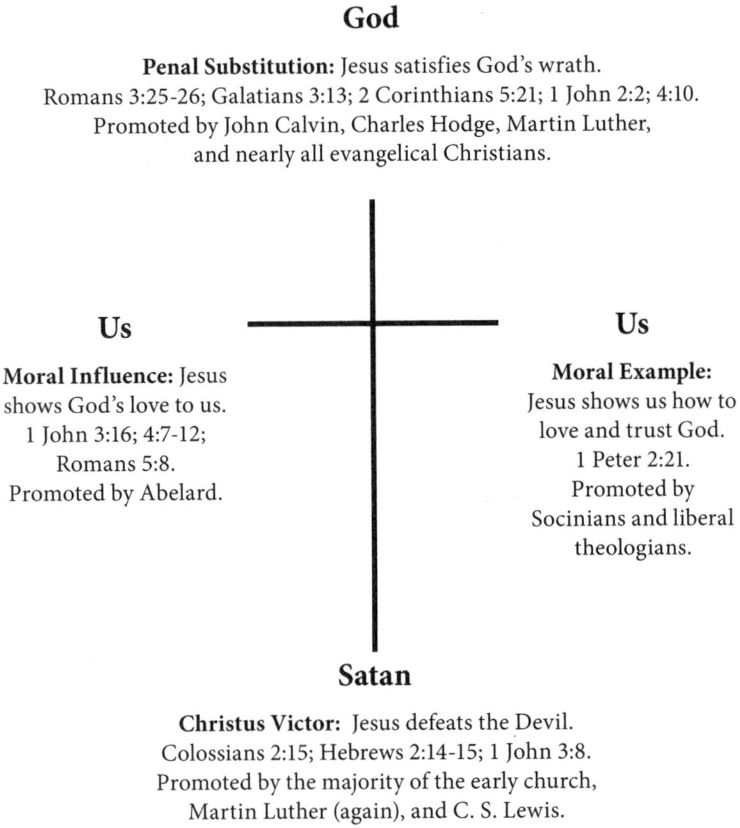

God

Penal Substitution: Jesus satisfies God's wrath.
Romans 3:25-26; Galatians 3:13; 2 Corinthians 5:21; 1 John 2:2; 4:10.
Promoted by John Calvin, Charles Hodge, Martin Luther,
and nearly all evangelical Christians.

Us

Moral Influence: Jesus
shows God's love to us.
1 John 3:16; 4:7-12;
Romans 5:8.
Promoted by Abelard.

Us

Moral Example:
Jesus shows us how to
love and trust God.
1 Peter 2:21.
Promoted by
Socinians and liberal
theologians.

Satan

Christus Victor: Jesus defeats the Devil.
Colossians 2:15; Hebrews 2:14-15; 1 John 3:8.
Promoted by the majority of the early church,
Martin Luther (again), and C. S. Lewis.

Fig. 6.1. Who Is the Target of the Cross?

Supporters of Christus Victor vary on precisely how the cross defeated Satan. Did Satan overstep his bounds by killing the God-man? Did Satan accept Christ's death as a ransom for the rest of humanity? Or as C. S. Lewis suggests, did Jesus' sacrifice of love accomplish a "deeper magic" that destroyed Satan's lawful power over us?[10] I will explain at the end of this chapter why this hole in Christus Victor is best filled by the penal substitution view, but for now note how Christus Victor adds an essential piece to our understanding of the atonement. Whatever else Christ accomplished, his main goal was to deliver us from the Devil and death.[11]

Other theologians tend to ignore the consequences of the cross on God and Satan and instead focus on its effects on us. The medieval theologian Abelard taught that the cross is God's way of showing how much he loves us, which in turn should motivate us to love him back.[12] Liberal theologians work from the opposite direction. Because they deny the deity of Christ, they do not believe the cross is God acting upon us. Rather, it is merely the act of a human Jesus who models how we should love and trust God even in our darkest hour.

While this subjective focus has biblical support — John writes that the cross is the ultimate demonstration of love, and Peter adds that Jesus has left "an example, that you should follow in his steps" — it is a mistake to make ourselves the primary object of the cross.[13] Those who do so create a gooey gospel that doesn't make much sense. In *Jesus: The Epic Mini-Series*, Jesus declares that he is going to the cross to "die for the everlasting kindness of the human heart, created by the Father, so that men will make his image shine once again, and those who will want to will find in me the strength to love until the end."[14]

Say what? If Jesus died merely to teach us how to love, then he is more foolish than kind. A man who gives his life to rescue a drowning child is a hero. A man who jumps into the swirling current when his child is dry and standing on the riverbank is an idiot, no matter how loudly he yells, "I love you," as he leaps. Likewise, the cross is only an act of love if it solves a real problem. We love God because he first loved us, defeating the Devil and death and satisfying the Father's wrath.[15] Since the cross's effect on us is a consequence of its effect on God and Satan, I consider the moral influence and example views to be second-tier atonement theories.

Nevertheless, our point here is that the atonement is larger than any one perspective can grasp. Limiting ourselves to only one theory is like watching a televised football game shot with a single camera. If mounted high enough, one camera may convey the gist of the action, but it will miss many important details on the field. Just as the NFL uses overlapping camera angles to capture every play from multiple perspectives, so we must view the cross of Christ from above (penal substitution), below (Christus Victor), and to a lesser extent, sideways (moral influence and example).[16]

2. Too Individualistic

Penal substitution is limited not only in its target (God) but also in its application. Gospel presentations from this perspective tend to limit salvation to the individual: Jesus died to forgive your sin. True enough, but didn't Jesus die for more than individual persons?[17]

What about the church? Jesus is not merely saving a smattering of isolated souls, but is building his church — an integrated community reconciled to God and each other. But since the gospel message they responded to focuses solely on them, many Christians think that the church exists only for their benefit. They attend church to hear an uplifting sermon, to be inspired by worship, to network with friends, or to educate their children. There is no need to join, or even keep going, if they can find similar help from other sources. And so the church moves to the edges of salvation. It is considered nice, but certainly not necessary, for the life of a growing Christian.

And what about creation? The individualized gospel of personal salvation scarcely hints at God's broader plan to restore his entire creation. Just as individual Christians find meaning by belonging to the church, so the church fulfills its mission by being the kingdom of God in the world. In the conclusion of this chapter, I will explain how this weakness in penal substitution — at least as it is commonly understood — may be shored up with insights from Christus Victor.

3. Too Soft on Sin

Penal substitution also is accused, with some merit, of being soft on sin. It emphasizes that the penalty of our sin is removed but says little about the sin itself. Most people figure out early in their Christian career that if God forgives them no matter what they do, then it does not really matter what they do. They might as well sin because their punishment is already covered.[18]

Martin Luther encountered this problem in Wittenberg. Once his congregation realized that Luther's gospel promised forgiveness for any and all sin, they stopped attending services and giving to the ministry and started indulging in greed, lust, and booze. A frustrated Luther threatened to go on strike if they did not change their ways. He declared, "You absolutely unthankful beasts, unworthy of the gospel; if you do not repent I will stop preaching to you." They did not and so he did, taking several months off from being "the shepherd of such pigs."[19]

Luther's irritation with his congregation continued throughout his life. One year before his death, he decided that he would not return to his sinful city and instructed his wife to sell their house. He declared that he would rather "eat the bread of a beggar than torture and upset my poor old age and final days with the filth at Wittenberg." Only an intervention by Luther's friends and his Wittenberg prince convinced him to return.[20] Again, I will explain at the end of this chapter how this weakness in penal substitution is fixed when combined with a corresponding strength in the Christus Victor view.

WORST PARENT EVER?

The most controversial objection to penal substitution, first stated by feminist and liberation theologians but now repeated in evangelical circles, is that this view of the atonement turns the cross into a form of divine child abuse.[21]

Steve Chalke suggests that penal substitution turns God into

> a vengeful Father, punishing his Son for an offence he has not even committed. Understandably, both people inside and outside of the Church have found this twisted version of events morally dubious and a huge barrier to faith. Deeper than that, however, is that such a concept stands in total contradiction to the statement "God is love." If the cross is a personal act of violence perpetrated by God towards humankind but borne by his Son, then it makes a mockery of Jesus' own teaching to love your enemies and to refuse to repay evil with evil.[22]

There seem to be two parts to this objection. First, why does a loving God require a sacrifice in order to forgive? Why does he demand "a kill" to satisfy his wrath? If God commands us to forgive without strings attached, then why doesn't he? Is our forgiveness more magnanimous than God's?[23]

LeRon Shults wonders whether God's demand to be paid undercuts the very idea of forgiveness. Just as a bank that forgives a bad loan does not ask to be paid back, so a God who truly forgives should not expect satisfaction. Shults writes: "If God arranged for the debt of humans to be fully paid (satisfied), then in what sense should we call this forgiveness? If a legal penalty or financial debt is forgiven, then it does *not* have to be satisfied. If God (or God the Son) has in fact already paid the debt (made full satisfaction), then there is no need anymore for God to forgive. If a payment is made, should we not speak of 'settlement' rather than forgiveness?"[24]

Second, not only does God demand blood — which sounds uncomfortably close to the ritual sacrifice of pagan religions — but he selects his perfect Son as the victim. What kind of despicable father would violate his innocent son for the sake of sinful outsiders? Like a high school coach who demands that his honor roll child trade test scores with his star quarterback, or a mafia don who orders his son to take the fall for his henchman's crime, so God's sacrifice of his Son seems to add to the injustice of his unwillingness to forgive.

Brian McLaren summarizes both questions: "If God was going to forgive us, why didn't he just forgive us? Why did Jesus have to die so that we could be forgiven? Having an innocent person die for guilty people did not seem to solve the 'injustice' of forgiveness — it only seemed to add to the injustice. So, why did Jesus have to die?"[25]

LOVE HURTS

Let's address these questions in reverse order. The question of divine child abuse mistakenly divides the unity of God into a vengeful Father who exploits his trusting, obedient Son. But Father and Son cannot be so easily divided. God is one. God offered himself on the cross, not some other, third party.[26] A proper understanding of the Trinity — God is both three and one — will prevent us from playing one person of the Godhead against another.

Even if we emphasize the distinction between the persons, any parent knows that the cross was much harder on the Father than the Son. What earthly father would not eagerly take the bullet to save his child from unnecessary suffering? And do we really think that our heavenly Father is any different? How excruciating to watch his beloved Son sweat blood in Gethsemane, to hear his bewildered cry, "Why have you forsaken me?" all the while knowing that, like father Abraham toward Isaac, it was he who held the knife!

This brings us to the fundamental issue: why does God demand payment for our sin? Why doesn't he simply forgive without strings attached?

The answer lies in the triune nature of God. We learned in chapter 3 that God is a community of self-giving lovers. This self-giving love is the definition of righteousness. Righteousness has never been about keeping rules, which is why Jesus did not think twice about healing on the Sabbath and why both he and Paul say that the purpose of the law is to show us how to love God and neighbor.[27] In the triune community of self-giving lovers, right is whatever promotes the other and wrong is whatever hurts the other. And because each divine person loves the other, they flourish and thrive. Nothing is more alive than this righteous community of love.

If self-giving love is righteousness that leads to life, then its opposite must be selfishness, which is sin that leads to death. This is a necessary fact, given the living, loving, and righteous character of God. God is not free to create a world in which sin causes no damage, where fallen creatures carry on without consequence. Sin cuts against the nature of God and any possible world that he could make. It inevitably and necessarily brings death (see fig. 6.2).[28]

| Self-giving Love | ⟶ | Righteousness | ⟶ | Life |
| Selfishness | ⟶ | Sin | ⟶ | Death |

Fig. 6.2. Two Paths to Two Destinies

God would violate himself if he ignored our sin that has poisoned his world. Reality would rupture if God turned a blind eye, pretended it didn't happen, or forgave without consequences. Sin must receive its due, and its payment is death. We know that God believes this, for when Jesus asked the Father if there was any other way to save us than the cross, he received a resounding no.[29]

But God himself stepped forward and paid the price, freeing us to forgive others without demanding payment in return. When we forgive without strings attached, we are merely passing on God's forgiveness, which cost his life. Since the only reason we can forgive without penalty is because God already has paid it for us, those who criticize God for being less magnanimous than them completely miss the point of the cross.

They forget that forgiveness requires satisfaction. While a legal or financial debt may not be satisfied by the person who is forgiven, it will be borne by someone. Someone always pays, whether it is the crime victim who absorbs injustice or the bank's shareholders who write off the bad loan. There is no free lunch, either in economics or salvation.

One troubling question remains: this talk of sacrifice and death assumes that God has a fair amount of wrath that needs satisfied. Is God equal parts wrath and love, and if so, doesn't his wrath make him less loving?

Scripture says that God *is* love and that he *has* wrath.[30] This means that love lies deeper than wrath in the character of God. Love is his essential perfection, without which he would not be who he is. Wrath is love's response to sin. It is God's involuntary gag reflex at anything that destroys his good creation. God is against sin because he is for us, and he will vent his fury on everything that damages us.

My children were graffiti artists. They wrote on our walls, our table, and even our new couch. Their budding artwork inspired a bit of wrath in me. Often it was because I liked my furniture, but in my better moments it was because I loved them too much to let them continue down the slippery slope from destructive toddlers to god-less graffiti nihilists. So I intervened, placing their tiny fingers in a soapy rag and gently compelling them to scrub until the wall came clean. The experience was painful for me and for them — especially them — but after a couple of times, they got the point and used their crayons only in their coloring books.

Likewise, God loves us too much to sweep our sin under the rug. He refuses to pretend that it is unimportant, for he knows that left unchecked it will turn us into people that neither he nor we want us to be. So God includes wrath as a vital piece of his salvation. A popular misunderstanding of penal substitution oversimplifies what happened on the cross. Many conservative Christians seem to separate God's love from his wrath, declaring that God poured his wrath on Jesus so we could go free. We receive grace and Jesus receives judgment. This is true as far as it goes, but closer inspection reveals a deeper reality. God's love and wrath are not so easily separated, and both Jesus and we receive a fair amount of each.

Jesus endured God's wrath when he bore the curse of sin, but he also experienced God's love, for the cross was a necessary step in crowning Jesus as Redeemer and Ruler of the world, the Lord whose exalted name forces every knee to the ground.[31] Similarly, though we receive unmerited grace from Jesus' passion, our old self of sin must die in order to rise to his new life of love. Eleven times in Romans 6:1 – 14 Paul declares that we have died with Christ. He states that "We were therefore buried with him through baptism into death in order that, just as Christ was raised from the dead through the glory of the Father, we too may live a new life."[32]

Karl Barth explains: "That Jesus Christ died for us does not mean, therefore, that we do not have to die, but that we have died in and with Him, that as the people we were we have been done away and destroyed, that we are no longer there and have no more future." Again, the cross means that "our hour has struck, our time has run its course, and it is all up with us."[33]

It is a mistake to separate God's love from his wrath and then assign his wrath to Jesus and charge God with divine child abuse. Every act of God flows from his love, even — and especially — those that demonstrate his wrath. This reconciliation of divine love and wrath is best explained by the penal substitution view, which makes it an essential perspective on what happened at the cross.

FULL ATONEMENT, CAN IT BE?

But penal substitution does not explain everything. A more complete understanding of the atonement combines the penal substitution perspective with Christus Victor. Many modern conservatives follow an oversimplified version of penal substitution: Jesus suffered the wrath of God so we could receive his love. Postmodern innovators rightly raise questions about this tidy gospel. Perhaps salvation is less like a business transaction — Jesus purchases our life with his death — and more like a cosmic battle between God and Satan. Maybe it is Satan rather than God who demands Christ's life. In that case the only wrath in the story belongs to Satan, and God is simply our loving rescuer from the Devil and death (see fig. 6.3).

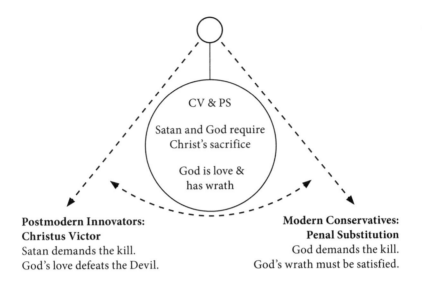

Fig. 6.3. Evangelical Perspectives on the Atonement

As we have seen in previous chapters, the best solution often is not to select one view or the other but to combine the insights of both. Christus Victor presents the big picture—Jesus came to wrest the world from the death grip of Satan, while penal substitution supplies the turning point of this story. Penal substitution is the heart of Christus Victor, for it explains how Jesus accomplished his mission.[34]

Here is one way to tell the story. Satan became the functional ruler of this world when he tempted Adam and Eve, God's appointed rulers of creation, to switch their allegiance to him. But God refused to let his world slip away that easily, and he promised Satan that one of Eve's children would someday crush his head.[35]

The early rounds went to Satan. God tried to establish a beachhead for his kingdom in this world, but his chosen nation Israel repeatedly rejected God and was taken into captivity—both literally and spiritually—by Satan and his evil empires. So God personally got involved, sending his divine Son into battle. This was the climactic campaign: God and Satan going all in, each taking his best shot for the control of creation.

Jesus won the initial skirmish. Three times Satan tempted him to switch sides — the last time offering to give back the world if Jesus merely tipped his hat and acknowledged that Satan was its rightful ruler. But Jesus knew that he would have to take back the world the right way — the hard way — or he would not take it back at all.[36]

Inspired by his initial victory, Jesus spent the next three years thoroughly thrashing Satan. He established the kingdom of God throughout Israel, proclaiming the good news of salvation and performing miracles that delivered the oppressed from Satan's power. The advance of his kingdom led Jesus to confidently proclaim that he had seen "Satan fall like lightning from heaven," for "now the prince of this world will be driven out."[37]

Satan's complete annihilation seemed inevitable. He wasn't merely losing contests; he wasn't even competitive. Soon he and his minions would be swept into the dustbin of history. But Satan had one last card to play. He had found someone on the inside, one of Jesus' most trusted disciples, who might be turned against his Lord. With his help Satan might be able to get Jesus before the religious establishment, whose jealous rage had reached fever pitch; the rulers of Rome, who feared another uprising in Judea; and the fickle crowd, whose interest in Jesus might be stoked into a mob frenzy if convinced that his presence threatened to bring down the hammer of Rome.

This evil brew exceeded Satan's expectations. He pulled the greatest comeback in human history, overturning three years of defeat in one very dark day. In less than twenty-four hours, he had Jesus arrested, tried, and executed. Game over. Satan had solidified his hold on the planet, and it had been surprisingly easy.

Too easy. In the ultimate plot twist, Jesus' defeat turned out to be his climactic victory, for by his death he defeated death. The cross satisfied the divine requirement that sinners must die (this is the insight of penal substitution), and Christ's resurrection freed him and us from the grip of sin and death. This one-two punch blindsided Satan's victory parade. He never saw it coming.

This is a beautiful aspect of the Christus Victor story. God did not conquer Satan in some heavy-handed way, using his omnipotent strength to slap him down. God beat Satan on a level playing field. He became a creature, vulnerable to Satan's attacks, and defeated the Devil through weakness rather than shock and awe. In this way he did not so much overpower Satan as he outwitted him. He showed Satan and his demons to be fools, for "having disarmed the powers and authorities, he made a public spectacle of them, triumphing over them by the cross."[38]

Satan should have known better. He knew that loving sacrifice — setting aside one's own interests for the sake of the other — defines the communal life of the triune God. He also knew that it sets the standard for creation — that in God's world right is whatever loves the other and wrong is whatever hurts the other. So it should not have been a surprise that loving sacrifice would also supply God's means of redemption. Jesus' death on the cross was not an unusual, out of character act for God. The same sacrificial love that existed before the world, the same love that created the world, was now saving the world.

As this story illustrates, we need both penal substitution and Christus Victor to properly understand Christ's atonement. Penal substitution explains the heart of Christus Victor — how exactly Christ defeats the Devil, and Christus Victor supplies the larger context for penal substitution.

Christus Victor informs us that salvation aims not merely at individuals but is for the entire world. God intends through Jesus "to reconcile to himself all things, whether things on earth or things in heaven, by making peace through his blood, shed on the cross."[39] Our personal salvation is part of something larger than ourselves. We belong to the church, the body of Christ that extends the kingdom of God in the world.

Christus Victor also corrects the tendency of penal substitution to go soft on sin. By itself penal substitution may encourage a sinful lifestyle, for who cares if sin is present so long as its penalty is removed? But Christus Victor reminds us that deliverance from the presence of sin — not just its penalty — is a vital part of the gospel. We can't easily claim to participate in Christ's victory if we remain bound to our sin. Anyone not making progress against sin should wonder whether he or she has truly joined the kingdom of God. There is no room for cheap grace here.[40]

Here is the point: conservatives have tended to reduce the work of Christ to an overly narrow gospel — say a prayer and the penalty of your sins will be forgiven. But we can enlarge this perspective without going to the other extreme and accusing penal substitution of endorsing divine child abuse. Such careless statements only discredit the speakers and alienate the conservatives they seek to help. We need all the theories — Christus Victor, penal substitution, and to a lesser degree, moral influence and example — to fully appreciate our great salvation.

This salvation plays out in and around the church. Just as modern conservatives and postmodern innovators debate different theories about how we are saved, so they disagree about when a person may belong to the church. Is the church a closed clique of converted Christians or an open community of questioning seekers? We will evaluate this controversy next.

CHAPTER 7

CAN YOU BELONG BEFORE YOU BELIEVE?

My conservative church is full of really nice people who care a lot about their non-Christian friends and family. We pray for them, look for opportunities to share our faith with them, and invite them to special meetings at church. But our efforts are spectacularly unsuccessful. Few of our friends ever "get saved" and fewer still join the church. Baptisms of new converts are as rare as happy endings in country-western songs.

Part of our problem may be that we are unintentionally uninviting. Many of us dress up to attend church — suits and ties for the guys and dresses and hose for the ladies — which probably sends the message that a visitor must pass a dress code just to get in the door. Our language may also be intimidating. We speak the inner lingo of covenants and Calvinism and sing about "raising our Ebenezers," whatever that means.

We may also be a bit overzealous on the two holidays when visitors do show up at church. We talk a lot about depravity on Christmas and Easter, hoping that something will register with our guests and convict them of their need for a Savior. But so much emphasis on sin and death can make even Easter feel like Good Friday, and so our discouraged friends stay away until Christmas, when we remind them that the reason for the season is not presents but the cross.

According to some postmodern innovators, my church's largest obstacle to faith may be that we require interested visitors to believe before they can belong. Those wanting to join our church must first testify to their faith in Christ. Wouldn't we be more welcoming, these postmodern leaders ask, if we accept people as they are, permitting them to participate in our community as a way of leading them to Christ? Rather than demand belief in Jesus at the outset, why not invite them to join our circle of friends, where they can learn firsthand about the Savior who inspires our love?

One pastor describes how his church allowed a non-Christian harpist to play during worship and a nominal Buddhist to join their drama team. Encouraged by the church's embrace, the harpist has since confessed her allegiance to Christ and the actor is considering it.[1] Other pastors are sharing the Eucharist with seekers.[2] A friend of mine related how his open-table policy helped lead one woman to Christ. Unlike at other churches, where she felt judged because non-Christians were not permitted to take the Lord's Supper, she reveled in the unconditional acceptance she found at his church and soon became a follower of Jesus.

This raises an important question that many Christians are asking: what is the proper order of believing, becoming, and belonging? In what sequence does someone join the body of Christ?[3]

BELIEVE, BELONG, BECOME?

Conservative churches typically arrange the three Bs in this order: *believe, belong,* and *become* (see fig. 7.1). *Belief* is far and away the most important of the three, and when it comes right down to it, the only one that really matters. Last week I attended the funeral of a man who had rarely if ever made time for God during his sixty years of life. But in his final days, as he put his affairs in order, he made sure to repent of his sin and "accept Jesus into his heart." On the strength of this prayer, his family and friends take comfort that his soul is now in heaven.

If he had lived longer or repented earlier — when he had some years left to offer the Lord — he may have moved on to the second step of *belonging*. He would have been told that joining a church is great for accountability, encouragement, and general growth in his Christian faith. Most committed Christians do it.

Yet given the low view of the church among many conservatives, he likely would have learned that belonging to a church is not mandatory. Many churches, especially the larger ones, have far more attendees than members. These are professing Christian families who travel to church alone, sit through the service alone, and then drive home alone. They mistakenly believe that their isolated and impersonal consumption of a worship product counts as going to church, when in fact they get no credit from God for even decades of such regular attendance. Going to church only counts when we *are* the church — when we know and belong to the people sitting beside us.

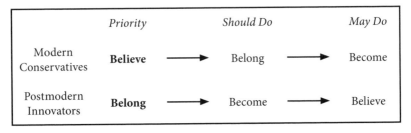

Fig. 7.1. How Do People Join the Church?

If conservatives consider belonging to be less important than believing, they deem *becoming* to be lesser still. Not that becoming doesn't matter. Conservatives worry a lot about purity, obedience, and loving our neighbor as ourselves. Their sermons regularly exhort listeners to resist temptation and do the right thing. But at the end of the day, the only thing that really counts is that we "invited Jesus into our heart" to forgive our sin. Backslidden believers may get fewer rewards than faithful followers of Christ, but they both escape hell and live forever with him. And isn't that what matters most?

Conservatives regularly remind themselves that it is possible to belong to a church and not be genuinely saved. It is even possible to become more righteous and loving and not be the real deal. But those who believe have crossed the threshold. They are inside the family of God whether or not they ever belong to a church or become holier.

BELONG, BECOME, BELIEVE?

Postmodern innovators react to this reductionism by heading in another direction. They lead with *belonging*. Rather than draw a border around our church that denies fellowship with those who believe differently, they argue that we should be missional Christians who use our Christ-centered faith to embrace rather than condemn outsiders.

Michael Frost and Alan Hirsch compare the two ways of doing church to digging a well and erecting a fence. Conservatives like fences that clearly separate those who are in from those who are out. But missional churches dig wells. They do not fret about who is on which side of the fence; they merely invite people to enjoy the life-giving water of Christ. Frost and Hirsch explain: "Rather than seeing people as Christian or non-Christian, as in or out, we would see people by their degree of distance from the center, Christ. In this way, the missional-incarnational church sees people as Christian and not-yet-Christian. It acknowledges the contribution of not-yet-Christians to Christian community and values the contribution of all people."[4]

Steve Chalke goes further, saying that how close people are to the center is not as important as which direction they are headed. There are Christians who are becoming less so and non-Christians who are becoming followers of Christ, even though they do not yet call themselves by that name. He writes, "As far as Jesus was concerned, it wasn't how close someone was to him at any given stage in their life that mattered as much as the direction in which they were traveling." A member of the inner circle like Judas could be moving in the wrong direction while a Gentile centurion, though distant from Christ, was moving toward him. Chalke explains that Jesus was interested in "the general direction in which a life was moving. And as far as he was concerned, the centurion showed great faith and was therefore a follower."[5]

Regardless how far people are from Christ and what direction they are headed, postmodern innovators want all people to feel that the church is a safe, hospitable community where they belong. One pastor says, "We provide space for people to belong before they come to believe. We build real relationships with people, regardless of the end result. We want to be able to share life with people, whether or not they choose to follow Jesus." Another declares, "We don't like rigid barriers between the ins and the outs. We will welcome everyone equally. We believe faith is a pilgrimage that we are all on."[6]

Once people belong to this community of faith, they may then embark on their journey of *becoming*. Becoming is important to postmodern innovators, especially becoming the kind of person who creates an inclusive, tolerant, and safe place for others to belong. They oppose racism, sexism, colonialism, and any other attitude that selfishly elevates ourselves above and excludes others. Brian McLaren says that since "the kingdom's purpose is to gather, to include, to welcome everyone who is willing (children, prostitutes, tax collectors) into reconciliation with God and one another," our task as citizens of the kingdom is to become people who "try to expand the borders of who is considered 'in' and worthy of dignity and respect."[7]

But much as conservatives consider becoming to be less important than believing, so postmodern innovators esteem becoming as less essential than their core value of belonging. Frost and Hirsch say that "the closer one gets to the center (Christ), the more Christlike one's behavior should become." However, "those who have just begun the journey toward Christ (and whose lives may not exhibit such traits) are still seen as 'belonging.' No one is considered unworthy of belonging because they happen to be addicted to tobacco, or because they're not married to their live-in partner. Belonging is a key value."[8]

If becoming is less important than belonging, then *believing* is even lesser still. Some postmoderns, such as Frost and Hirsch, do value right beliefs (and so differ in an important way from what I am calling postmodern innovators). They write that missional churches "must have a very clear set of beliefs, rooted in Christ and his teaching. This belief system must be nonnegotiable and strongly held by the community closest to its center."[9] But as we discovered in chapters 2 and 3, others suggest that requiring allegiance to the central doctrines of the Christian faith is unnecessary at best and unloving at worst.[10]

Unlike conservatives, who rejoice that their loved one said the sinner's prayer before he died, Spencer Burke took comfort that his dying father had enough faith not to mess with it. Burke writes, "Instead of making sure my father was 'right with God,' I found myself telling him that maybe saying any prayer or performing rites and rituals wasn't what it was all about after all." Rather than urging his father to believe the right things so he could go to heaven, Burke says that they discussed how to "make the most of life today" by loving others and caring for the needy.

Burke concludes that "I all but saw my dad die, and there was an amazing sense of peace about it all. He lived an amazingly full life, and he wasn't worried about trying to get into heaven at the end. He had this sense ... that God's grace and love were great enough. Bigger, really, than anything religion could comprehend."[11]

KEEP ON GOING OR TURN AROUND?

Modern conservatives and postmodern innovators disagree about the sequence of believing, belonging, and becoming because they diagnose differently the human condition (see fig. 7.2). Conservatives tend to focus on the Fall. They emphasize that people are sinners who need to repent, which, as just about any conservative churchgoer could tell you, comes from a Greek word that means to change your mind about sin and head in the opposite direction. This conversion requires truth — for how else will you know where to head and how to live? This truth is found in the Bible, where it is discovered and authoritatively proclaimed by a preacher to believers who come each week to learn and obey God's will.

Those who have converted intuitively recognize that they differ from others who have not, and so they tend to view their community as an exclusive fellowship with clear boundaries between the church and the world. They are apt to have a pure church — no unbelievers are allowed to join — but their hierarchical structure, with the pastor leading the congregation and the congregation seeking to convert the lost, often seems too arrogant to attract outsiders.

	Modern Conservatives	Postmodern Innovators
Our Condition	Fallen Sinners	Created Seekers
	↓	↓
Our Goal	Conversion	Journey
	↓	↓
Our Means	Find Answers/Truth	Ask Questions/Wonder
	↓	↓
Our Ministry	Confident, Authoritative, Hierarchical	Humble, Democratic, Mutual
	↓	↓
Our Church	Exclusive/Bounded Set Pure Church, but Few Converts	Inclusive/Centered Set Many "Converts," but Still Church?

Fig. 7.2. Why Different People Do Church Differently

Postmodern innovators emphasize Creation. They view people more as seekers than sinners — or as Frost and Hirsch say, at least "see everyone as equally fallen" — which leads them to emphasize our common journey rather than our need for dramatic conversion.[12] One leader explains, "Evangelism or mission for me is no longer about persuading people to believe what I believe.... It is about shared experiences and encounters. It is about walking the journey of life and faith together, each distinct to his or her own tradition and culture but with the possibility of encountering God and truth from one another."[13]

Dave Tomlinson, a self-described "post-evangelical" in Great Britain, writes, "The world is not a place where Christians are over there on the right and non-Christians are on the left, with evangelism being the task of moving people from one side to the other. It's much more helpful to think of people as being on a spiritual journey where God is at work and waiting to be recognized."[14]

And Steve Chalke interprets Jesus' words about being born again, not as a need for a stunning reversal, but merely that Nicodemus should continue "the journey [he] was already on." Jesus "wasn't about bringing people to a point of crisis in order to get them saved." Instead, he was concerned that "they understood his message — even if only dimly — and were heading in his direction." Nicodemus "is already searching, asking questions. He is catching some of the fire, but he wants to get closer."[15]

Since postmodern innovators view the Christian life more as a journey than a sudden conversion, they allow plenty of room for questions that wonder at the mystery of God. Answers are essential for conservatives who think that people are headed in the wrong direction and need to turn around. But if we are already traveling on the right path, then questions are all we need to get on down the road. As one pastor believes, "So long as we are asking questions, we are on the journey and okay with God."

If the conservative concern for answers lends itself to authoritative and hierarchical forms of ministry, the postmodern focus on questions produces a humble, democratic way of doing church. Many postmodern churches practice open, fluid leadership, where anyone may take a turn leading in their area of passion.[16] Others are replacing the traditional thirty-minute sermon with a "progressional dialogue." Rather than passively listen to a monologue, the congregation contributes to a running conversation that establishes both the content and application of the week's message.[17] Postmodern innovators are especially humble toward outsiders. Note the quotes above on the purpose of evangelism, which now seems content to converse with non-Christians rather than convert them.

The postmodern emphasis on our common human quest to discover the meaning of life produces an inclusive view of the church. No longer dividing people into in- and out-groups, the church invites all comers to actively participate in its life and fellowship. This minimalist approach will likely attract many visitors to the group, but it may also threaten the identity of the church. How does an all-inclusive church differ from any other gathering of good people? If there is no significant difference between Christian and non-Christian, then there is no clear difference between the church and the world. So why bother joining a church? Why not hang out with friends, as some are doing, and call it good?[18]

In this way postmodern innovators are dangerously close to repeating a modern mistake. At the turn of the nineteenth century, a liberal theologian named Friedrich Schleiermacher defended the Christian faith to his skeptical romantic friends. In *On Religion: Speeches to Its Cultured Despisers*, Schleiermacher told them that Christianity, like all religion, was merely a human effort to express in words the deep yearning that every person feels for the divine. And since romantics cared most about feeling, mystery, and the imagination, Schleiermacher informed them that they were already religious and just didn't know it.[19]

Isn't this the upshot of the postmodern turn toward belonging before believing? If being a child of God means nothing more than setting off on a journey to find him, then anyone who asks thoughtful questions is already on the inside, whether or not they have hit on any of the right answers. Just as Schleiermacher dumbed down religion so that it was nothing more than nineteenth-century romanticism, so postmodern innovators risk redefining Christianity into a mirror image of twenty-first-century postmodernism.

POSTMODERN PILGRIMS

Both the modern conservative and postmodern paradigms are inadequate by themselves. The postmodern order of belonging before believing is too permissive — few if any beliefs are out of bounds as long as you tolerate, accept, and include others. The conservative sequence of believing before belonging is often stifling and oppressive. It is hard to join a church — and easy to get kicked out of one — when membership requires signing on to a detailed doctrinal statement, many of which include precise beliefs about the mode of baptism, the use of sign gifts, and the sequence of events at Christ's return.

But what if we combined the insights of both, so that the strengths of each covered the weakness of the other? What if, rather than view these as mutually exclusive options, we arranged them in chronological sequence? The gracious, inviting nature of the postmodern order would describe the pre-Christian journey to faith, while the conservative emphasis on truth would remind us that this journey is not open-ended, but has a destination in the committed Christian life (see fig. 7.3).

Pre-Christian Journey to Faith			*Christian Journey in Faith*		
Belong ➡ **Become** ➡ **Believe**			**Believe** ➡ **Belong** ➡ **Become**		
welcoming acceptance	change by common grace	grow toward God	change by special grace	church membership, participation	grow in Christ

Fig. 7.3. Combining Modern and Postmodern Views of Church

For starters, who can deny that the church should embrace non-Christians, loving them as they are whether or not they ever clean up their act? It is hard to argue with Brian McLaren, who says that the church should send visitors this message: "We are a community bound together and energized by faith, love, and commitment to Jesus Christ. Even though you don't yet share that faith, love, and commitment, you are most welcome to be with us, to belong here, to experience what we're about. Then, if you're attracted and persuaded by what you see, you'll want to set down roots here long-term. And even if you don't, you'll always be a friend."[20]

McLaren correctly contends that we should stop viewing people as embodied souls whom we befriend with the sole purpose of saving. Instead, we should love them as whole people who are worthy of our friendship, regardless of whether they ever convert. The former impersonally treats people as means to some higher goal. We feign friendship in order to save their souls, but when that happens, or looks like it will never happen, we move on to the next target of our evangelism. How much better to love people as ends in themselves! We will still share our faith with them, but now because we love them rather than merely want to convert them. We will give them a place to *belong*, whether or not they ever join our faith.

As these non-Christian friends hang around the people of God, their lives should *become* better. Through hearing the Word of God and interacting with God's people, they should improve how they serve their spouse, raise children, handle money, perform jobs, and love their neighbor. The church's influence should help them to flourish in every facet of their human life.

They may also begin to *believe*. If initially they were skeptical about religion or Christianity, their experience of a loving, righteous community of God's children should at least make belief in God seem plausible. They may never go all the way and convert, but at least they will understand why a person would.

Thankfully, the journey of faith need not stop here. The same God whose common grace enables our non-Christian friends to markedly become and believe better may also intervene in special grace to give them new birth. We learned in chapter 2 that this conversion requires truth, for sinners must *believe* something specific about God and themselves in order to be saved. Although questions about God and the journey of faith do not stop — indeed, for thinking Christians, must never stop — here is one place where some answers are required. It is not enough to raise provocative questions. We must know and rely on the truth about Jesus to experience the radical change of regeneration.

Once we are born again, we are able to more fully *belong* to the church than before we were saved. No longer merely a friend or frequent attendee, we now must join and actively serve an organized community of God's children. The notion that church membership is optional for Christians is a novel idea. Until recently, most Christians believed Cyprian's famous saying that "outside the church there is no salvation."[21] In case someone thinks that this statement is too Roman Catholic for Protestants to accept, ask yourself whether it is possible to belong to Christ if you pointedly choose not to belong to his church. Can you be connected to the head if you are not part of the body?[22]

Belonging to the church is a vital aspect of *becoming*. Conservatives sometimes give the impression that the journey of faith is over once someone "accepts Jesus into their heart." They have crossed the finish line, they know the important answers and have few if any remaining questions, and their only job now is to confidently share these answers with others as they await Christ's return.

McLaren corrects this shortened view of life when he observes that coming to Jesus is a starting line rather than a finish line.[23] The journey of faith does not end when we trust Jesus; it just begins to get interesting. Our pilgrimage never completely ends, not even in John Bunyan's celestial city. Even on the new earth, when we are dwelling with God in our perfect world, we will still have more questions than answers. We will not understand everything in the sweet by-and-by, for God's infinity will always dwarf our limited creaturely minds. We will know God better than we do now, but every fresh insight into his unfathomable nature will prompt new questions, an unlimited number of which we will never be able to answer.

To summarize: both modern conservatives and postmodern innovators will improve their understanding of the church if they listen to rather than demonize the other. When we combine both models in the way we do church, we will gladly admit that Christian and non-Christian alike are on a journey, but we will emphasize the turning point of repentance and faith to get on track. We will clasp the clear, life-giving answers of Christianity in one hand and raise a hand for questions with the other. We will expect new Christians to grow in love and righteousness, and we will compassionately embrace those who struggle. We will limit membership in the body of Christ to those who believe but welcome and make room for those who do not.

Of course, this distinction between Christian and non-Christian implies that it matters a lot whether a person believes in Jesus. But many Christians today are not so sure. They wonder whether salvation is limited to the few who follow Jesus, or if the kingdom of God includes people of other religions, such as Buddhists, Hindus, and Muslims. To this question we now turn.

CHAPTER 8

DOES THE KINGDOM OF GOD INCLUDE NON-CHRISTIANS?

Conservative Christians know missions. Our prayers ask God to bless four things: food, family, friends, and the missionaries. Our churches host annual missionary conferences, featuring exotic food from far-off lands, flags from foreign nations, and multiple renditions of "People Need the Lord." And we send our teenagers on missionary trips — smaller churches settle for a vacation Bible school in Kansas while larger ones head to the Philippines or Koh Samui.

Closer to home, conservative Christians talk a lot about personal evangelism. We celebrate preachers who regale us with stories of their evangelistic exploits. One speaker from my college days seemed to lead every person he had ever met — and a few he hadn't — to the Lord. He told us how he wrapped tracts in red cellophane and tossed these gospel bombs at unsuspecting bystanders as he drove down the street. Some people got mad, especially the mechanic who, thinking the missile was a firecracker, banged his head on his car's bumper as he jumped out of the way. But before our speaker had turned the corner, the mechanic had opened the unexploded tract and given his heart to Christ.

Until recently it was easy for conservatives to hold this straightforward view of salvation. We sent missionaries around the world and witnessed to our friends nearby because we feared that anyone who did not repent of their sin and trust Jesus would spend forever in hell. But now a growing number of Christians are not so sure.

The world is smaller. We readily believed that Buddhists, Muslims, and Hindus were going to hell when our only contact with them was through missionaries who told us so. But now we are connected by airplanes, telephone, and the Internet. Many of them are our neighbors. We shop with them, go to school with them, and outsource our jobs to them. We know them. And it is hard to accept that these kind and decent people may be forever damned just because they do not believe that Jesus died and rose to forgive their sin.

We are also humbler. Christianity has long been the dominant religion in the world's most dominant country. America's super-power status — and Christianity's role in her success — instilled confidence that our country and our religion were the best. We believed that other nations should convert to our form of government, a free democracy that flows best from belief in the biblical God.

But worry over terrorism and the war in Iraq has caused many to reconsider America's role in the world. We are less confident that our country is always right and will always win, and so we are less sure about the religion used to justify our actions. Rather than impose our will upon others, we now seek to listen and learn from the perspectives of other nations and religions. We live in a diverse, multicultural world, where being right seems less important than getting along with others.

Our humility has led to a new openness toward other religions. Billy Graham once traveled the world warning people to avoid hell by believing in Jesus. When asked recently "whether he believes heaven will be closed to good Jews, Muslims, Buddhists, Hindus, or secular people," Graham replied: "Those are decisions only the Lord will make. It would be foolish for me to speculate on who will be there and who won't.... I don't want to speculate about all that. I believe the love of God is absolute. He said he gave his [S]on for the whole world, and I think he loves everybody regardless of what label they have."[1]

Many postmodern innovators are moving beyond Graham's ambivalent position and claiming that people from other religions probably do belong to the kingdom of God. Brian McLaren asks a series of rhetorical questions to imply that members of other religions may become better kingdom citizens than Christians. He writes:

> Wouldn't it be fascinating if thousands of **Muslims**, alienated with where fundamentalists and extremists have taken their religion, began to "take their places at the feast," discovering the secret message of Jesus in ways that many Christians have not?

Could it be that Jesus, always recognized as one of the greatest prophets of Islam, could in some way be rediscovered to save Islam from its dangerous dark side? Similarly, wouldn't there be a certain ironic justice if Jesus' own kinsmen, the **Jewish people**, led the way in understanding and practicing the core teaching of one of their own prophets who has too often been hijacked by other interests or ideologies? Or if **Buddhists, Hindus,** and even **former atheists and agnostics** came from "east and west and north and south" and began to enjoy the feast of the kingdom in ways that those bearing the name *Christian* have not?[2]

Why does McLaren use the term "former" to describe atheists and agnostics but not Buddhists, Hindus, Muslims, and Jews? Is he saying that people may enter the kingdom without leaving their non-Christian religions behind?[3]

One leader explains: "My understanding is that if the kingdom is what God is about, then God might be involved in other faiths.... We very much see our work in relation to the unique person and work of Christ. If other religions are involved in that work, that is fine."[4]

Another says, "We partner with others who seem to embody kingdom values and are doing kingdom work, even if they are not 'orthodox' Christians. We collect cans with Unitarians, work at blues festivals, and work with secular organizations in Pittsburgh. The urban challenges are so great that groups need to work together wherever possible."[5]

This postmodern turn raises two important questions that this chapter will address: are people in other religions "saved," and if not, may they still contribute to the kingdom of God?[6]

HOW BROAD IS THE WAY?

1. *Universalism.* Not many postmodern innovators seem to believe in full-fledged universalism — the idea that all people everywhere will be saved (see fig. 8.1). The most compelling reason to be a universalist is that an all-loving and all-powerful God will override our choices and not allow any rejection of him to stand.[7] But this disrespects human freedom too much for postmodern innovators, who detest anything that smacks of coercion. A leading character in McLaren's trilogy explains: "Maybe God's plan is an opt-out plan, not an opt-in one. If you want to stay out of the party, you can. Nobody will force you to enjoy it."[8]

Even Spencer Burke, who claims that grace and spirituality transcend all religions, so that no one has "to convert to any particular religion to find God," reserves the right for people to reject God's grace if they wish. Burke paradoxically calls himself "a universalist who believes in hell," by which he means "We're in unless we choose to be out. That is how grace works. We don't opt in to it — we can only opt out."[9]

Nevertheless, since it is difficult for Burke and the protagonists in McLaren's story to imagine someone staring the God of grace in the face and still opting for hell, they do seem to lean toward universalism. Like many postmodern innovators, they believe that God's love embraces everyone except those potential few who knowingly insist on sabotaging their salvation.[10]

The problem with universalism is its tendency to downplay the righteous judgment of God and our sin that provokes it. As we saw in chapter 4, self-described universalists like Burke no longer speak of sin and disobedience but only of our brokenness and fragmentation. Burke correctly observes that we are broken, but he forgets that this felt need is a symptom of a deeper problem. Unless we lay down our weapons and repent of our rebellion, we cannot be made whole.

Pastors who routinely define sin as brokenness rather than rebellion against God are, perhaps unwittingly, laying the foundation for universalism. After all, if people are merely broken and bleeding, why wouldn't a loving God heal and forgive them? But if people are injured by their sinful revolt against God — an uprising in which they stubbornly persist — then their restoration becomes complicated. It is difficult to repair and reconcile with insurgents who continue to fight. I will say more about this in my response to inclusivism.

2. Pluralism. Few if any postmodern innovators admit to believing in pluralism. This popular view in our culture declares that every religion is a legitimate road to God (or nirvana, in the case of atheistic Buddhism) and all who faithfully follow each path will eventually arrive there. Spencer Burke appears to hold a version of this position, for his church "celebrates other traditions ... as beloved children of God." His church not only visited a Buddhist temple, but they participated in a guided meditation with the Buddhist family in their congregation.[11] Indeed, Burke easily would be a pluralist if he believed that individual religions actually mattered. But since he believes that everyone begins life already accepted by God, he does not think they need to take a religious path to get to him.[12]

The problem with pluralism is that it ignores God's revelation in Jesus Christ. If Jesus Christ accurately reveals God, then other religions are incomplete at best and, where they differ from Jesus, plainly wrong. Any pluralist who embraces these religions as viable alternatives is not a Christian in any historical, intelligible sense of the word. Most postmodern innovators are aware of this, and few so far have fallen into the pluralist trap.[13]

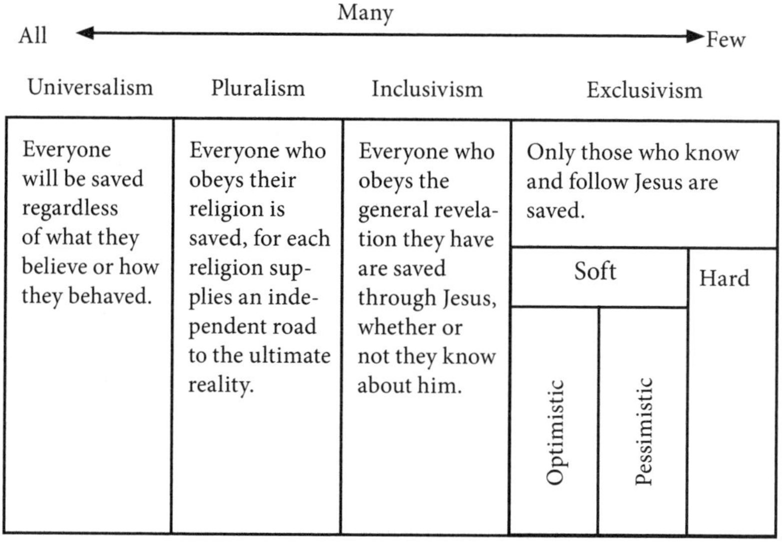

Universalism	Pluralism	Inclusivism	Exclusivism		
Everyone will be saved regardless of what they believe or how they behaved.	Everyone who obeys their religion is saved, for each religion supplies an independent road to the ultimate reality.	Everyone who obeys the general revelation they have are saved through Jesus, whether or not they know about him.	Only those who know and follow Jesus are saved.		
				Soft	Hard
			Optimistic	Pessimistic	

All ←————————— Many —————————→ Few

Fig. 8.1. How and How Many Are Saved?

3. *Inclusivism.* If their belief that people may *opt out* of God's plan prevents postmodern innovators from becoming full-blown universalists, their belief that people do not need to *opt in* commits them at least to a heightened form of inclusivism.

Traditional inclusivists — which includes a rising number of evangelicals — believe that it is possible for members of other religions to be saved.[14] They argue that all saved people are saved through Jesus, but they do not need to know and believe in Jesus to receive this benefit. Jesus' life, death, and resurrection may cover people who have never heard of him.[15]

Inclusivists begin with God's unbounded love for the entire world. They insist that their gracious God would not damn people who never had an opportunity to accept or reject Christ. After all, it is not their fault that lazy or selfish Christians failed to send missionaries to tell them the gospel.[16] A just and loving God would not hold people accountable for what they did not know, but only for what they did.[17]

This leads inclusivists to conclude that people may be saved if they rightly respond to God's general revelation. Anyone who looks at themselves and their world can deduce that all this was created by a good and powerful God. If they submit to and serve this general notion of God, they will be saved, whether or not they know about the cross and resurrection of Jesus.[18]

This inclusive view is now the position of the Roman Catholic Church. In 1964 its Council of Vatican II announced: "Those who, through no fault of their own, do not know the Gospel of Christ or his Church, but who nevertheless seek God with a sincere heart, and, moved by grace, try in their actions to do his will as they know it through the dictates of their conscience — those too may achieve eternal salvation."[19]

Notice that the sincerity of faith counts more than its content. Inclusivists claim that it does not matter how much a person knows but how they respond to what little they do know. Clark Pinnock asserts, "According to the Bible, people are saved by faith, not by the content of their theology.... People are judged on the basis of the light they have received and how they have responded to that light."[20]

Even if what people believe about God is wrong, they are still accepted as long as they respond to their idea of God with worship and obedience. C. S. Lewis closed his Chronicles of Narnia with Aslan accepting the well-intended worship offered to a false god. Aslan spoke: "Child, all the service thou hast done to Tash, I account as service done to me.... Therefore, if any man swear by Tash and keep his oath for the oath's sake, it is by me that he has truly sworn, though he know it not, and it is I who reward him."[21] Elsewhere Lewis explained, "I think that every prayer which is sincerely made even to a false god ... is accepted by the true God and that Christ saves many who do not think they know him."[22]

Thus, as we saw in chapters 2 and 3, inclusivists tend to value ethics over doctrine. It is more important that people *mean* well than that they *know* well, more important that they *do* the right thing than that they *believe* the right thing. In this way inclusivists claim that even virtuous pagans may be saints, their good behavior either making them "anonymous Christians" or pre-Christian believers accepted by God.[23]

But postmodern innovators go even further and hold to a heightened form of inclusivism. Traditional inclusivists assert that people must do something to be saved. They need not know and believe in Jesus, but they must, as Vatican II suggested, "seek God with a sincere heart, and, moved by grace, try in their actions to do his will as they know it through the dictates of their conscience."

Now postmodern innovators appear to have lowered the bar even more. Not only do people not need to believe in Jesus, but also they do not need to reach toward and obey the God they know. They do not need to believe or do anything to be saved, for in Burke's words, "We're in unless we choose to be out." As long as we do not reject God's grace, we will enjoy his salvation forever. Traditional inclusivism said that we must believe or do *something*, however minimal, to be saved. This postmodern version says that we are saved even if we believe or do *nothing*. We are born already on the inside.

Both forms of inclusivism are attractive. Who doesn't want to believe that regardless of who they are or where they live, everyone has the opportunity to receive salvation by obeying or at least by not rejecting however much they know? Shouldn't we expect our loving and sovereign God to make salvation available to everyone?

HOW NARROW IS THE WAY?

There is just one problem. What if, as we discussed in chapter 4, people are born broken, bent on having their own way rather than submitting to what they know about God? Then they will likely squelch and try to ignore what God has revealed about himself in the world. This is what the apostle Paul says everyone does.

Paul begins his letter to the Romans with an argument for the universal sinfulness of the human race. He declares that all Jews sinfully disobey God's special revelation in the Law and all Gentiles culpably suppress God's general revelation in the world. Since everyone is either a Jew or a Gentile, Paul confidently concludes that "all have sinned and fall short of the glory of God."[24]

Because we are discussing the salvation of those unacquainted with the gospel, we will focus on what Paul says every Gentile knows about God. Paul declares that "since the creation of the world God's invisible qualities — his eternal power and divine nature — have been clearly seen, being understood from what has been made, so that men are without excuse." After citing a list of sins that people routinely commit, Paul adds, "Although they know God's righteous decree that those who do such things deserve death, they not only continue to do these very things but also approve of those who practice them."[25]

Paul says that every person knows — whether innately or by looking at nature — that God exists and that he is all powerful and righteous (almighty and "alrighty"). The next thing that everyone should immediately recognize is that they are not. Their sin has landed them in trouble with a holy God. They need help. Not just a little bit of help, not just a push in the right direction, but the whole shebang. They need complete salvation, a rescue that from start to finish comes entirely from God.

Isn't it telling that there is only one candidate for this job? Jesus Christ is the only God who offers redemption entirely from grace. Every other religion that promises salvation adds human works to the mix.[26] Their members strive to become better in hopes that their god will relent and accept them. But given what Paul says everyone knows about the righteous God, these worshipers must realize that their tiny contribution cannot begin to close the gap. So why do they persist?

Because they are rebels. Paul observes that although people know certain things about God, they can be counted on to "suppress the truth by their wickedness."[27] They stubbornly want to play God, so they create religions that tip their hat to God's righteous power but leave plenty of room for human pride.

For example, Islam reduces the religious life to a set of unchallenging rules that anyone may easily keep. Muslims may earn salvation simply by tithing a mere 2.5 percent of their income, traveling once to Mecca, fasting during the daylight hours of Ramadan, attending mosque on Friday, and offering prayers five times per day.

And even if they should fail at these five pillars of Islam, they may believe that their attempts have likely produced enough good works to merit Allah's acceptance. Muslims never humble themselves before God and confess that they are desperate, helpless sinners. They acknowledge God's majesty, but in an undemanding way that neither crimps their pride nor calls for costly sacrifice. So long as they are moral, they may assume that God is pleased with them.[28]

Left to themselves everyone would choose a religion like this, which, if it concedes God's existence, keeps him and his demands at arm's length. This is why everyone needs the Holy Spirit to initiate salvation, overcoming their suppression and effectually empowering them to repent of their sin and throw themselves on the mercy of Jesus Christ.

How does the Holy Spirit do this job? In chapter 2 I argued that he uses special revelation — the Word of God proclaimed by human preachers — to give new birth. This fact is the driving force behind the exclusivist position.[29] Exclusivists believe that since the Holy Spirit uses truth to regenerate sinners, knowledge of the gospel is required for salvation. As Paul says, "Faith comes from hearing the message, and the message is heard through the word of Christ."[30] The flip side, and what many find distasteful, is that those who do not know and believe in Jesus cannot be saved.

Exclusivists respond to this dark side of their view in different ways.[31] Hard exclusivists unabashedly announce that the unevangelized cannot be saved, while soft exclusivists hold out various degrees of hope. Soft exclusivists gladly concede that it is theoretically possible for anyone to rightly respond to general revelation, and if they do, God will find a way to get them the special revelation they need to be saved, whether by missionary or the unusually direct method of a dream or vision.[32]

Some are pessimistic about this possibility, since sinners need the Holy Spirit to overcome their suppression, and the Holy Spirit seems to operate in tandem with the Word of God. How probable is it that the Holy Spirit will initiate salvation in general revelation, using knowledge of the Creator to whet a person's appetite for redemption?

Some believe that this is likely and will cite stories — perhaps urban legends — of devout pagans deep in Muslim lands who received divine dreams urging them to believe the gospel of Christ.

This optimistic soft exclusivism is neighbor to inclusivism, for both assert that many are responding in faith to general revelation and being saved. The difference is that inclusivists believe that salvation may come through general revelation alone, while optimistic exclusivists say that salvation comes only through special revelation, which is given as a reward for obeying general revelation.[33]

I am a soft exclusivist who is pessimistic about the fate of those in other religions. Though anything is possible and I wish for the best, I believe that apart from the saving grace of the Holy Spirit, which in Scripture always comes from hearing the Word, everyone will sinfully push down and distort what little they know about God. It is hypothetically possible for anyone to obey God's general revelation and receive more light. But given the depths of our depravity, I doubt that anyone does.

IS THERE A MIDDLE WAY?

Nevertheless, my traditional evangelical belief that non-Christians are excluded from the kingdom of God need not imply that they may never contribute to it. Conservatives tend to err on this extreme, limiting the kingdom of God to one aspect of one segment of the population (what believers in Jesus enjoy when they gather as a church to receive the Word and Sacrament).[34] Liberals head in the opposite direction, declaring that anyone who contributes to the common good in the world is a member of the kingdom of God, regardless of what they believe.[35] As before, I prefer not to opt for either extreme but take a nuanced view that retains the best elements of both (see fig. 8.2).

The kingdom is God's rightful rule over his world as its Creator and Redeemer.[36] The God who created all things will rescue all things from the destruction of Satan and sin.[37] This kingdom, established by Jesus at his first coming and consummated at his return, is now centered in his church.[38]

The church is the heart of God's kingdom on earth, for it is where rebellious sinners, nourished by the Word, baptism, and the Lord's Supper, lay down their weapons and submit to the lordship of Christ. Jesus is destroying Satan's kingdom, not primarily through Christian schools, bookstores, or televangelists (especially not them), but by his church, which he promised would storm the gates of hell.[39] We cannot stress enough the importance of the body of Christ. It plays the starring role in extending God's reign on earth.

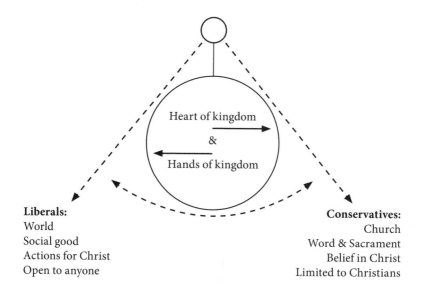

Fig. 8.2. Where Is the Kingdom of God?

But though God's kingdom is headquartered in his church, it is larger than the gathering of God's people. Citizens of God's kingdom seek to exhibit his reign over every area of life, not only in their weekly worship but also in their homes, jobs, hobbies, and entertainment. Christians who have given their hearts to Christ naturally want to become his hands in the world. Just as Jesus established his kingdom by exorcising demons and healing the sick, so we reveal the rule of God when we root out the many ways sin has contaminated our world.[40]

We contribute to the kingdom in everyday matters when we refuse to spin the truth to our own advantage, patiently listen to another's case before we share our side, stick to our word even though it hurts, and turn the channel rather than be entertained by sin. We extend the kingdom in dramatic ways when we care for children orphaned by AIDS, rescue young girls from sex trafficking, discover a cure for colon cancer, and influence governments to stop genocide.

Now if these acts are "kingdom work" when performed by Christians, what should we say when non-Christians do them? What should we call Oprah building a topflight school for disadvantaged girls, Angelina Jolie adopting an assortment of poor children from around the world, George Clooney calling attention to the genocide in Darfur, and Warren Buffett and Bill and Melinda Gates donating $67 billion dollars to fight disease in Africa and reform education in America?[41]

These are not kingdom acts per se, for they are not motivated by love for Christ and his reign. But inadvertently they still contribute. We should not disparage such efforts because they are insufficiently Christian, but we should applaud the givers' generosity and seek to team up whenever possible. Say the Bill and Melinda Gates Foundation donates truckloads of malaria tents and AIDS cocktails to sub-Saharan Africa, where you work as a medical missionary. Do you refuse the help because it comes from a non-Christian source, or do you rejoice that through common grace the Holy Spirit inspires even non-Christians to pitch in and battle some of the effects of sin?

Cornelius Plantinga wisely observes that "God needn't employ only Christian organizations to push forward the cause of his kingdom. God can use all kinds of groups and persons to further his purposes, including groups and persons that are uninterested in God or even opposed to God.... A person does not have to believe in Christ in order, unconsciously, to do a part of Christ's work in the world."[42]

George Whitefield was close friends with Ben Franklin. Initially a business relationship — Whitefield wanted publicity from Franklin's newspaper and Franklin needed Whitefield to sell papers — they soon became such good friends that Franklin invited Whitefield to stay in his home when his revival came to Philadelphia. Whitefield attempted to encourage his deist friend by thanking him for his kind gesture on behalf of Christ. But Franklin would not bite. "Don't let me be mistaken," he replied. "It was not for Christ's sake, but for your sake."[43]

Franklin's hospitality was not a kingdom act, and yet indirectly he contributed much to the cause of Christ, publishing Whitefield's sermons and hosting the greatest evangelist of the eighteenth century. Augustine called this "plundering the Egyptians," a reference to Israel leaving Egypt with lots of pagan silver and gold with which they built the tabernacle.[44] Just because non-Christians themselves do not belong to the kingdom of God does not prevent them from unknowingly contributing to its cause. Like Whitefield and Israel, we may accept their efforts even as we redirect them to a higher end.

You may be thinking that it is slim solace to count non-Christians' labor as indirectly contributing to the kingdom of God if they themselves remain outside of it. What will become of them? This raises the subject of the next chapter and one of the hottest debates of our day: what should we believe about hell?

CHAPTER 9

IS HELL FOR REAL AND FOREVER?

Conservative Christians fixate on the afterlife. Our favorite evangelistic icebreaker is "Do you know where you would spend eternity if you were to die tonight?" And we wonder why we aren't invited to more parties! We fill our evangelistic sermons with stories of cancer, crashes, and kidnappings and then warn our listeners to "get right with God" in case something similar should happen to them. Even our emphasis on evangelism (rather than discipleship) indicates that we think where people live in the next life is more important than how they live in this one. All things considered, we would rather be selfish losers who repent moments before death than a good person who "stepped into a Christless eternity" for having never said the sinner's prayer.

The sheer length of the afterlife threatens to dwarf the significance of our life here and now. Many Christians believe that their brief life on earth is merely practice for their real life that begins when they die. A bestselling book supports this popular sentiment:

> Life on earth is just the dress rehearsal before the real production. You will spend far more time on the other side of death — *in eternity* — than you will here. Earth is the staging area, the preschool, the tryout for your life in eternity. It is the practice workout before the actual game; the warm-up lap before the race begins. This life is preparation for the next. At most, you will live a hundred years on earth, but you will spend forever in eternity.[1]

Many postmodern innovators resist this hegemony of the afterlife by trying to reclaim the importance of this one (see fig. 9.1). Rather than promote salvation as preparation for death, they present following Jesus as the best possible way to live. They rephrase the evangelistic icebreaker into the more challenging question, "If you knew that you were going to live tonight, wouldn't you want to live for Jesus?"

Some postmodern innovators go even further, claiming that we will never overcome our obsession with the afterlife until we get over our hang-ups on hell. Brian McLaren asks: "And doesn't the preoccupation with hell tempt us to devalue other things that matter? In other words, isn't hell such a grave 'bottom line' that it devalues all other values? It so emphasizes the importance of life after death that it can unintentionally trivialize life before death."[2]

McLaren worries that we often become so preoccupied with avoiding hell that we forget to do God's will on earth. As Pastor Dan explains in McLaren's story, many Christians believe that "this world will soon end, so why worry about justice *here and now*? All that counts is where you will end up *then and there*, in the afterlife. Your status there depends on religious piety — on prayer and Bible study and worship, not deeds of compassion and social justice."[3]

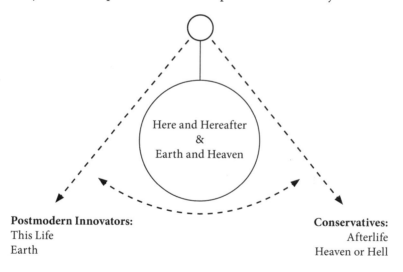

Postmodern Innovators:
This Life
Earth

Conservatives:
Afterlife
Heaven or Hell

Fig. 9.1. Which Life Matters?

McLaren has a point. Some Christians may become so consumed with securing salvation for the next life that they neglect to serve God and others now. And yet, as previous chapters have shown, postmodern innovators who try to steer out of a conservative slide tend to overcorrect. McLaren is not content to balance a traditional view of the afterlife with a robust concern for seeking the kingdom of God now, but he attempts to recover the importance of our present life by questioning our assumptions about the next one. What follows is his bold attempt, in his words, to "deconstruct our conventional concepts of hell."[4]

GET THE HELL OUT

McLaren argues that the traditional view of hell turns God into "a deity who suffers from borderline personality disorder or some worse sociopathic diagnosis." Christians tell others that "*God loves you and has a wonderful plan for your life, and if you don't love God back and cooperate with God's plans in exactly the prescribed way, God will torture you with unimaginable abuse, forever.*" McLaren thinks this view of God has produced some "dysfunctions of the Christian religion," which he seeks to correct by reexamining Jesus' perspective on hell.[5]

The heroes of his story, Neil and Pastor Dan, wonder why Jesus spoke so much about hell if the Old Testament was mostly silent about the afterlife.[6] What sources was Jesus drawing from? They surmise that Jesus had probably heard about hell from the Pharisees, who, having picked up the concept from other religions, were now threatening sinners with it.[7]

Neil reminds Dan that the Pharisees were a legalistic bunch who longed for the Messiah to come and liberate Israel from the crushing power of Rome. They figured the Messiah had not come yet because too many Jews were wallowing in sin and refusing to live up to the law's high standards. In order to encourage them to try — and thereby speed the Messiah's coming — the Pharisees warned that any unrepentant sinner would burn forever in the flames of hell.[8]

This insight leads Neil and Dan to their breakthrough discovery. They determine that Jesus may not have believed in hell but was merely using hell as a rhetorical device. Jesus heard the Pharisees threaten drunks and prostitutes with everlasting torment, and he said, "Wait a minute. You self-righteous arrogant boors are the real sinners. If anyone is going to hell it's you." Jesus was practicing theological jiujitsu, turning the Pharisees' argument back on them.[9]

Neil and Dan conclude that it doesn't matter whether hell is real. Jesus is not necessarily describing an actual place, but is merely using the idea of hell to warn the Pharisees to stop excluding the weak and the ugly from the family of God. Neil explains:

> The Pharisees used hell to threaten sinners and other undesirables and mark them as the excluded out-group, hated by God. Their rhetorical use of hell made clear that God's righteousness was severe and merciless toward the undeserving. Jesus turned their rhetoric upside down and inside out and used hell to threaten those who excluded sinners and other undesirables, showing that God's righteousness was compassionate and merciful, that God's kingdom welcomed the undeserving, that for God, there was no out-group.[10]

Then Dan offers a stunning application. He declares that religious conservatives are the new Pharisees, using hell to threaten nonconformists to get in line and believe like them. Dan says, "Our problem is that we use the idea of hell precisely the way the Pharisees did, exactly the opposite of the way Jesus did. We say everyone not of our elite party — the party of people who believe in certain doctrines, however they're defined — are excluded and will face not only our rejection in this life but also God's eternal rejection and scorn forever."[11] If Jesus were to return today, he would welcome the compassionate and the outcast and warn conservatives — those who insist that certain beliefs are necessary for salvation — that they are headed for hell.

Yikes! Since I am on record saying that sinners should believe some specific truths to be saved (see chap. 2), I would like to find a flaw in this argument and so save myself from hell, whether real or rhetorical. My first question is why Neil and Dan limit their discussion of hell to Jesus. Why don't they include John's detailed description in Revelation 19 – 20? This is a significant oversight for a book that leaves the distinct impression that hell is a rhetorical device rather than a real place.[12] While different Christian traditions disagree about various aspects of Revelation, the majority believes that the hell John describes is real. Neil and Dan's failure to discuss how the biblical story ends undercuts the force of their argument.

Even if we limit ourselves to the sayings of Jesus, we are still struck by the volume and the detail of what Jesus said about hell. He often warned his listeners to avoid being thrown into outer darkness, where they will gnash their teeth amid raging fires and flesh-eating worms. His story of the rich man and Lazarus, though probably a parable, does specifically say that those in hell are desperate for a drop of water on their tongues to cool their "agony in this fire."[13]

Here is my second question: did Jesus wink when he repeated these warnings? Small children who believe in Santa often warn each other to be good to avoid getting coal in their stockings. Sometimes overmatched parents play along, using their child's belief in Santa to control her behavior. They may say, "Stop screaming right this minute! I mean it! Okay, now I'm counting — o-o-o-ne, two-o-o-o, thre-e-e-e. That's it! No presents from Santa!" The parent will wink to other adults in the room when she mentions Santa because (1) of course her little brat is going to get presents, and (2) she doesn't really believe in Santa Claus.

What would we make of a parent who seemed to think that her threat actually had teeth? What if she droned on about Santa and how tragic it would be if he bypassed her house, as if she actually believed it? Wouldn't you be tempted to call the child protection hotline?

And what should we make of Jesus, who spoke long and often about hell as if he believed it was a real danger? He warned about following the broad way that leads to destruction, not because, as Neil suggests, there are many ways "to get into trouble with the Romans" (huh?) but because he thought our final destiny depended on what we do now.[14]

And what about John, who seems to have missed Jesus' wink and taken the joke too far? His vision of the end declares that Jesus' warning comes true, so that "if anyone's name was not found written in the book of life, he was thrown into the lake of fire."[15] Either Jesus and John believed in a real hell or they were extremely cynical.

Ironically, it is Jesus' belief in hell that supplies the rhetorical punch that Neil and Dan are after. I laugh when my little Alayna clenches her fist and jokingly asks if I want a piece of her. Her rhetoric has no bite because she can't inflict much damage. I would take the question more seriously if it came from Evander Holyfield, for his punches hurt a lot more.

So I wonder why we must choose between a real and rhetorical use of hell. I agree that Jesus used hell rhetorically. He warned about hell to persuade the Pharisees to stop sinning and avoid a terrible fate. But his rhetoric is most convincing, both to Jesus and his audience, if they believe that the danger of hell is real. Anything less has too many winks to be taken seriously.

WHAT A DUMP

But saying that hell is real does not explain what kind of reality it is. Scholars agree that the standard term for hell in the New Testament is *Gehenna,* which refers to an infamous valley southwest of Jerusalem. A place of child sacrifice during the reigns of kings Ahaz and Manasseh, it was turned into a garbage dump by King Josiah.[16] Isaiah and Jeremiah gave it apocalyptic significance when they declared that it would be the location of God's coming judgment. Isaiah ends his prophecy with the divine announcement that this valley will hold the "dead bodies of those who rebelled against me; their worm will not die, nor will their fire be quenched, and they will be loathsome to all mankind."[17] So Jesus was following a long tradition when he compared hell to the garbage dump in Gehenna. He said that hell will be pretty much like what we find there, a putrid place of outer darkness, undying worms, and unflagging fire.[18]

In McLaren's story, Neil cites Jesus' allusion to Gehenna as a reason to dismiss a literal interpretation of hell. He notes the difficulty of believing in worms that never die and the coexistence of fire and utter darkness. So rather than take Jesus' words literally, Neil thinks that Jesus is merely warning us not to waste ourselves on the garbage heap of life. Observing that Jesus' garbage analogy suggests "waste, decay, regret, and sorrow," he continues:

> Isn't that what anyone would feel if he spent his whole life on accumulating possessions or wealth or knowledge or power but missed out on life to the full in the Kingdom of God? He would have wasted his life! He would have failed to become the glorious person he could have become and instead become something crabby and cramped and ingrown and dark and shabby and selfish. Wouldn't that make you weep and gnash your teeth? Isn't a garbage dump the perfect imagery to use for that kind of waste? It sounds to me like hell is one image Jesus uses among others.[19]

While waste and regret are certainly a significant part of hell, Neil seems to reduce everlasting punishment to nothing more than being disappointed with ourselves. When Dan challenges him on this point, Neil fires back:

> What could be more serious than standing in front of your Creator — the Creator of the universe — and finding out that you had wasted your life, squandered your inheritance, caused others pain and sorrow, worked against the good plans and desires of God? What could be more serious than that? To have to face the real, eternal, unavoidable, absolute, naked truth about yourself, what you've done, what you've become?[20]

Dan quickly concedes the point. Compared to facing the truth about ourselves, "fire and brimstone are ... mere metaphors." They are "mere word pictures to help us imagine what it would feel like to come clean, to face the truth, to be found out, in the presence of God.... Nothing could be more serious than that."[21]

I am not as optimistic that autonomous sinners will ever fully "come clean" and "face the truth" about themselves. This week I saw a young man busted on national television for attempting to have sex with a fourteen-year-old girl. His response to getting caught was not remorse and repentance but simply "Now everyone is going to label me a loser for the rest of my life!" Implied: "I am not a loser, but now others will wrongly think that I am."

Sinners curved in on themselves will always find a way to exonerate their behavior. Bill Clinton spun his fornication in the Oval Office into a positive, saying that other young people may be inspired by the way he overcame adversity and survived impeachment. Richard Nixon was not shamed by Watergate, but blaming a legion of foes — both real and imaginary, defiantly flashed his double victory sign and insisted, "I am not a crook." Rare is the person, who, caught red-handed in despicable sin, willingly takes responsibility for blowing up his own life and hurling shrapnel into the lives of others.

Sinners may find it harder to hide when they stand before the piercing flame of God's judgment, but never underestimate the ability of autonomous people to let themselves off the hook. Every knee will bow before God, but many, if not most, will be forced to the ground. Sinners will fight to the end to preserve a shred of dignity and self-respect. They did it their way, and though they may admit mistakes, they wouldn't have it any other way.

Not only is it unlikely that sinners will own the waste they have made of their lives, but it would not be enough if they did. Their subjective sorrow cannot make up for the objective damage their sin has inflicted on God, others, and the world. I hope that anyone who smashes into my car will feel sorry about it, but I won't be satisfied until they buy me a new one. Objective damage requires objective satisfaction. Sinners who refuse Christ's satisfaction on the cross must pay it themselves. The cost is suffering in hell regardless of whether they express regret. Thus, because sinners will never concede the whole truth about themselves, and even if they did, their subjective sorrow would not satisfy the objective demands of justice, hell must be more than mere feelings of regret and disappointment.

The torment in hell is objectively real, and it lies beyond what our minds can comprehend. Jesus used the most loathsome sight in his day — a burning refuse pile crawling with worms — to indicate a bit of what hell must be like. Just as the new heaven and earth confounds our categories — expect it to be even better than John's superlatives of golden streets and pearly gates — so we can expect hell to be much worse.

Hell may not have literal worms, fire, and blackness, for as Calvin observes, God must use items from our world to describe another one.[22] But this does not mean that hell's torment is only spiritual. If the entire person, both body and soul, is guilty of sin, then the entire person, both body and soul, should suffer its consequences. Jesus warns that one's "whole body" may "be thrown into hell," and this is a danger that we must not ignore.[23]

FOREVER IS A VERY LONG TIME

But how long does hell's torment last? An increasing number of evangelical theologians are suggesting that sinners quickly perish in the flames of hell rather than stay alive to suffer forever.[24] They argue that the everlasting torture of the damned violates both God's love and justice. What could sinners possibly have done to deserve such a fate, and even if they did, how could a loving God allow it? If sinners must go to hell, wouldn't God mercifully permit them to burn up rather than languish for an exceedingly long time?[25]

They find evidence for this in Scripture, which calls hell a place of death and destruction. Isaiah's description of Gehenna, which

Jesus quotes in his warning about hell, declares that the undying worms and fire will feed on "dead bodies" rather than live ones.[26] Those who carefully read Scripture will realize that it is the flames, smoke, and worms that last forever, not necessarily the sinners who are sent there.[27]

These theologians allege that the Christian tradition missed this because it smuggled the Platonic belief in the immortality of the soul into its reading of Scripture. If the human soul cannot die, then of course those in hell must suffer forever. But if, as Scripture teaches, the human soul and body are made from nothing, then both are able to die and return to nothing. And nothing would annihilate them faster than a blazing fire.[28]

Although attractive to those with non-Christian friends and family, this hope for the annihilation of the lost cuts against the Christian tradition. The church fathers did not make the annihilationists' subtle distinction between everlasting fire and temporary torment. They seemed to think that the suffering in hell lasts forever, not because they agreed with Plato that a soul is inherently indestructible, but because they believed that the New Testament says it will.[29]

The fathers noticed that Jesus never corrected the Pharisees' belief in everlasting torment, informing them that hell's fire lasts longer than its inhabitants. Instead, Jesus told stories, like the rich man and Lazarus, which implied that the damned experience conscious, ongoing torment in hell. They read Revelation 20:10, which unequivocally declares that God will throw the Devil, the Beast, and the False Prophet "into the lake of burning sulfur," where they "will be tormented day and night for ever and ever." They assumed that if Satan will survive the flames of hell and suffer forever, then the same fate awaits his human followers who are thrown into the same lake.[30] They found support for this in Revelation 14:11, which says that "there is no rest day or night for those who worship the beast and his image," but "the smoke of their torment rises for ever and ever."

So Scripture and tradition seem to teach the everlasting, conscious torment of the wicked.[31] But what about the annihilationists' main concern: can we reconcile such unimaginable suffering with a just and loving God? How could our good God allow it? I respond with three points.

First, the existence of hell is a mystery. Anything connected to the Fall will never make sense, for the Fall is the one part of the biblical story that does not fit. We will never fully comprehend why God allowed Adam and Eve to sin, why he permits unthinkable tragedies to happen to uncommonly good people, or why he does not empty hell and save everyone. If we could understand the Fall and its consequences, wrap it up with a bow and say, "Oh, I get it, that's why this happened," then it would cease to be evil. Evil, precisely because it is evil, is not supposed to make sense.

This is what Paul concludes in Romans 9 – 11 when he asks why God saved Jacob and not Esau. Paul boldly answers that God is not unjust, but he does not say why. He simply says that God's ways are not our ways, and "who are you, O man, to talk back to God?" He continues, "Oh, the depth of the riches of the wisdom and knowledge of God! How unsearchable his judgments, and his paths beyond tracing out!"[32] Rather than fix the problem of hell by reducing it to subjective disappointment or temporary punishment, Paul declares that hell, like everything connected to the Fall, is a mystery not meant to be solved.

Second, it is important to remember that God does not hold anyone in hell against his or her will. Philosophers tell us that addicts have first and second order desires. On a secondary level, a chain smoker may want to quit smoking because he knows it is killing him, yet on a primary level he craves another nicotine fix. Just as he is conflicted, both wanting and not wanting to quit at the same time, so sinners are torn in their addiction to autonomy. On one level everyone in hell wants out, for their torment is more than they can bear. Yet, apart from the grace of the Holy Spirit, none are willing to do the one thing that could theoretically gain their release: repent of their autonomy and serve God rather than themselves.[33]

C. S. Lewis remarked that hell is locked from the inside. He wrote, "There are only two kinds of people in the end: those who say to God, 'Thy will be done,' and those to whom God says, in the end, '*Thy* will be done.' All that are in Hell, choose it."[34] This fact alone does not solve the problem of hell, for we may still wonder why a sovereign God does not lovingly yet noncoercively change the hearts of the damned so they submit to him.

However, while this is a fair question, no one is in a position to ask it. The damned are in hell because they choose to be independent from God. They can hardly blame God for giving them what they want. Neither can the redeemed justly question God, for the only reason they are not in hell is because God changed their minds so they would choose him. There is only one person who may raise the question of hell, and he did.

Jesus did not receive an answer when he cried from the cross, "My God, my God, why have you forsaken me?"[35] But his suffering offers a third insight. We may not know why God does not save everyone from going to hell, but we do know that God himself has gone there. The Apostles' Creed states that Jesus descended into hell. In that eternal moment when the perfect Son was intolerably forsaken by his Father, God himself experienced the worst torments of hell. This does not tell us why God permits hell to exist, but it does assure us that God is love. He may not get everyone out of hell, but he has allowed hell to get to him.

Ultimately, I believe that we should want God to empty hell. I cringe when dour theologians callously claim that the redeemed will take delight in the damnation of the wicked.[36] Such sentiments aren't Christian. They aren't even normal. I wish that God would save everyone from going to hell, though I can't say that I hope so. Biblical hope springs from what God has revealed. I hope for my resurrection and the redemption of the world because Jesus has promised to do both when he returns. But he has never promised to empty hell or prevent people from going there, and so I can't say I hope for it. But I do wish it. And so should you.

THE PRESENCE OF THE FUTURE

So far I have argued that the suffering in hell is objectively real and forever, against Neil and Dan's view that it amounts to subjective regret and the annihilationists' belief that its inhabitants will go out of existence. But what about the initial concern that began this chapter? Even if I am right, doesn't my concern for avoiding hell in the next life distract me from living for the kingdom of God in this one?

It would if I am trying to earn salvation. Then I must spend all of my time doing the sorts of religious practices that gain God's approval. But what if, as I explained in chapter 3, I realize that my salvation is already secure in Christ? As Luther said, then I would be free to "give myself as a Christ to my neighbor, just as Christ offered himself to me. I will do nothing in this life except what I see is necessary, profitable, and salutary to my neighbor, since through faith I have an abundance of all good things in Christ."[37]

Far from being a distraction, a right understanding of the afterlife — and what Jesus has achieved for us there — is the only Christian motivation for this life (see fig. 9.1). The best workers in the kingdom realize that they have been blessed "in the heavenly realms with every spiritual blessing in Christ."[38] Those who have received the most can give the most, and there is nothing better than knowing that our final destiny is settled.

And nothing is more loving than to warn others about the danger that lies ahead. Against Dan's charge that people like me are self-righteous Pharisees for telling people that they must believe certain things to avoid hell, I respond that we are not unloving if what we say is true. As I argued in chapter 2, if everyone needs the Holy Spirit to give them new birth and if the Holy Spirit uses truth to do this job, then knowledge of some facts is required to be born again and escape the terrors of hell. It is not unloving to share this with others. It would be unloving not to.

But this need to know something to be saved assumes that knowledge is possible. This brings us to a fundamental dispute between modern conservatives and postmodern innovators. What do we know, and how do we know it? We will examine this controversy next.

CHAPTER 10

IS IT POSSIBLE TO KNOW ANYTHING?

Conservative Christians believe that God's Word can solve most any problem. When I was a child, my pastor told us that the Bible contains the cure for cancer. It may lie deep within the Old Testament — likely buried in Leviticus — but we could find it if we knew where to look and what we were looking for. We're still looking.

Of course, having the Answer Book can breed a bit of arrogance. Recently I met conservatives who, when discussing alternate views on women in ministry and God's knowledge of the future, confidently declared that their opponents simply "don't believe the Bible." As if their interpretation of the Bible was the only possible way to read it![1]

Sometimes their arrogance makes conservatives unteachable. Not long ago a fellow walked out near the start of my sermon and, when asked about it later, replied that he had some Bible knowledge and would not condone my message by his presence. I wonder how this man will ever learn a new thing if he rejects every idea the first time he hears it. I also wonder how he could object to my completely orthodox sermon!

Conservatives often leave the impression that it is not enough to have the right answers if they do not say them forcefully. They must leave no doubt about what they believe, not only in foundational doctrines but also when it comes to more tangential topics like baptism, female pastors, and events surrounding Christ's return. Any hedging — saying "perhaps" or "quite possibly" rather than "Thus saith the Lord" — or appreciation for another point of view smacks of weakness that leads to liberalism.

Unlike conservatives, whose greatest fear is not knowing the right answer, postmodern innovators dread being caught without a good question. They leap at every opportunity to get lost in the mystery of God. One leader explains: "I grew up thinking that we've figured out the Bible, that we knew what it means. Now I have no idea what most of it means. And yet I feel like life is big again — like life used to be black and white, and now it's in color."[2]

While conservative Christians are reluctant to express doubts for fear of being judged weak or out of the faith, postmodern innovators tend to outdoubt each other in vulnerable competitions of "keeping it real." Where conservative preachers might stress the proofs for God's existence, postmodern pastors are likely to confess the various times they doubted God or his Word.

While their honesty is refreshing, some postmoderns can be so humble that they mumble. After hearing them share their doubts and questions about the Christian faith, one might wonder what they still believe. What are we to make of a preacher who says, "For all we know, the tomb is empty"? Or a teacher who questions the biblical account of Jesus because of something he read in the Gnostic gospels? It is one thing to acknowledge that God is larger than our conservative box; it is another to suggest that our core beliefs are up for discussion.

It doesn't help when postmodern innovators punt many of the important questions into the inscrutable realm of mystery. Earlier this year I attended a conference on the missional church. When asked for a definition of the term *missional,* a leader of the conference mysteriously proclaimed that the concept was too lofty for him to explain. Then he asked us to accept his inability to define it as proof that he understood it, implying that anyone who could put words to it would prove that they did not get it. So if we think we know, we don't; and if we don't know, we do. At this point I realized that I had just lost two days of my life to a cause that even the leaders knew little about!

This chapter will explain why modern conservatives and postmodern innovators disagree so strongly about the value of questions and answers. We will examine the difference between modern and postmodern perspectives on truth and then combine the best insights of both into a biblical way forward.[3]

HOW FIRM A FOUNDATION

The modern world desperately wanted a solid foundation for knowledge. They had just endured the wars of religion (1618 – 48), where various denominations destroyed each other over their differing interpretations of the Christian faith. Roman Catholics killed Calvinists and Lutherans, Lutherans and Calvinists fought the Catholics and each other, and everyone beat up on the Anabaptists, who had the misfortune of being pacifists.

Weary Europeans realized that their religious wars were a dead end. Those committed to their denominations ultimately agreed to disagree, but the majority of Europeans sought to unite everyone around what they shared in common. And they could if they began with human reason rather than divine revelation. Because the Christian groups disagreed about where to find revelation and how to read it, starting with revelation would only end in more battles. But if they began with what every mind could discover, they might find enough common ground to transcend their petty squabbles and get along.

Europe's quest for shared knowledge assumed that its target must be objective rather than subjective, universal rather than local, and absolute rather than relative, changeable, and uncertain. These modern thinkers would consider a belief to be true only if they were absolutely sure that it was true for all people. Anything less would leave room for relativism and land Europe back in its religious mess, where each tradition thought that its truth was better than the rest.

This high bar for knowledge prompted modern philosophers to place a lot of weight on proof. Only by proving their beliefs beyond all doubt could they say with certainty that they were acquiring knowledge that transcended Europe's religious divisions. They achieved this certainty by paying attention to the foundation of their knowledge. Led by René Descartes, who emphasized reason, and John Locke, who stressed what people learned through their five senses, the modern world said that we should begin our quest for knowledge with beliefs that are self-evident, incorrigible, or evident to the senses.

Self-evident beliefs are things that are obviously true, such as $2 + 2 = 4$. Most people do not count on their fingers or mentally do the math when they hear this equation, for it is self-evidently true for them. Incorrigible beliefs are beliefs that cannot possibly be doubted. One such belief occurs when you dismount from a Tilt-a-Whirl. As the world chases its tail in ever tightening circles around you, only one belief remains constant: you're dizzy, and you know it. Dizziness is one of life's few incorrigible beliefs, for unlike most beliefs, it is awfully hard to deny when it comes.

Besides these rational starting points, modern philosophers said that we may also begin from an empirical foundation. While making allowances for the limitations of our senses (e.g., we know that the straw in our soda is not really as bent as it appears through the side of our glass), we nevertheless believe that what our eyes and ears report is reliable. And so besides beliefs that are self-evident and incorrigible, moderns say that we may also believe anything that is evident to our senses.

From this secure foundation, we may infer other beliefs, such as the sky is blue, a triangle has three sides, and if your wife is unhappy, it's probably your fault. If we can logically trace each one of these beliefs back to our foundation, and if our foundation is indubitably true, then we can declare with confidence that we know them (see fig. 10.1).[4]

Fig. 10.1. The Modern Structure of Knowledge

Unfortunately, modernity's need for rational and empirical proof led many to dismiss belief in God. They could not prove God, for his existence did not seem self-evident, indubitable, evident to the senses, or deducible from this foundation. No one had ever seen God, and the presence of evil gave reason to doubt him. Since anything that could be doubted should be, many modern philosophers concluded that they had no choice but to give up belief in God.

Modern Christianity responded in two vastly different ways. Liberal theologians like Friedrich Schleiermacher rescued belief in God by grounding it in religious experience. He declared that God is nothing more than our subjective "feeling of absolute dependence." Everyone is aware that they depend on something for their existence, and this feeling is what it means to be religious. Schleiermacher said that people may express their feelings in different ways — for example, Judaism speaks of retribution and Christianity emphasizes redemption — but at bottom everyone is describing the same ineffable God.[5]

Modern conservatives realized that Schleiermacher's emphasis on feeling recovered belief in God at the expense of allowing anyone to believe anything they felt about him. Princeton theologians Charles Hodge, Alexander Archibald Hodge, and B. B. Warfield returned to modernity's "objective" foundation, but this time they argued that reason actually proves key elements of Christianity. They thought that modern thinkers were right to believe only what they could prove but wrong to believe that the Christian faith lacked proof. The followers of Warfield and the Hodges developed logical arguments that should persuade any rational, honest person that God exists and that the Bible is his revelation. In this way they hoped to meet and defeat modernity's skepticism on its own terms, demonstrating beyond reasonable doubt that the Bible was the objective, universal, and absolute Word of God.[6]

KEEPING IT REAL

Postmodern innovators are not impressed. They shake their heads at modernity's arrogance. Did modern thinkers — both secular and Christian — really presume to prove their beliefs? How could they forget that we are finite? Because our perspective is limited, we can never be certain that we know the absolute truth about things. And that is a good thing, for as we witnessed during the modern world, those "in the know" often used their superiority to oppress others.[7]

Postmodern innovators counter this dangerous hubris of modernity with a humble emphasis on the subjective, local, and relational nature of knowledge (see fig. 10.2). Against the modern idea that we directly perceive the world as it is, postmodern innovators correctly observe that everything we see and hear is filtered through our unique perspective. We are unable to get outside of our skin and see the world in the raw, but we must interpret whatever we know.[8]

For example, consider the evidence of global climate change. People may agree that polar ice caps are melting, but some disagree sharply about what that means. Most conclude that the world is warming and that if we do not stop polluting the atmosphere with carbon emissions, we will suffer catastrophic consequences. A few others suggest that the present warming may be cyclical, and even if it is not, global warming may produce enough benefits to offset its problems.[9]

This diversity of opinion prompts postmodern innovators to concede that all knowledge is local. Just as members of the Sierra Club interpret global climate change differently than the bosses of Exxon Mobil, so our knowledge of everything is to some extent determined by our community. Black people see the world differently than whites, men than women, Christians than Muslims, and wealthy Westerners than the poor in the developing world. Knowledge does not come in one size fits all, but like a good suit, is tried on and tailored to each community's taste.

There are some obvious benefits to this postmodern perspective on knowledge. First, it reminds us of the Christian teaching that we are finite and fallen, and so we should be suspicious of all claims to knowledge. Scripture warned of our sinful tendency to oppress others long before postmoderns discovered that "Power is knowledge."[10] Second, it supplies a harsh remedy for those who use the power of being "in the know" to victimize others. Few things are more unsettling to an oppressor than to learn that his views are so conditioned by his culture that others need not concede his superiority.

However, there is also great danger. If modernity was overconfident—"we can know whatever we can prove"—postmodern innovators often lack confidence — "since we can't prove anything, we really don't know anything." If everything we claim to know is interpreted through our own unique viewpoint, how can we know whether our interpretation is correct? How can we tell whether our perspective breaks through the clutter of competing claims to connect with reality, describing the world as it really is? At the end of the day, aren't we left with only our interpretations of reality rather than reality itself?[11]

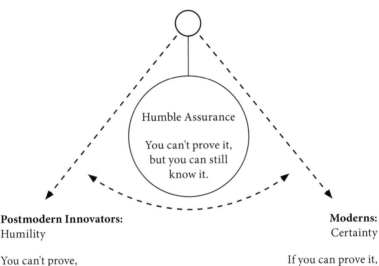

Postmodern Innovators:
Humility

You can't prove,
so you can't know it.

Truth is 1) Local
2) Relational
3) Subjective

Moderns:
Certainty

If you can prove it,
you can know it.

Truth is 1) Universal
2) Absolute
3) Objective

Fig. 10.2. How Do You Know?

Perhaps revelation can solve our problem. We may not be able to rise up and apprehend reality, but God may stoop to our level and reveal the truth to us. Some postmodern innovators insist that this does not get us off the hook, for there is no way to tell whether any purported revelation is really from God. According to John Caputo, all we know for sure is that we believe that we have received a revelation. But this belief conflicts with the beliefs of other faith communities, many of whom doubt our revelation. So we should humbly concede that our supposed revelation does not give us a corner on the truth but is merely one perspective among many.[12]

Even if revelation could prove itself, postmodern innovators remind us that it does not accurately describe God. Because God transcends us in every way, he must accommodate his revelation to what our limited minds can grasp, using small concepts and bite-sized words to convey his unfathomable majesty. This infinite distance between God and us leads John Franke to conclude that "even revelation does not provide human beings with a knowledge that exactly corresponds to that of God."[13] Franke elaborates on what he means by "not … exactly corresponds" with an illustration from Merold Westphal, who explains the gap between God and his revelation with a "homely example":

> I tell my son not to suck on quarters, and he asks why. He has no access to my language about viruses and bacteria, so I break through into his language with a message he needs: "There are little bugs on coins, so small you can't see them, but they can make you very sick if they get inside you." This account does not correspond to the real as I understand it, but it is the "truth" so far as he is able to receive it, and he ought to believe it and act on it. My teacher, Kenneth Kantzer … told us, "The Bible is the divinely revealed *misinformation* about God."[14]

While I appreciate Franke's and Westphal's emphasis on divine transcendence, doesn't their "high view" of God unintentionally land us in pious agnosticism? If what I know does not exactly correspond to what God knows and if his revelation amounts to misinformation, then I cannot say that I know anything about him. Peter Rollins pursues the logical outcome of their claim and concedes the point. Because our words are *"never speaking of God but only ever speaking about our understanding of God,"* Rollins recommends "believing *in* God while remaining dubious concerning what one believes *about* God."[15] When "asked how I could possibly believe that my own religious tradition was true," Rollins replied that "the only answer I could give to this question was, 'I don't.' … I was quite confident in asserting that my own religion was not true."[16]

Perhaps this is why, as we saw in chapters 7 and 8, some postmodern innovators are not eager to evangelize those in other religions. If you are not confident that your beliefs are truer than anyone else's, then you wouldn't want to press them upon others.

One leader explains: "Is our religion the only one that understands the true meaning of life? Or does God place his truth in others too? Well, God decides, and not us.... People are rightfully afraid of any religion that will not accept its place at the feet of the Holy Mystery. If the Christian God is not larger than Christianity, then Christianity is simply not to be trusted."[17]

Granted that modern Christians are overconfident in their ability to prove the truth, but must postmodern innovators eat so much humble pie? Is there a third, more biblical way between these two extremes, one that is appropriately modest yet claims to know specific truths about God and his world?[18] Against the modern project, I concede that there is no way to irrefutably prove my beliefs to anyone else. But against what many postmoderns assume, this does not leave me without access to universal, true-for-everyone knowledge. I possess truth even though I can't prove it. Here's why.

TRUTH WITHOUT PROOF

Modern thinkers (both secular and Christian) and postmodern innovators make the same mistake: they start with themselves. Both groups claim to know only what their minds can prove. They differ in that, while moderns naively suppose that they can prove a lot, postmodern innovators recognize that our limited minds cannot prove anything.

Neither group leaves enough room for God. Many moderns are nontheists because they cannot deduce God from their rational and empirical foundation. Some moderns do believe in God, but only because they mistakenly think that their arguments prove his existence. Postmodern innovators also *believe* in God, but they are so bothered by the limitations of their perspective that they do not seem to *know* much about him.[19]

But why begin with ourselves? If starting with ourselves leads either to naive arrogance or humble ignorance, perhaps we are beginning in the wrong place. What would happen if, rather than start with ourselves and attempt to reason up to God, we made God the foundation of our knowledge?

According to C. S. Lewis, placing God in our foundation is the only way to know anything. Lewis said that if there is no God, then the history of the world is a series of random, chance events. But chance is irrational (we chalk things up to chance when there is no reason for them). If, like everything else in the world, my mind is the product of chance, then why should I trust it? I would be foolish to rely on a rationality that rested on irrationality. Thus, belief in God is the only reason to trust my reason.[20]

Alvin Plantinga restates the argument in a positive way. He observes that true beliefs need warrant to count as knowledge. It isn't enough to be right about what we believe; we also need a credible reason for what we are right about. For instance, consider a hurricane that was successfully predicted by a weatherman and a witch. Although it turns out that both were correct, most Westerners would say that only the weatherman had knowledge of the event, for Doppler Plus Next Rad Storm Team radar supplies a stronger (and overhyped) reason for belief than a crystal ball.

What warrant does Plantinga suggest we need for our beliefs? Simply this: if we have good reason to believe that our minds and sensory equipment are functioning properly and that we are in a suitable environment for them to detect truth, then we may justifiably believe whatever we perceive in the world. And what reason do we have to believe this? Our belief in God. Only if we believe that there is a God who made us to flourish in this world do we have warrant to trust what our eyes and ears report is going on around us. According to Plantinga, those who do not believe in God cannot claim to know anything at all.[21]

But how can I start with belief in God? Isn't this fideism? In case you have misplaced your Introduction to Philosophy notes, I remind you that "fideist" is the worst thing you can call a thinking person. It's like saying "liberal" to a conservative, "right-wing fundamentalist" to a liberal, or "Hello, waiter" to an Ivy Leaguer. Fideism means that you're flying blind, that your faith is a wishful leap into the abyss. Fideists don't have any good reason for believing what they do; they just believe and hope for the best. They may get dumb lucky and guess right, but the odds are heavily stacked against them.

Is my foundational belief in God a desperate stab in the dark? No, for I do not merely wish that God exists. I know it. And so does everyone else. Despite the arguments that skeptics raise against God's existence, the apostle Paul declares in Romans 1:18–20 that everyone knows there is a God, and any who claim ignorance "are without excuse."

When I lived in Beijing, I tried for two years to persuade my Chinese friend to believe in God. I told Sun Yi that there must be a wise and powerful Creator who made our beautiful world and grounds our concept of right and wrong. But her atheistic upbringing had conditioned her to deflect my best arguments. If the complexity of the world demands a world-maker, then doesn't the grandeur of God require a God-maker? If God is necessary to ground morality, then why is communist China less corrupt in some ways than "Christian" America?

Our conversations ended in stalemates, leaving me frustrated that I couldn't come up with better arguments and Sun Yi smugly confident that she had held her own. Then my Bible study led me to Romans 1, where I learned that all people have some basic knowledge of God. "Hmm," I thought, "maybe I've been going at this all wrong." So the next time she asked why I believed in God, I simply turned the question back on her.

"Sun Yi," I said, "it doesn't matter why I believe in God. But tell me, why do you?" I'll never forget her response. "Oh," was all she said, but her smiling eyes met mine, and we both knew the game was up. Romans 1 had called her bluff.[22]

Here is the point: our foundational belief in God — which according to Romans 1 everyone shares — supplies the necessary and sufficient reason to trust our deliverances of reason. Because we are finite and fallen, we must critically evaluate whatever we think we know, but these limitations do not prevent us from learning much about the world. While we could be wrong — and so we remain open to correction — we are justified in believing that water freezes at thirty-two degrees Fahrenheit, autumnal trees shed their leaves in a blaze of color, and listening to Mozart is more inspiring than the opening rounds of *American Idol*. Regardless of how many people might disagree, our belief in God justifies our inclination to believe that what our minds report is actually true. As Lewis and Plantinga made clear, without this prior belief in God, we would lack warrant to know anything at all (see fig. 10.3).

A WORD FROM GOD

But how do we know that Romans 1 is true? And what about our many beliefs that transcend what our minds can discover? For these we need a second foundational belief, this time in revelation. As with God's existence, I cannot prove that the Bible is God's Word, but then again, I do not have to. John Calvin wrote that Scripture is self-authenticating, by which he meant that "it carries with itself its own credibility in order to be received without contradiction, and is not to be submitted to proofs or arguments."[23]

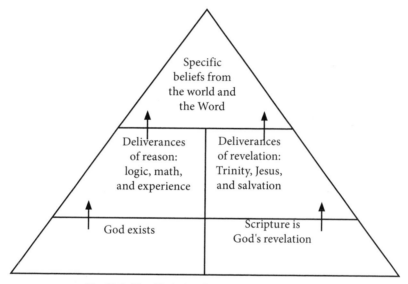

Fig. 10.3. The Christian Structure of Knowledge

Calvin believed that the Bible proves itself to be God's Word, that "Scripture exhibits fully as clear evidence of its own truth as white and black things do of their color, or sweet and bitter things do of their taste."[24] Just as snow is obviously white and sugar is indisputably sweet, so those who read Scripture should recognize that it is the Word of God.

However, our sinful condition prevents us from perceiving the voice of God, which is why Calvin says that God sends his Spirit to overcome our blindness and enable us to believe what we should have seen all along. He writes: "For as God alone is a fit witness of himself in his Word, so also the Word will not find acceptance in men's hearts before it is sealed by the inward testimony of the Spirit. The same Spirit, therefore, who has spoken through the mouths of the prophets must penetrate into our hearts to persuade us that they faithfully proclaimed what had been divinely commanded."[25]

Here is the point: because everyone should recognize that Scripture is the Word of God, I am justified in believing what it tells me about God, Jesus, and the way of salvation. I do not need to play the modern game, withholding belief until I produce an objective, universal, and absolute argument that the Bible is God's Word. Neither need I succumb to postmodern timidity, humbly mumbling that my perceived revelation is not necessarily truer than any other. I can justifiably know that the Scriptures are God's Word, for when I read them, the Holy Spirit opens my ears to hear the voice of God. That is reason enough to believe, even without proof that can go public.[26]

But what about the postmodern objection that God's transcendence prevents me from rightly understanding him through his revelation? I agree that I will never completely comprehend God or his revelation, but this does not prevent me from knowing God truly. Calvin said that God speaks to us like a mother talks to an infant, with lots of coos and aahs and goochie goos.[27] There is much about a mother that lies beyond what an infant can comprehend, and yet what a child does understand — that he or she is cared for by a loving adult — he or she knows correctly. Likewise, though God will always exceed the grasp of my finite mind, there remains much about him that I do understand. The perfect must not become the enemy of the good.

In summary, moderns are right to say that an objective, real world exists, while postmoderns are right to counter that no one has clean and unfettered access to this world. When we combine the insights of each, we conclude that though we interpret everything from our finite and flawed perspective, we are still able to accurately, though incompletely, access this real world.[28] We may self-critically believe what our minds and senses tell us because we justifiably believe that we and our world are made by God. And we may self-critically believe what we learn from Scripture because we believe that it is inspired by God. Rather than give in to the modern extreme of arrogant certainty or the postmodern extreme of uncertain timidity, we may with humble assurance declare that even though we can't prove it, we do know much.

But perhaps we glossed too quickly over the role of Scripture in our foundational beliefs. Some postmodern innovators are wondering whether it belongs there, and many are raising questions about its truthfulness and in what sense it is written by God. We will study this controversy next.

CHAPTER 11

IS THE BIBLE GOD'S TRUE WORD?

My friend's house burned down last month. Besides thanking God for sparing his life, we noted with interest that his Bible had not caught fire. When my friend mentioned this fact to his insurance adjuster, the Christian agent replied that in over twenty years of settling claims, he had never seen a Bible burn (really, not even a Gideon's?). Apparently God protects his Word by making its pages flame retardant, though as my friend discovered, God could do better at preventing water damage.

This mystical reverence for the Bible is common in conservative churches, where our esteem for its divine authorship often obscures its human side. So rather than study Scripture's context to learn what its human authors meant, we often blithely misapply the words of Scripture directly to our own lives. I have heard national leaders say that they marched around a piece of property seven times to claim it for God (only do this if you're going to demolish the building anyway), that I would be healthier and happier if I followed the Maker's Diet laid out in Leviticus, and that I should follow the example of Abraham's servant if I wanted a wife like Rebekah (go where the girls are and wait for a sign).

At least these were attempts to understand the Bible. Some conservatives do not even try. I know of a long line of preachers who begin each sermon by reading a verse of Scripture. But rather than explain what the passage means, they use the text as a springboard to tell stories about their life with God. They may read Mark 14:34, where Jesus tells his disciples in Gethsemane, "Tarry ye here, and watch," and then spend the next thirty minutes telling of the many times and various ways they tarried. These preachers may gush about their high regard for Scripture, but in fact they merely use it as a supernatural talisman to bless their very human sermons.

If conservative Christians believe that God inspires chapter and verse (why else would someone preach on the 3:16s of the Bible?), postmodern innovators stress Scripture's human element. One leader asserts that we should not assume that "the Bible is a divine product, dropped out of the sky by God." Rather, "people wrote some things down, and the 'God' element came later."[1] Another takes Karl Barth's view that Scripture is not revelation but is a witness to Jesus Christ, who alone is God's revelation.[2]

I respond to these statements in their respective endnotes. Here I have space enough only to address the postmodern innovators' two main objections to the conservative view of Scripture. They think that conservatives make two modern mistakes: we use the Bible as our foundation for knowledge, and we believe that it was written without error.[3]

One comment expresses both concerns. In a seminar I attended, an evangelical theologian warned against placing the Bible in our foundation lest we find an error in it and our entire house of beliefs come crashing down. Better to think of our beliefs as an interrelated web with the Bible contributing an important part. Then if we find errors in Scripture, we can merely reconfigure our web rather than suffer complete collapse.

This chapter will lay out these postmodern objections, provide a conservative response, and conclude with what we may learn from our postmodern friends.

WHAT'S YOUR AUTHORITY?

Many postmodern innovators reject modernity's focus on the foundations of knowledge. As I explained in chapter 10, modern philosophers thought they could prove their beliefs if they started from an objective, indubitably certain foundation and reasoned up from there. But their search for universally accessible, indisputable facts ended in failure. Postmoderns now realize that people come from too many different perspectives to ever completely agree on anything.

So rather than pretend that we have constructed the perfect house of knowledge on an unshakable foundation, some postmodern innovators argue that we should think of our beliefs as an interrelated web. This nonfoundational approach to knowledge asserts that rather than reason from the bottom up, inference between beliefs runs in multiple directions. Most important, since no beliefs are foundational, then none are immune from criticism. No belief finds acceptance with everyone, and none comes with 100 percent logical certainty. We must admit that we could be wrong.[4]

While I appreciate this humble reminder that my beliefs could be wrong, I wonder how I can tell whether any of them are right. If my beliefs are not built on a solid foundation, then how do I know they are true?

In their important book *Beyond Foundationalism*, Stanley Grenz and John Franke claim that we do not need a foundation — whether from reason, experience, or even Scripture — to access truth. They argue that our source and final authority for knowledge is "the Spirit speaking in or through Scripture" to our Christian community.[5] The Spirit uses the original meaning of Scripture to communicate his will, but "we must never conclude that exegesis alone can exhaust the Spirit's speaking to us through the text.... The Spirit appropriates the text with the goal of communicating to us in *our* situation, which, while perhaps paralleling in certain respects that of the ancient community, is nevertheless unique."[6]

If the Spirit's speaking goes beyond the original meaning of a biblical text, how can we tell whether what we think he is saying is true? Grenz and Franke reply that there is safety in numbers. Our authority is not what we believe the Spirit is saying to us as private individuals but what he is saying to our gathered community.[7]

But what if our entire community gets it wrong? Grenz and Franke respond that the goal of the Spirit's speech is to empower his church to construct a world that reflects God's purposes for creation. If our interpretation of the Spirit's voice enables us to do that — if our "theological vision provides the framework for the construction of true community" — then we may confidently declare that our understanding of what the Spirit says is true.[8]

Grenz and Franke, who are more theologically conservative than many postmodern innovators, emphasize the Spirit's role in our use of Scripture because they want to protect the sovereignty of God. They defend God's claim as our final authority from all challengers, whether that be tradition, reason, or even Scripture. In his prequel to *Beyond Foundationalism*, Franke writes that "the ultimate authority in the church is not a particular source, be it *Scripture*, tradition, reason, or experience, but only the *living God*."[9] The Bible is not authoritative in its own right, but only "because it is the vehicle through which the Spirit speaks."[10]

THE ERRORS OF INERRANCY

Besides claiming that conservatives mistakenly place the Bible in their foundation of knowledge, postmodern innovators also allege that the conservative commitment to biblical inerrancy is idolatrous, outdated, unbiblical, and compromised by modern science.

1. *Bibliolatry.* Postmodern innovators frequently suggest that conservatives have elevated Scripture above the God who inspired it. They have not only placed the Bible rather than God in their foundation of knowledge, but their insistence on an inerrant text has led them to worship words instead of God. Carl Raschke levels the charge: "Inerrancy is an idolatry of the text. It is bibliolatry plain and simple, inasmuch as it cannot see beyond the logical lattice of the text to encounter the Other who is ever calling us into his kingdom and before his throne."[11]

Raschke contends that the conservatives' concern for biblical inerrancy prompts them to turn the Bible into a list of propositions that can be checked for factual accuracy. Was there a great flood? Did ten plagues strike Egypt? Did Jesus feed thousands with five loaves and two fish? Raschke says that this preoccupation with impersonal facts causes conservatives to miss the larger point that the Bible is God's promise to us. Because we cannot verify a promise until it comes true, we should stop fretting over how to prove the facts of Scripture and instead focus on hearing and obeying God's voice in the text. In so doing we show that Scripture is God's authoritative Word, whether or not it is inerrant.[12]

2. *Compromised by modern philosophy.* Other postmodern innovators argue that biblical inerrancy is an outdated concern of the modern world. They say that when modern liberals built their beliefs on the foundation of religious experience, modern conservatives countered by grounding their beliefs on an inerrant Bible. In this way conservatives could justifiably claim that they possessed sure and infallible truth that could compete with the beliefs of modern liberals and secularists. But now that we have outgrown the

modern fixation with foundations, we no longer need an inerrant Scripture to ground our beliefs.[13]

3. *Unbiblical.* Some postmodern innovators go further, claiming that grounding our beliefs in an inerrant Bible is not only unnecessary but also unbiblical. As Neo tells Pastor Dan, Scripture says that "the church is the foundation of the truth.... But, unless I'm mistaken, the Bible never calls itself the foundation."[14] Brian McLaren explains, "Interestingly, when Scripture talks about itself, it doesn't use the language we often use in our explanations of its value. For modern Western Christians, words like *authority, inerrancy, infallibility, revelation, objective, absolute,* and *literal* are crucial.... Hardly anyone notices the irony of resorting to the authority of extrabiblical words and concepts to justify one's belief in the Bible's ultimate authority."[15] Dave Tomlinson adds that a "fundamental problem with the doctrine of inerrancy ... is that the Bible makes no such claim for itself."[16]

In an interview on this question, a leading postmodern innovator declared that the idea of biblical inerrancy is driven by a modern rather than biblical question: whether the Bible is scientifically or empirically trustworthy. He said that Scripture's faithfulness does not depend on its every jot and tittle being scientifically true, for the truth of Scripture transcends what science can prove. Besides, trying to correlate Scripture with science is a losing game, for what science believes continually changes as we learn more about the world.

4. *Compromised by modern science.* A final objection to biblical inerrancy is that besides being idolatrous, outdated, unnecessary, and unbiblical, it also seems to capitulate to the criteria of modern science. Dave Tomlinson writes, "The evangelical notion of inerrancy is based on the view that Scripture must have the same sort of accuracy in reporting past events that an objective modern history or science text possesses."[17] Theologian John Perry agrees: "Specifically, for most of the twentieth century, there was a steadily increasing concern among conservative American Christians that Scripture is accurate in all matters, including the precise wording of detailed historical events and matters of science."[18]

Because they thought that Scripture must follow modern standards for writing history, some conservative Christians worried about how to reconcile contrary accounts in the Gospels. Luke says that Jesus stood during the Sermon on the Mount, while Matthew says he sat.[19] Luke writes that Jesus healed a blind beggar on his way into Jericho, while Matthew and Mark say that he healed the man on the way out.[20] Mark declares that Peter denied Jesus three times before the rooster crowed twice, while other Gospels only say that the rooster crowed once.[21]

How can both sets be true? Some conservatives resolve the conflict by adding the stories together. They conclude that Jesus must have both sat and stood during different parts of his sermon (seems probable), that he healed the blind man as he left Old Jericho and entered the new city (sounds plausible), and that Peter must have denied Jesus in two sets of three, with a rooster crowing after each set (*what?*).[22]

This last case illustrates why some say biblical inerrancy surrenders too much to modern science. Must we resort to such interpretive gymnastics to preserve our belief in Scripture? Isn't there a way to believe in biblical inerrancy without succumbing to these postmodern objections? Despite the impression given above, some conservative Christians have thought deeply about the meaning and value of biblical inerrancy. Here is what we believe.

THE TRUTH ABOUT INERRANCY

1. *Bibliolatry?* For starters, contrary to Raschke's comment that conservatives are guilty of bibliolatry because they "cannot see beyond ... the text to encounter the Other," I have never met anyone who places the Bible above God. Like a lover who reads and rereads letters from his beloved, every conservative I know reads the Bible not for its own sake but because it is where we hear the voice of God.

Just as any lover knows that there is more to his beloved than she can express in words, so every Christian recognizes that the living God transcends his Word. Conservatives agree with others that God is more than what his words can express, but we also insist that he is not less.[23] Our belief that God's Word accurately conveys truth about him does not imply that we think it captures him.

But while we may not elevate the Bible above God, Raschke is right that our focus on the facts of Scripture may distract us from pursuing the Person who wrote them. I will address this temptation at the end of this chapter, but for now note that while biblical inerrancy is essential, it is not everything. We must never forget that the Bible is more than merely true — it is also the Word of God.

2. *Unbiblical and modern?* What about the charge that inerrancy is a modern idea? Earlier Christians may have believed that Scripture was true and trustworthy, but they did not directly say that it was without error in all matters until the modern period. Doesn't this prove that biblical inerrancy is a modern belief—perhaps appropriate for that time but no longer meaningful to postmodern people? If the inerrancy of Scripture is so important, then why wasn't it clearly stated until recently?[24]

a. *Why inerrancy arrived late.* The reason inerrancy arrived late is because it wasn't needed. Doctrine typically develops in response to heresy. The church states what it believes when it must refute what it doesn't. Until modern people began denying the accuracy of Scripture, it never occurred to anyone to insist on biblical inerrancy.

In 1689 it was enough for Baptists to claim that the Bible is "the certain and infallible rule" for "the knowledge, faith, and obedience that constitutes salvation."[25] This powerful declaration is inadequate today, for in the intervening three centuries, some have said that the Bible may be trusted about matters of salvation but not when it speaks to other, lesser areas of history and science.

Conservative Christians realized that the spirit of their earlier confessions required that they go beyond them. So evangelicals meeting in 1978 went further, claiming in their Chicago Statement on Biblical Inerrancy that "Scripture is without error or fault in all its teaching," not only when it tells us how to be saved, but also when it addresses "God's acts in creation," "the events of world history," and "its own literary origins."[26]

Thus, like everything else the church believes, the doctrine of biblical inerrancy was a timely correction of a bad idea. The fact that this correction occurred in the modern period does not count against it, anymore than we may discount the doctrine of the Trinity because it was not developed until the fourth century, justification by faith alone because it was not determined until the sixteenth century, or the extent of God's foreknowledge because it was not debated until the last decade.

b. *Why inerrancy is not the property of modernity.* But doesn't belief in biblical inerrancy commit us to the outdated view of modern foundationalism? Not necessarily. Postmodern theologians like Grenz and Franke object to what is known as *strong foundationalism.*

This was the dominant way of knowing in the modern world, which, as explained in chapter 10, seeks to ground every belief in an indubitably certain foundation that cannot possibly be wrong.

Most everyone now realizes that this modern dream was hopelessly naive. In its place many Christians favor what is known as *weak foundationalism*. It is considered weak because it is less strict about what beliefs may belong to one's foundation. Rather than demand absolute certainty, weak foundationalism allows us to start on any foundation that seems plausible.[27]

My Christian structure of knowledge from the last chapter is an example of weak foundationalism, for although I cannot prove my belief in God or prove that Scripture is God's Word, I am permitted to start there. I must be prepared to defend these beliefs against any and all objections, but I do not need to withhold belief until I prove them. Thus, I am able to ground my beliefs in Scripture without succumbing to Grenz and Franke's charge that I am too modern.[28]

c. *Why weak foundationalism is better than nonfoundationalism.* I prefer the authority of Scripture to Grenz and Franke's reliance on "the Spirit speaking in or through Scripture," for despite their careful argument, they leave us wondering how to determine whether any particular message is from God. It seems possible for an entire church to misunderstand what the Holy Spirit is saying through the Bible. Even if everyone agrees and what they agree on seems to work, there is no guarantee that they have correctly heard the Spirit's voice.[29]

The problem worsens when Grenz and Franke realize that, having separated the Spirit's authoritative speaking from the text of Scripture, there is nothing to prevent the Spirit from speaking authoritatively through other means. So besides listening for the Spirit's direction through Scripture, they assert that the church must also "listen intently for the voice of the Spirit" in "the world, bubbling to the surface through the artifacts and symbols humans construct."[30] It is hard enough for the church to agree on what the Spirit is saying through Scripture; imagine the difficulty of hearing his voice in the diverse world of human culture![31]

Because the community may easily stray, it seems better to place our trust in the settled Word of God. Of course we will often misinterpret its texts, but this only gives us more reason to start there. If we know that error will inevitably creep into our understanding of God's will, why should we not do all we can to confine it to the stage of interpretation? Better to have a fixed source of knowledge (Scripture) and a fallible interpretation than to have both a variable source (who decides where and what God is speaking?) and interpretation (who decides what it means?).[32]

And contrary to what Neo told Pastor Dan, there is biblical support for using Scripture as our foundation of knowledge. Paul declares that the church is "built on the foundation of the apostles and prophets, with Christ Jesus himself as the chief cornerstone."[33] The church has long held that "apostles and prophets" here represents their writings, or Paul's way of saying that the church is founded on the truth of Scripture.

d. *Why inerrancy is believed.* Whether or not foundationalism is correct is actually beside the point, for contrary to what some allege, foundationalism is not why conservatives believe in biblical inerrancy.[34] We believe that Scripture is inerrant not because we need to prop up our foundation with indubitable certainty but because we believe that the Bible is the Word of God. Expressed as a syllogism, we believe the following:

> Major premise: The Word of God is without error.
>
> Minor premise: The Bible is the Word of God.
>
> Conclusion: Therefore the Bible is without error.

Those who deny our conclusion must either deny that the Bible is God's Word or question in what sense the Bible is without error. The former view, held by Karl Barth and increasingly popular among evangelicals, is devastating for biblical authority and our knowledge of God's will.[35] The latter is often a source of confusion, so let me clear up what we mean when we say that the Bible is inerrant.

NOTHING BUT THE TRUTH

The premodern authors of Scripture did not always write with the objective precision that we expect today. Because the modern world privileges science and facts, modern historians attempt to reproduce verbal photographs of the past, reporting exactly who said what and what happened next in precise order.[36]

By this standard the Gospels are riddled with errors, for they do not always agree even on the basic order of events. Luke says that

Jesus called Matthew before the Sermon on the Mount while Matthew puts his calling afterward.[37] Luke declares that Satan offered Jesus the world before tempting him to jump from the temple, while Matthew reverses this order.[38] According to modern criteria, these accounts can't all be true.

Or consider the quotations found in the Gospels. When Jesus asked his disciples who they thought he was, Peter said either "You are the Christ" (Mark 8:29), "The Christ of God" (Luke 9:20), or "You are the Christ, the Son of the living God" (Matthew 16:16). According to modern standards, at least two of these gospels carelessly recorded Peter's words, and thanks to their sloppiness, we will never know what Peter actually said.

But just as we would object if some future historian corrects us for not writing according to his criteria, so we should not hold the first-century authors of the New Testament to our twenty-first-century standards. Premodern authors were more interested in *what* than *when*, the significance of the event than its chronology. They shaped, modified, and rearranged their material in ways that modern historians never would.

For example, Matthew organized his gospel around five major speeches of Christ. Perhaps he placed his own calling after the Sermon on the Mount (first speech) so that it appears near Jesus' commissioning of the twelve disciples (second speech). Luke lists the selection of the twelve disciples before the Sermon on the Mount, so it would make sense for him to include Matthew's calling there.

Likewise, it is appropriate that Matthew would end Christ's temptations with Satan's offer of the world, because his gospel emphasizes that Jesus came to take back the world. Matthew begins with Jesus refusing Satan's offer of the world and ends with the resurrected Christ declaring, "All authority in heaven and on earth has been given to me."[39] Alternately, Luke may close with the temptation on the temple because it occurred in Jerusalem, which is the geographic focus of his gospel.[40]

Just as the Gospels saw no need to follow a strictly chronological order of events, so they felt free to paraphrase what was said rather than limit themselves to direct quotes. Whereas Mark has Peter say that Jesus is the Messiah, Luke makes it more emphatic by adding that Jesus is "the Messiah of God." Matthew teases out the logical implications of Peter's confession and, with a messianic title common in his gospel, has Peter declare that Jesus is also "the Son of the living God."[41]

Thus, when we say that the Bible is inerrant, we do not mean that it tries to meet modern standards for historical reporting. But neither do we mean, as some believe, that the Bible is only true when it speaks to salvation and is potentially false when it addresses lesser subjects, such as "geology, meteorology, cosmology, botany, astronomy, geography, etc."[42]

Instead, we mean that everything the Bible affirms — when understood according to its premodern, Eastern, and commonsense view of the world — is entirely true and without error. So we take Joshua's statement that the sun stood still, not as scientific proof that the sun moves around the earth, but merely as a description of how things appeared to him.[43] We read Jesus' statement that the mustard seed "is the smallest of all your seeds" not as a scientific statement about the smallest possible seed but as a general observation that illustrates a spiritual point.[44]

We interpret Jesus' prophecy that "not one stone" of the temple "will be left on another" not as a precise statement that must be literally fulfilled but as a descriptive promise of the temple's destruction. Despite the continuing presence of the temple's western wall, we may say that Jesus' words came true.[45]

And we avoid the temptation to cram the Creation story into our modern mind-set, concocting reasons why the light of Day 1 precedes the sun on Day 4 and saying, like the visiting preacher in my town, that anyone who does not agree with his scientific reading of Genesis 1 is a liberal who does not believe the Bible. Instead, we read Genesis 1 for what it is, a literary narrative that describes God's creation of our good world.[46]

Inerrancy does not mean that Scripture will address all of our contemporary concerns or answer every question we put to it. It simply means that when properly understood within its own genre and purpose, each passage of Scripture speaks the truth about whatever it affirms.

Here is a helpful way to think about inerrancy. The human authors of Scripture surely held some wrong beliefs. Some may have thought that the earth is flat and the center of the universe, that women are inferior to men, and that bleeding is a terrific way to flush out disease (it wasn't that long ago that our best doctors bled

George Washington to death). Inerrancy reminds us that the Holy Spirit prevented these mistaken views from entering Scripture. He wrote the words of Scripture with and through the human authors so that they included only what is true.[47]

ESSENTIAL BUT NOT EVERYTHING

As with previous chapters, so here we can eliminate the extreme ends of the postmodern and conservative continuum and settle on a biblical perspective that balances the concerns of both (see fig. 11.1).

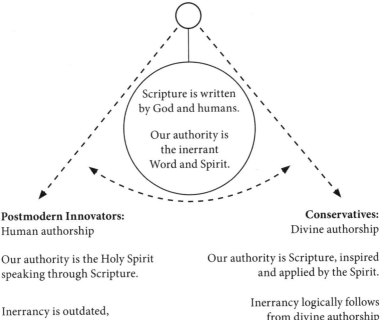

Scripture is written by God and humans.

Our authority is the inerrant Word and Spirit.

Postmodern Innovators:
Human authorship

Our authority is the Holy Spirit speaking through Scripture.

Inerrancy is outdated, is naive, and turns Scripture into an idol.

Conservatives:
Divine authorship

Our authority is Scripture, inspired and applied by the Spirit.

Inerrancy logically follows from divine authorship and supplies confidence to trust the Scriptures.

Fig. 11.1. The Battle for the Bible

First, conservatives stress Scripture's divine side and postmodern innovators emphasize its human element. Why not say that Scripture is fully authored by both God and men? God is the primary author of Scripture — for "all Scripture is God-breathed" and "men spoke from God as they were carried along by the Holy

Spirit" — but God's initiative does not reduce the human authors to passive participants.[48]

Unlike B. B. Warfield, who said that the human authors of Scripture were nothing more than stained glass through which God's light passed, it seems that they actively joined the Spirit of God when they wrote Scripture.[49] Luke was not merely a window pane through which God wrote the story of Christ and his church, but he "carefully investigated everything from the beginning" for his gospel and Acts. Likewise, it was Paul who saluted his friends in the last chapter of Romans, not merely God sending greetings through Paul.[50] Just as Jesus is both wholly God and man, so we must not slight either the divine or human authors of Scripture.

Second, against the conservative temptation to emphasize Scripture more than the Spirit and Grenz and Franke's postmodern attempt to emphasize the Spirit more than Scripture, I believe that our authority is the Word *and* Spirit. We learned in chapter 2 that the Spirit and Scripture are inseparably united, so it would be a mistake to elevate one at the expense of the other. Scripture receives its authority from the Spirit, and the Spirit speaks authoritatively through Scripture. We cannot have one without the other.

Finally, postmodern innovators rightly note that inerrancy is not the greatest thing we can say about the Bible. It does not even apply to Scripture's most important parts. The Bible contains commands ("Do it all for the glory of God"), questions ("Which is the greatest commandment?"), prayers ("Lord, save me!"), and praise ("Who can proclaim the mighty acts of the LORD or fully declare his praise?").[51] None of these are true or false, for none describe a state of affairs that can be checked. Commands, questions, prayers, and praise are deeply meaningful, but we would not say that they are true.

This reminds us that the Bible is much more than a true book. Many books are true — I hope this is one — but only one is the Word of God. As such, Scripture is far more than a storehouse of facts about God and the world. It is the living Word that uses its higher categories of command, promise, prayer, and praise to create and nourish our life with God. We must never let our spirited defense of Scripture's truth distract us from its main point.

And yet, though inerrancy does not capture the highest peaks of Scripture, it does supply the foundation on which they rest.

Commands, praise, prayers, and questions may not be directly true or false, but they do depend on more foundational facts that are. "Do it all for the glory of God" and "Praise the LORD" are meaningless unless God exists, "Lord, save me!" is pointless if Jesus cannot help, and asking which command is greatest is futile if God has not revealed his will to us. God's Word is more than true, but it cannot be less.[52]

Postmodern innovators correctly say that we cannot prove that the Bible is inerrant, for we cannot go back in time and verify its historical claims. It is too late to prove that Jesus walked on water, healed a leper, and arose from the dead.[53] But as we saw in chapter 10, we do not need proof to claim truth. Unless we have good reason to think otherwise, we are justified in believing that God's Word — because it is *God's Word* — does not err.

And we must, for how can we believe any part of Scripture if another part is wrong? How can we trust the higher truths of Scriptures if its lower claims are false? If we must believe the Word of God in order to be saved, then the inerrancy of Scripture plays a vital role in our salvation. It would be hard to have faith without it.[54]

Many postmodern innovators disagree with this last statement, in part because they think that they are forging a new faith for which the old rules do not apply. My final chapter challenges this assumption, arguing that those who ignore the mistakes of history will probably repeat them. We are inevitably shaped by history, especially when we are least aware of it. In the words of William Faulkner, "The past isn't dead. It isn't even past."

CHAPTER 12

THE FUTURE RUNS THROUGH THE PAST

Last Easter an evangelical website posted a blog that attempted to persuade liberal Christians to believe in the resurrection. This is a tough sell, given that full-blown liberals do not believe in miracles, much less a miracle that involves a person rising from the dead.

But the author, Diana Butler Bass, had a liberal in her corner. She quoted a Bishop Corrigan, who, when asked whether he believed in the resurrection, replied "Yes. I believe in the resurrection. I've seen it too many times not to."

This agreeable response actually ducks the issue. The parishioner wondered whether Bishop Corrigan believed in the *physical* resurrection of Jesus and his followers. Because he did not want to admit that he did not, Corrigan simply changed the subject. He has seen evil people become good, so yes, he does believe in a *moral* resurrection.

Rather than confront his evasion, Butler Bass suggested that Corrigan's comment provides a way past the liberal-conservative divide and "points to a different way of embracing, of believing, the resurrection." Against liberals, who turn the resurrection "into an allegory or a spiritual metaphor" and conservatives, who attempt to prove that Jesus rose from the dead, we can believe in the resurrection because of changed lives. Thus, the resurrection has historical evidence — as conservatives believe, and it has personal significance — as liberals emphasize.

Butler Bass concluded, "The evidence for the resurrection is all around us. *Not in some ancient text,* Jesus bones, or a DNA sample. Rather, the historical evidence for the resurrection is Jesus living in us; it is the transformative power of the Holy Spirit, bringing back to life that which was dead. We are the evidence."[1]

Although Butler Bass claimed to have found a third way beyond the liberal-conservative impasse, her argument seems to give too much away to the liberals. It's not clear whether she agrees with Bishop Corrigan's redefinition of the resurrection or is merely using it as a conversation starter with liberal Christians. Either way, it does not work, for the former guts the heart of the Christian faith and the latter says that our moral change rather than Scripture ("some ancient text") is the reason we believe that Jesus is alive.

Before conservatives cluck too self-righteously, remember the many times we have joyfully sung, "You ask me how I know he lives? He li-i-ives within my heart!" We say that Jesus is alive because "He walks with me and talks with me along life's narrow way."[2] How does this hymn differ from Butler Bass's argument? Both seem hopelessly subjective. Warm hearts and changed lives cannot prove that Jesus rose from the dead. After reading 1 Corinthians 15, can anyone imagine the apostle Paul defending the resurrection with either of these arguments?

While Butler Bass's argument is not persuasive, her desire for a new option is shared by many postmodern innovators. Brian McLaren recalled being introduced at a youth workers' convention, where, upon asking how many people considered themselves to be liberal or conservative, the speaker (Mark Oestreicher) asked, "And how many of you wish there could be a third alternative, something beyond the confining boxes of liberal and conservative?" McLaren wrote that "the room erupted with applause and cheers. Then Mark very kindly said that I was a pilgrim in search of that third alternative."[3]

This chapter will examine this desire to transcend the polarized camps of liberal and conservative Christianity. I will establish the liberal-conservative baseline of the modern world, explain how postmodern innovators attempt to overcome this divide, and then conclude with a better, third way forward.

THROUGH THE PAST

Christianity in the modern world was divided between liberals and conservatives. Because liberals did not believe in the supernatural claims of Scripture, they reduced the Christian faith to the moral principles behind the stories. They did not believe that Jesus fed more than five thousand people from a boy's lunch, but the story does illustrate the importance of sharing. If we follow the boy's example and share what we have, then others will share too until all are fed.

Liberals did not believe that Jesus rose bodily from the dead, but they thought they still embraced the point of the resurrection. Just as Jesus cried out in faith from the cross and was rewarded with a "resurrection," so we may follow his example and entrust ourselves to God in our darkest hour.[4] The resurrection reminds us that spring is coming, when the power of new life is felt in the fresh breezes that blow across our greening world and sprouting tulips.

Immanuel Kant pioneered the liberal tendency to turn the miraculous stories of Scripture into universal ethical principles. In his *Religion within the Limits of Reason Alone* (1793), Kant said that Jesus is not God and he did not die and rise again for our sins. But rather than discard the wildly embellished story of Jesus, Kant said that we should follow his example as we seek to become better people. It does not matter what we believe about Jesus, whether we pray, are baptized, or receive the Lord's Supper. As long as we are becoming better people, we are fulfilling the point of the Christian religion.[5]

The leading liberals at the end of the nineteenth century were Albrecht Ritschl and Adolf Harnack. Both thought that historical criticism had disproved the deity of Christ, his physical resurrection, and other fantastic miracles. By peeling away the husk of these supernatural claims, Ritschl and Harnack believed that they could uncover the kernel of the Bible's message. According to Harnack, this unchanging core amounted to three points: the coming of the kingdom of God, the infinite value of the human soul, and the command to love one another.[6]

This liberal concern for love and ethics was powerfully expressed in Walter Rauschenbusch's 1917 lectures, *A Theology for the Social Gospel*. Rauschenbusch argued that traditional Christianity had focused so much on an individual's relationship with God that it had forgotten its most important social aspect. Rather than fixate on specific doctrines, individual acts of piety, or what might happen in the next life, Rauschenbusch said that the whole point of the gospel was to improve social conditions now. Jesus showed the way by bearing on the cross such social evils as religious bigotry, political injustice, mob frenzy, and class contempt. When we confess our participation in these social evils, we will be shamed by our complicity in Christ's death and will seek to bring his kingdom to earth.[7]

The liberal disregard for traditional doctrines provoked a backlash from conservatives. Their leading thinker, J. Gresham Machen, responded in 1923 with his classic book *Christianity and Liberalism,* in which he declared that "modern liberalism not only is a different religion from Christianity but belongs in a totally different class of religions."[8] Machen allowed that individual liberals may be saved, for only God knows "whether the attitude of certain individual 'liberals' toward Christ is saving faith or not. But one thing is perfectly plain — whether or not liberals are Christians, it is at any rate perfectly clear that liberalism is not Christianity."[9]

Machen noted that it was difficult to deal with liberals because they kept their beliefs intentionally vague.[10] Liberal pastors acknowledged that they were serving congregations in which many still believed the miracle stories of Scripture. These pastors said that they must choose, either becoming "truthful traitors" who honestly explained their modern skepticism and then left to become Unitarian ministers, or "loyal liars" who said what their people wanted to hear but meant something different by it. Like Bishop Corrigan who redefined the resurrection, liberals who chose to become "loyal liars" could remain in their churches and slowly work to modernize the faith of their people.[11]

Machen's fellow conservatives thought the "loyal liars" were the most dangerous kind of liberal, and they sought to smoke them out by declaring five fundamental doctrines that every Christian must believe:

1. the inerrancy and infallibility of Scripture (against liberalism's use of higher criticism to challenge the truthfulness of the Bible);
2. the virgin birth and deity of Jesus Christ (against the liberal view that Jesus was only human);
3. Christ's substitutionary atonement (against the liberal position that Jesus saves by supplying a moral example);
4. the literal, physical resurrection of Jesus (against naturalism, which led liberals to dismiss the supernatural events in Scripture as mere symbols of a spiritual truth);

5. the literal, physical return of Jesus (against naturalism again).[12]

Liberals refused to bite. They simply returned to their emphasis on social ethics and repeated their slogan "Doctrine divides; love unites." This liberal strategy of duck and hide infuriated the conservative "fundamentalists," for they could not avoid being cast as the aggressors. Their doctrinal interrogations seemed needlessly divisive. Why wouldn't they leave the peace-loving liberals alone?

Many fundamentalists came to embrace their combative role. One history of fundamentalism — written by a fundamentalist — shows a Bible with a fist on its cover. The author describes his movement as "the *militant* exposure of all non-biblical affirmations and attitudes."[13] Fundamentalists published newspapers like *The Sword of the Lord* and gave their preachers macho nicknames like "Fighting Bob," "Duke," and "The Texas Tornado." As historian George Marsden shrewdly observed, "A Fundamentalist is an evangelical who is angry about something."[14]

By 1930 the "Fighting Fundies" had frightened so many that they were forced to leave their denominations and start their own. For the next few decades they licked their wounds, founding schools, mission agencies, and radio programs that were fiercely separate from the world. Then in the 1950s, with the help of Billy Graham, conservatives mounted a comeback.[15] They called themselves "evangelical" to distance themselves from the previous generation of fundamentalist street fighters. They started schools, such as Fuller Seminary, whose academic quality won the respect of outsiders. They created an influential magazine called *Christianity Today*, a gathering place for conservative scholarship in the Evangelical Theological Society, and a powerful voting bloc known as the Religious Right.

And then they took the White House. In 1976 *Newsweek* magazine put Jimmy Carter on its cover and proclaimed the "Year of the Evangelical." Every president since has claimed to be "born again," biblical code for evangelicals that he is one of them.

But now many are wondering whether this conservative movement has run its course. Afraid that conservatives have compromised their faith by identifying Jesus with the platform of the Republican Party and wanting a Christianity that will unite people rather than drive them apart (are you for or against gay marriage, abortion, and embryonic stem cell research?), many are looking for a third way that will bring together the best that liberals and conservatives have to offer.[16]

IN THE PRESENT

The first move to the middle was made by a family of theologians known as *postliberals*. These thinkers, loosely associated with Hans Frei and George Lindbeck from Yale Divinity School, are erstwhile liberals who want to move beyond their tradition's typical disregard for Christianity's conventional doctrines.[17]

Like other strong foundationalists of the modern period, classical liberals sought universal truths that everyone believed. They did not think that they could find this foundation in doctrine — since there were too many disagreements — but they could ground the Christian faith in either religious experience (Schleiermacher) or morality (Ritschl, Harnack, and Rauschenbusch). Since everyone has a feeling of absolute dependence and/or a sense of right and wrong, liberals argued that everyone could embrace a Christian faith that was reduced to these concepts.

Postliberals rightly reject this attempt to gain universal acceptance by conforming the gospel to the prevailing culture. Rather than reduce the Christian faith to those few principles that everyone would accept, postliberals claim that Christians must first and foremost be faithful to the biblical narratives and their unique perspective on God.

Like other nonfoundationalists of the postmodern period, postliberals believe that truth claims are local rather than universal. They argue that the Christian faith does not state timeless truths that are readily apparent to everyone but simply shares the story of Scripture as the Christian view of the world. Since the biblical story consists of historical events that cannot be proved, we should not expect others to automatically accept our interpretation of reality.

Instead, postliberals claim that Christian beliefs function like the rules in a game. Just as basketball players must follow the rules when they play the game of basketball, so those who participate in the Christian game must follow the rules established by Christian beliefs. A person who runs with the ball and tackles other players is not playing basketball, and a person who denies the Trinity and the deity of Christ is not participating in the Christian faith.[18]

While this emphasis on the role of doctrine is a large improvement over classical liberalism, postliberals leave us wondering to what extent our Christian beliefs are true. If our beliefs merely supply the rules for playing the Christian game, how can we tell whether our game is truer than another?[19] Does the Christian faith merely describe our view, or does it accurately depict the way things are in the world? Are Jesus and the story of Scripture true for all people or just Christians? How do the beliefs of our faith relate to the rules of other religions?

George Lindbeck asserts that Christian beliefs need not conflict with the views of other religions. Each religion comes with its own set of rules for playing its own game. Just as we would not criticize a basketball player for disregarding the rules of baseball, so we should not fault a Muslim or Buddhist for failing to play by the beliefs of Christianity. In this way Lindbeck hopes that postliberalism may foster interfaith dialogue, for rather than seek to convert others, "the missionary task of Christians may at times be to encourage Marxists to become better Marxists, Jews and Muslims to become better Jews and Muslims, and Buddhists to become better Buddhists (although admittedly their notion of what a 'better Marxist,' etc., is will be influenced by Christian norms)."[20]

While conservative theologians debate whether and to what extent postliberalism falls into relativism (do they believe that Christianity is merely one game or the only true game in town?), some are joining postliberals in what Hans Frei calls a "generous orthodoxy."[21] These *postconservatives* use the insights of postliberalism to overcome the perceived problems of their conservative past and move to the center (see fig. 12.1).

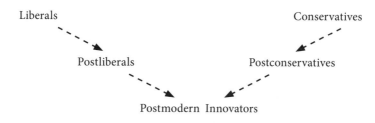

Fig. 12.1. How We Got Where We Are

First, because the game itself is more important than its rules, postconservatives replace the conservative focus on doctrine with a renewed emphasis on Christian piety. They rightly say that the point of the Christian life is not merely to believe the right things but to use our beliefs to draw close to God and live for him. Second, postconservatives agree with postliberals that the Bible is more than a collection of eternal truths illustrated with stories. The principles in Scripture are important, but they exist to explain the Bible's grand narrative, which is the main thing.

Third, postconservatives replace conservatism's modern quest for certainty with postliberalism's emphasis on language games. Rather than attempt to prove the Christian faith with universally accessible, indubitably certain arguments, postconservatives concede that their faith can only be properly understood and evaluated from within their Christian community.

This admission of finitude leads postconservatives to their most important characteristic. Unlike conservatives, who tend to denounce anything that deviates from their tradition, postconservatives argue that we must be willing to correct and move beyond tradition when necessary. In this way they are "reformed and always reforming," ever ready to embrace whatever new light may break upon them as they read Scripture in their community of faith.[22]

There is much to appreciate here: Scripture is narrative, our faith is communal, doctrine is not an end in itself, and Scripture must judge our tradition. Yet it seems that some postconservatives — the ones I am calling postmodern innovators — are going too far. In their desire to unite with postliberals, are these postconservatives falling into old liberal habits?[23]

WITH THE PAST IN THE PRESENT

Many postmodern innovators are leaders in Emergent Village, a network of friends committed to finding a new way of Christianity that transcends liberal and conservative categories. Emergent Village recently published its long awaited *An Emergent Manifesto of Hope*, a book in which its leading pastors and thinkers wrote brief chapters on various aspects of their new way of doing church. While I found much in this book to applaud and apply, I was perplexed that several authors suggested — as did modern liberals — that it does not matter whether we believe in Jesus as long as we live like him.

The most disturbing passages come from Samir Selmanovic, who begins his essay by describing an Indian chief's reluctance to convert to Christ. The chief refused to put his trust in Christ, for he did not want to go to paradise if the rest of his family went to hell. Selmanovic said that the chief's decision was "moved by the Holy Spirit," for though he did not pledge "allegiance to the name of Christ," the chief did "want to be like him and thus accept him at a deeper level." Because Jesus is love, the chief's choice not to believe in Jesus, out of love for his family, is more "Christlike" than if he had accepted "the name of Christ."

So the chief followed Christ by not believing in him? Besides wondering how Selmanovic would interpret Jesus' stern warning "Anyone who loves his father or mother more than me is not worthy of me; anyone who loves his son or daughter more than me is not worthy of me," this story illustrates the dismal end of liberal thought.[24] Once we concede that sinners need not believe in Jesus to be saved, there is nothing in principle that will prevent us from concluding, like Selmanovic, that some may be saved by not believing in Jesus!

But Selmanovic is not done. He describes his friend Mark who refused to become a Christian because he thought it "would be a moral step backwards." Yet Mark did believe that life was a gift. He thought that "there is a transcendent sweep over our existence" that "humanity has been squandering." Mark continued: "But in the midst of this mess, I see grace of a new beginning all around me. And within me. I often fail to respond to it. I participate in the madness instead. Whenever in my inner life I do turn to this grace to look for a second chance, I am always granted one. I think I want to spend the rest of my life being a channel of that same goodness to others."

These vague introspective thoughts somehow lead Selmanovic to surmise that though Mark does not believe in Jesus, he does have a "doctrine of creation, sin, salvation, and new life. That's Christ, embedded in the life of Mark, present in substance rather than in name." Then Selmanovic draws the logical conclusion, writing that the stories of the chief and Mark "leave us wondering whether Christ can be more than Christianity. Or even *other than Christianity.*"[25]

Statements like these suggest that for all their talk about a third way that transcends the liberal-conservative divide, some postmodern innovators are presenting merely postmodern versions of modern liberalism. While there are important differences — most postmodern innovators do not deny the deity of Christ, divine revelation, or the miracles of Scripture — yet they make the liberal leap from "doctrine matters less than ethics" to the view that the specific, historic doctrines of the church may not matter at all.[26] Indeed, many of their "new" ideas were already addressed more than eighty years ago in Machen's *Christianity and Liberalism* (1923).

HAVEN'T WE SEEN THIS BEFORE?

In chapters 2 and 3 we learned that some postmodern innovators teach that it matters more that we love like Jesus than that we believe in him. At any rate we should not exclude good people from the kingdom just because they do not believe our Christian faith. Machen wrote that the liberals in his day insisted that "Christianity is a life, not a doctrine," and that conservatives should focus on "the weightier matters of the law" (Christian ethics) rather than use the "trifling matters" of doctrine to divide the church.[27]

Machen responded that doctrines such as Christ's "vicarious atonement for sin" is not "trifling" and that Christ is not merely "an example for faith" but is "primarily the object of faith." He explained: "The religion of Paul did not consist in having faith in God *like the faith* which Jesus had in God; it consisted rather in having faith *in Jesus*.... The plain fact is that imitation of Jesus, important though it was for Paul, was swallowed up by something far more important still. Not the example of Jesus, but the redeeming work of Jesus, was the primary thing for Paul."[28]

Chapter 4 explained that some postmodern innovators believe that people are basically good and free from serious sin. Likewise, Machen observed that the defining belief of modernity was its "supreme confidence in human goodness." He wrote that "according to modern liberalism, there is really no such thing as sin. At the very root of the modern liberal movement is the loss of the consciousness of sin." This absence of sin led Machen to wryly observe that the liberal church "is busily engaged in an absolutely impossible task — she is busily engaged in calling the *righteous* to repentance." Machen countered that the gospel must begin with sin, for "Without the consciousness of sin, the whole gospel will seem to be an idle tale."[29]

Chapter 6 examined the objection of some postmodern innovators to the traditional understanding of the cross: Why does
God demand the sacrifice of his innocent Son to satisfy his wrath?
Machen noted that modern liberals raised the same issue. He wrote:
"Modern liberal teachers ... speak with horror of the doctrine of an
'alienated' or an 'angry' God," for this implies that God is "waiting
coldly until a price be paid before He grants salvation." Liberals
deny that "one person" may "suffer for the sins of another," and
they "persist in speaking of the sacrifice of Christ as though it were
a sacrifice made by some other than God." They insist that a loving
God would forgive without penalty.[30]

Machen replied that "the modern rejection of the doctrine of
God's wrath proceeds from a light view of sin." He observed: "If sin
is so trifling a matter as the liberal Church supposes, then indeed
the curse of God's law can be taken very lightly, and God can easily
let by-gones be by-gones." But "if a man has once come under a true
conviction of sin, he will have little difficulty with the doctrine of
the Cross." Machen added that God does not punish someone else
for our sin, but "God Himself, and not another, makes the sacrifice
for sin.... Salvation is as free *for us* as the air we breathe; God's the
dreadful cost, ours the gain."[31]

Chapter 7 explored the concern of postmodern innovators to
break down the walls between Christians and non-Christians and
emphasize our common journey with God. Machen agreed that
"the Christian man can accept all that the modern liberal means
by the brotherhood of man. But the Christian knows also of a relationship far more intimate than that general relationship of man to
man, and it is for this more intimate relationship that he reserves
the term 'brother.' The true brotherhood, according to Christian
teaching, is the brotherhood of the redeemed."[32]

Chapter 8 explained the postmodern tendency to extend salvation to include those who have not believed in Christ. Machen said
that liberals in his day wanted "a salvation which will save all men
everywhere, whether they have heard of Jesus or not, and whatever may be the type of life to which they have been reared." He
replied that such openness would remove the offense of the gospel and change its historic meaning. He wrote: "What struck the
early observers of Christianity most forcibly was not merely that
salvation was offered by means of the Christian gospel, but that

all other means were resolutely rejected. The early Christian missionaries demanded an absolutely exclusive devotion to Christ.... Salvation, in other words, was not merely through Christ, but it was only through Christ."[33]

Chapter 9 reported the desire of some postmodern innovators to focus on this life rather than the afterlife. Machen said that liberals in his day believed that concern for the next life is "a form of selfishness." Consequently, "the liberal preacher has very little to say about the other world. This world is really the centre of all his thoughts; religion itself, and even God, are made merely a means for the betterment of conditions upon this earth."[34]

Machen responded that we must not treat Christianity "as a mere means to a higher end.... Christianity will indeed accomplish many useful things in this world, but if it is accepted in order to accomplish those useful things it is not Christianity." Those who seek first the kingdom of God will find that "all these things shall be added unto you. But if you seek first the Kingdom of God and His righteousness *in order that* all those other things may be added unto you, you will miss both those other things and the Kingdom of God as well."[35]

Machen agreed that our Christian faith must change the way we live here and now, but he insisted that "there can be no applied Christianity unless there be 'a Christianity to apply.' That is where the Christian man differs from the modern liberal. The liberal believes that applied Christianity is all there is of Christianity, Christianity being merely a way of life; the Christian man believes that applied Christianity is the result of an initial act of God."[36]

Thus, Machen would probably disagree with the postmodern innovators who suggest that simply being postmodern enables them to transcend the modern liberal-conservative controversy.[37] Instead, Machen would likely argue that these postmoderns repeat too many of the mistakes of modern liberalism to get very far past it. Their "third way" is too much like the old way to become a new way. Here is a better way forward.

TO THE FUTURE

We can transcend the liberal-conservative controversy if we incorporate the best insights of each. Liberals emphasize ethics and conservatives defend the specific, historic doctrines of the Christian faith. Don't we need both? Is it even possible to have one without the other? (see fig. 12.2).

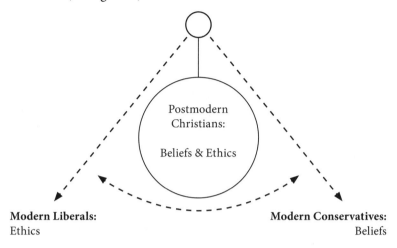

Modern Liberals:
Ethics

Modern Conservatives:
Beliefs

Fig. 12.2. A Third Way Forward

1. *Ethics require beliefs.* While the history of liberalism might imply that Christian ethics are possible without traditional Christian beliefs, this is only because liberals have not thought through the implications of what they believe. If Jesus did not rise from the dead, then we will not rise either. And if we will not live forever, then why bother being good now? If everyone's life ends in eternal nothingness, then does it ultimately matter whether we have fought injustice or fed the poor? As the apostle Paul concludes: "If the dead are not raised, 'Let us eat and drink, for tomorrow we die.'"[38]

The devastating effect of liberal belief on ethics is memorably portrayed in the fictional but realistic story, *The Flight of Peter Fromm.* Peter Fromm was a passionate Pentecostal teenager from Oklahoma who enrolled at the University of Chicago to destroy this bastion of liberalism from the inside out. He planned to embarrass his professors, rescue the souls of his fellow students, and polish his debating skills for a lifetime defense of fundamentalism. Unfortunately, Peter quickly fell beneath the spell of a liberal professor, and the rest of the book describes his descent into ethical chaos. He quickly lost his virginity — for sexual purity was unimportant in the situation ethics of liberalism — and he eventually lost his mind during a climactic Easter sermon.

Peter began his sermon as a "loyal liar," informing his congregation that "the secret of Easter is the Christian assurance of the triumph of life over death." But then he transitioned into a "truthful traitor," telling his audience that it is Jesus' spirit rather than his body that is alive. Like Bishop Corrigan, Peter said that the spirit of Jesus is present whenever people love one another, seek justice, and search for truth. Regardless of how bleak the present seems, we must remember that morning always follows the darkest night, that spring comes after winter, and that good arises from evil, for Jesus is alive.

And then Peter chuckled. He realized the absurdity of saying, "Jesus is alive," when he did not mean it. Where is the hope if the tomb is not empty? Then he laughed. Derisively, mockingly, maliciously. The crowd gasped, and several of them walked toward the platform to lead him away. Peter shoved them back and knocked them down. He ripped off his clothes, ran over to the organist, and urinated on her instrument. His ordeal mercifully ended when he was clocked by a candelabra and fell atop the organ in "a burst of discordant, unearthly music."[39]

Most liberal preachers do not meet Peter's demise, but this is only because they have not reflected deeply enough upon the implications of their beliefs. Those who do not believe in the historical truth of the Christian story will find it hard, if not impossible, to logically justify their life of good works.[40]

2. *Beliefs require ethics.* Just as we cannot have Christian ethics without Christian beliefs, so we do not genuinely believe if we are not living our faith. In *The Religious Affections,* Jonathan Edwards observed that costly sacrifice is the surest sign of true faith. He wrote, "Passing affections easily produce words; and words are cheap; and godliness is more easily feigned in words than in actions. Christian practice is a costly, laborious thing.... Hypocrites may much more easily be brought to talk like saints, than to act like saints."[41]

Hypocrites seek maximum press with minimum effort. They shy away from anything that demands a price. If you want to know whether your faith is genuine, consider how much it costs you. Do you resist temptation? Love the people you live with? Give your best to others? Those who believe in Christ — who have placed their whole weight on the promises of his gospel — will naturally look for ways to share his love.

Scott and Amy Vogel were pursuing the American dream when God intervened. Scott was hanging out with old friends when he realized that for the first time it bothered him that they were probably headed for hell. What was he doing to reach them? Then his pastor preached on God's command to serve those in greatest need. Scott responded by going on a guided hike through the hood, visiting crack houses, soup kitchens, and people living in abandoned buildings.

Scott and Amy decided to take a radical step. They would be the first to say that this is not for everyone, but they sold their landscaping business and began a ministry in the inner city. While they were restoring a former drug house, they met a couple of kids whom they brought to their church's Saturday night service. Pretty soon these children asked to bring along their friends, and in short order the Vogels were throwing their own Saturday night gym party and Bible lesson for two hundred urban children. Today their organization, Urban Family Ministries, has expanded into schools and neighborhoods, supplying tutors and mentors for children and home repair and cleanup for their parents.

I asked Scott to respond to the postmodern innovators' objections. Does his concern for where people will live in the next life distract from his efforts to improve how they live in this one? And does his narrow view that salvation requires trusting in Jesus make it hard to embrace those who do not believe?

Scott said that he sees a direct connection between this life and the next one, for "the only way people's lives can change now is through a relationship with Christ." The same Person who secures their future supplies salvation in the present. This strong conviction does not stop Scott from serving those who do not believe, for Scott promises that whether or not people repent and follow Christ, "I'm still going to be your friend and love you. I will serve you even if you reject God."

As it should be. Far from being an obstacle to good works, traditional Christian beliefs are the best — and I would argue the only — way that we can love others. Genuine Christians never stop serving, because they never stop loving, and they never stop loving, because they never stop believing.

A QUESTION THAT ANSWERS A LOT

I can summarize the point of this book with a question about two stories. First, consider Christine — a hardworking, loving wife and mother who cheerfully volunteers for most any need. She has built several homes for Habitat for Humanity, given gallons of blood to the Red Cross, led a Girl Scout troop and her PTA, served as Big Sister to at-risk girls in her community, tutored latchkey kids after school, and adopted three orphans who were abandoned by their drug-addicted parents. In her free time, she knits mosquito nets for the children of Burundi. However, despite making Mother Teresa look like a slouch, Christine has never repented of her sins and believed in Jesus.

Now consider Jack, an American missionary who lives with his wife and five children in Uscamistan (pronounced Û-scam-i-stan). Because Jack is an ordained minister who receives the majority of his pay as housing allowance, his taxable income places his family below the poverty line of Uscamistan. So, despite his comfortable salary and million-dollar house, Jack applies for and receives fifty thousand dollars per year in welfare checks from the Uscamistani government (ten thousand dollars for each child). When you ask Jack whether it is appropriate to take fifty-thousand dollars per year that he does not need from people whom he professes to love, he tells you that he has done nothing illegal and that you should mind your own business.

Here is the question: Which person is more likely to avoid hell and live forever with Jesus? Modern conservatives, while appalled by Jack's conduct, would likely give the nod to him, for his trust in Jesus forgives any sin he could ever commit. Postmodern innovators would probably prefer Christine, for a loving God would surely show more pity to a caring person like her than a hypocritical swindler like Jack.

The point of this book is that both are in trouble. James says that *faith without works is dead,* for how can we claim to believe in God if we do not pass on his love and serve our neighbor?[42] Paul adds the other side, declaring that *works without faith are vain.* Works without faith give us reason to brag — look what we did — but they are useless in earning any part of our salvation. Paul explains, "If, in fact, Abraham was justified by works, he had something to boast about — but not before God."[43]

Rather than emphasize beliefs *or* ethics, can't we agree that following Jesus demands *both* faith *and* practice? Conservatives should admit Jack's perilous position, without worrying that they are conceding too much to liberalism's emphasis on social ethics. And postmodern innovators should acknowledge that Christine's works are not enough to save her, without worrying that they are minimizing the value of her charity or conceding too much to conservatism's emphasis on right beliefs.

It is tempting to chase the pendulum as it swings from side to side. Postmodern innovators react to conservatives' focus on faith by stressing how we live, while conservatives respond to the new emphasis on ethics by accenting what we believe. Both tend to push each other to opposite extremes, so that postmodern innovators suggest that beliefs and conservatives imply that works are not necessary to be saved.

Let's stop the pendulum and embrace both sides. God commands us "to *believe* in the name of his Son, Jesus Christ, and to *love* one another as he commanded us."[44] Genuine Christians never stop serving because they never stop loving, and they never stop loving because they never stop believing.

EPILOGUE

I have written this book as a theologian, attempting to state as objectively as possible what I perceive to be the merits of my view. Now I would like to say a few words as a Christian who loves the church of Jesus Christ.

This postmodern generation is asking thoughtful and penetrating questions, questions that compose the outline of this book. I believe that they are raising these issues not to be difficult but because they honestly want answers. So unlike postmodern innovators, who respond to their questions with more questions, or some conservatives, who cut off their questions with prefabricated conclusions, I endeavor to supply answers even as I hear — and learn from — their questions.

I believe this is important because — not to be overly dramatic about it — individual lives and whole churches are at risk. Many postmodern innovators grew up in conservative churches that anchored their faith in the historic doctrines of Christianity. But many of their followers have not. What will become of this next generation? They have been told that the Christian life amounts to doing good works and asking good questions. While both of these are valuable, they are not enough to sustain the Christian faith.

I fear that, despite their best intentions, many postmodern innovators are unwittingly secularizing the church. What makes our Christian faith unique is not its aptitude for good works or good questions but its distinctive belief in a divine Father who sent his Son into our world to live, die, and rise again so that all whom the Spirit empowers may believe the Story, repent of their sin, and live forever. If we lose the need for this Story — if we fill our churches with people who either do not know the Story or why they must believe it — then we will lose our Christian identity.

Although it never runs from questions, the Christian faith is grounded in truth. God never instructs his children to open their minds to the beauty and insights of other religions. He did not tell

Israel that since "all truth is God's truth," they should investigate the religion of Egypt or glean insights from the worship of Baal. Rather, he commanded them to "throw away the gods your forefathers worshiped beyond the River and in Egypt, and serve the LORD."[1] Likewise, Paul said, "We demolish arguments and every pretension that sets itself up against the knowledge of God, and we take captive every thought to make it obedient to Christ."[2] This is why Paul did not thank the Athenians for enlarging his view of God with their anonymous altar but told them about the resurrection and their need to repent.[3]

Postmodern innovators often point out that, unlike their conservative counterparts, they are not preoccupied with defending their faith. But perhaps they have this luxury because they are rarely criticized by those outside the faith. And perhaps they are so seldom attacked because they rarely if ever say anything that would offend a typical postmodern person. We should not seek to antagonize, but neither should we avoid proclaiming the scandalous aspects of the gospel. Those who conceal its offensive parts may become popular, but they will cease to be Christian.

I am uncertain whether this book will persuade many postmodern innovators, for they may be too deeply invested in their new brand of Christianity to turn back now. But I hope to convince their followers that Christian belief matters as much as (but not more than) the Christian life. I want this not only for their sake but also for the benefit of my children, who will soon begin to explore the center and the boundaries of their Christian faith. I pray that they will be surrounded by peers who value both questions and answers, both belief and practice. May they — and all of God's children in every generation — never stop wondering, loving, or believing.

I value your thoughts about what you've just read.
Please share them with me. You'll find contact information
in the back of this book.

NOTES

Introduction

1. For those who missed the joke, many postmodern Christians are unhappy with D. A. Carson's criticism in his book *Becoming Conversant with the Emerging Church* (Grand Rapids: Zondervan, 2005). While the postmodern top ten list is entirely my creation, most of the conservative list I received in an email long ago, and I am unable to locate its source.

2. Stanley J. Grenz and Roger Olson, *Twentieth-Century Theology* (Downers Grove, Ill.: InterVarsity, 1992), 15 – 23.

3. I will follow the lead of David Wells and James Smith and limit my focus to postmodernity — the popular and often unconscious expression of the age — rather than postmodernism, the application of postmodern ideals to the high end of culture, such as art, architecture, and literature. See David F. Wells, *Above All Earthly Powers* (Leicester: Inter-Varsity; Grand Rapids: Eerdmans, 2005), 64; James K. A. Smith, *Who's Afraid of Postmodernism?* (Grand Rapids: Brazos, 2006), 20.

4. Helpful introductions to postmodernism include the following: Heath White, *Post-modernism 101* (Grand Rapids: Brazos, 2006); Smith, *Who's Afraid of Postmodernism?*; Robert C. Greer, *Mapping Postmodernism* (Downers Grove, Ill.: InterVarsity, 2003); Stanley J. Grenz, *A Primer on Postmodernism* (Grand Rapids: Eerdmans, 1996); Richard Appignanesi and Chris Garratt, *Introducing Postmodernism* (New York: Totem, 1995); Steven Best and Douglas Kellner, *Postmodern Theory: Critical Interrogations* (New York: Guilford, 1991); and *The Postmodern Turn* (New York: Guilford, 1997). In *Above All Earthly Powers*, pp. 75 – 79 and 91 – 124, David Wells argues that the pluralism of postmodernity is not only motivated by compassion for the oppressed but also by consumerism with its plethora of choices and immigration with its new religious imports.

5. See, e.g., the explanation in Diana Butler Bass, *The Practicing Congregation* (Herndon, Va.: Alban, 2004), 72 – 76.

6. Summaries of the theology of Schleiermacher and his liberal successors appear in Grenz and Olson, *Twentieth-Century Theology*, 39 – 62; and James C. Livingston, *Modern Christian Thought*, 2nd ed. (Minneapolis: Fortress, 1997, 2006), 1:93 – 105, 270 – 98.

7. Learn more about this fundamentalist movement in Livingston, *Modern Christian Thought*, 1:299 – 326; 2:387 – 416; and Joel A. Carpenter, *Revive Us Again* (New York: Oxford University Press, 1997).

8. Observe the titles of these books by a leading postmodern innovator: Brian McLaren, *A New Kind of Christian* (San Francisco: Jossey-Bass, 2001), and *Everything Must Change: Jesus, Global Crises, and a Revolution of Hope* (Nashville: Nelson, 2007). Of course, there is diversity of opinion among postmodern innovators. I do not mean to imply that postmodern innovators agree completely on every issue, but only that they share a common perspective on church and theology.

9. Postmodern innovators also reject some conservative beliefs as the product of modernity, such as the inerrancy of Scripture and the penal element of Christ's substitutionary atonement.

Chapter 1. A New Kind of Christian

1. Though not equally balanced — 80 percent of this book will argue for right belief and 20 percent for right practice. I have slanted the argument this way for several reasons. First, some leaders are suggesting that it is no longer necessary to believe the specific, historic beliefs of the church, but few if any argue that it is unnecessary to practice the Christian life. Second, the former group is capturing the imagination of our next generation, and so it seems important to examine their claims. Third, the solution to a failure in right living seems simple and straightforward: practice what you preach, while the arguments for and against our beliefs are difficult to sort out and so require more time. Fourth, though authentic Christianity requires both right belief and right practice, the former seems foundational for the latter (it is impossible to apply what you do not know). Thus, the present conversation about the necessity of Christian belief threatens to eliminate the possibility of practicing the Christian life.

2. The Cappadocian fathers were among the first to recognize that doctrine develops over time. As they hammered out the deity of the Holy Spirit, something not specified until the fourth century, Basil noted that they were commenting on issues "passed over in silence by earlier generations," and Gregory of Nazianzus observed, "You see lights breaking upon us gradually." See Basil, *Epistle* 159 and Gregory of Nazianzus, *Orations* 31 in *Creeds, Councils, and Controversies*, ed. J. Stevenson (London: SPCK, 1966; rev. 1989), 83, 85.

    Cf. Karl Barth, *Church Dogmatics*, ed. G. W. Bromiley and T. F. Torrance, trans. G. W. Bromiley, vol. 1, pt. 1 (Edinburgh: T. & T. Clark, 1975), 15 – 16: "The task of dogmatics, therefore, is not simply to combine, repeat, and transcribe a number of truths of revelation which are already to hand, which have been expressed once and for all, and the wording and meaning of which are authentically defined.... Hence dogmatics as such does not ask what the apostles and prophets said but what we must say on the basis of the apostles and prophets."

3. Martin Luther, "Table Talk," in *Luther's Works*, ed. Theodore G. Tappert and Helmut T. Lehmann, trans. Theodore G. Tappert (Philadelphia: Fortress, 1967), 54:359: "Whoever wants to be clever must agree with nothing that others esteem. He must do something of his own. This is what that fellow does who wishes to turn the whole of astronomy upside down. Even in these

things that are thrown into disorder I believe the Holy Scriptures, for Joshua commanded the sun to stand still and not the earth [Josh. 10:12]."

4. Ephesians 6:5; Colossians 3:22; 1 Timothy 6:1 – 2; Titus 2:9 – 10; and Philemon 10 – 18. Other purported biblical support for slavery included Noah's curse on Ham, the practice of the Old Testament patriarchs to own slaves, and the regulation of slavery in the law. See Kevin Giles, "The Biblical Argument for Slavery: Can the Bible Mislead? A Case Study in Hermeneutics," *Evangelical Quarterly* 66, no. 1 (1994): 3 – 17; and Larry R. Morrison, "The Religious Defense of American Slavery before 1830," *Journal of Religious Thought* 37 (1980 – 81): 16 – 29.

5. Anselm, "Proslogion, Chapter 8," in *Anselm of Canterbury: The Major Works*, ed. Brian Davies and G. R. Evans (New York: Oxford University Press, 1998), 91.

6. John 11:35.

7. Other influential developments in culture include mathematics and philosophy. Regarding mathematics: Einstein's demonstration of the close relationship between space and time has inspired some theologians to revise how God relates to time. Theologians have always said that God is both immanent and transcendent when it comes to space: he is both here and everywhere. If God is both immanent and transcendent when it comes to space, then why not also in his relation to time? Instead of choosing between a temporal or atemporal God, why not say that he is both? In his immanence God experiences time with us, and in his transcendence he simultaneously continues to exist outside of time.

   Regarding philosophy: Many philosophers are replacing the ancient definition of *person* as "rational substance" with a contemporary view that person denotes a being who is in relationship with other persons. This new perspective has unleashed exciting and significant breakthroughs in our understanding of God, who is now more accurately conceived as a community of three relational persons rather than a solitary thinking substance. In this way the church is rediscovering the biblical God as the model for our relationships.

8. Jesus is called the *logos*, or *Word* of God, and the Trinity is defined as consisting of one *ousia* (generic essence) and three *hypostaseis* (individual, personal essences).

9. Augustine, *Confessions*, trans. Henry Chadwick (New York: Oxford University Press, 1991), 3.

10. For a polemical critique of this Greek view of God, see Clark Pinnock, *Most Moved Mover* (Grand Rapids: Baker, 2001), 65 – 111.

11. Proof that the evangelical church remains under the spell of Plato is found in chapter 6 of the immensely popular *Purpose-Driven Life*. See Rick Warren, *The Purpose-Driven Life* (Grand Rapids: Zondervan, 2002), 47 – 52. For a non-Platonic explanation of the meaning of life, see Michael Wittmer, *Heaven Is a Place on Earth* (Grand Rapids: Zondervan, 2004).

12. Even Augustine was persuaded by this logic. He argued that coercion, such as leveling fines and exiling his Donatist opponents, was acceptable because

it inspired many to convert and join the Roman Catholic Church. See Augustine, "Letter XCIII to Vincentius," in *The Nicene and Post-Nicene Fathers,* first series, ed. Philip Schaff (Edinburgh: T. & T. Clark; repr., Grand Rapids: Eerdmans, 1991), 1:382–401.

13. Frederick C. Copleston, *A History of Medieval Philosophy* (1972; repr. Notre Dame, Ind.: University of Notre Dame Press, 1990), 104–24, 150–59, 176–98.

14. Diogenes Allen, *Philosophy for Understanding Theology* (Atlanta: John Knox, 1985), 152–69, explains how these modern philosophers and scientists eroded the Aristotelian worldview.

15. Heiko A. Oberman, *Luther: Man between God and the Devil* (New York: Image, 1992), 203.

16. I thank Richard Muller for explaining this term and its significance.

17. Kenneth Woodward, an astute religious observer, believes that Bill Clinton's sexual sins were rooted in his freedom to interpret the Bible as he saw fit. Woodward argues that Clinton was merely following the Baptist creed, "Ain't nobody but Jesus goin' to tell me what to believe." See "Sex, Sin, and Salvation," *Newsweek,* November 2, 1998, 37. For a persuasive rationale for knowing the church's rich tradition, read D. H. Williams, *Retrieving the Tradition and Renewing Evangelicalism: A Primer for Suspicious Protestants* (Grand Rapids: Eerdmans, 1999).

18. I believe this was Mark Bailey in my hermeneutics class at Dallas Theological Seminary.

19. Note Jesus' words to his Father in Gethsemane: "... yet not my will, but yours be done" (Luke 22:42).

20. Brian McLaren describes this fundamentalist view in *The Last Word and the Word after That* (San Francisco: Jossey-Bass, 2005), 136: "On judgment day, all God will care about is opening up our skulls and checking our brains ... to see if we had the right notion of salvation by grace through faith in there somewhere."

21. I thank my friend Robert Reyes for this illustration.

Chapter 2. Must You Believe Something to Be Saved?

1. David Van Biema, "The 25 Most Influential Evangelicals in America," *Time,* February 7, 2005, 45; and Debra Rosenberg, with Karen Breslau and Michael Hirsh, "Church Meets State," *Newsweek,* November 13, 2006, 38.

2. Brian McLaren, "The Method, the Message, and the Ongoing Story," in *The Church in Emerging Culture,* ed. Leonard Sweet (Grand Rapids: Zondervan, 2003), 218–20.

3. Brian McLaren, *The Last Word and the Word after That* (San Francisco: Jossey-Bass, 2005), 121. It is important to note that the views expressed by the characters in a story are not necessarily the beliefs of the story's author. On the other hand, we should assume that the author is telling his story to communicate some message, and that the best place to look for his point is in the speeches of his protagonists, or heroes of the story. So while we can

not say with certainty that McLaren holds the same views as Pastor Dan or Markus, neither should we assume that they are vastly different.

4. Ibid., 136. Cf. Dave Tomlinson, *The Post-Evangelical* (Grand Rapids: Zondervan, 2003), 70: "Ultimately, our church pedigrees, spiritual experiences, or creedal affirmations do not impress God. St. Peter will not be asking us at the pearly gates which church we belonged to or if we believed in the virgin birth."

5. McLaren, *Last Word*, 138.

6. Ibid., 85. Cf. p. 138, where Markus summarizes McLaren's view: "Salvation by grace, judgment by works."

7. Brian McLaren wrote the foreword for this book.

8. Spencer Burke and Barry Taylor, *A Heretic's Guide to Eternity* (San Francisco: Jossey-Bass, 2006), 131 – 32.

9. Ibid., 61. Cf. p. 206: "As I've said, grace is an opt-out issue, not an opt-in one. God wants us at his party, just because we exist." McLaren hints at the same idea when he has Markus say, "Maybe God's plan is an opt-out plan, not an opt-in one. If you want to stay out of the party, you can. Nobody will force you to enjoy it" (McLaren, *Last Word*, 138).

10. Ibid., 195. Burke explains: "I'm not sure I believe in God exclusively as a person anymore.... The truth is that seeing God as spirit more than person doesn't destroy my faith.... A panentheist view points to the radical connectedness of all reality and infuses the world with the idea that all life is sacred and therefore to be nurtured and cherished."

11. Ibid., 197.

12. John 14:6.

13. Brian McLaren, *A Generous Orthodoxy* (Grand Rapids: Zondervan, 2004), 70.

14. Brian McLaren, *More Ready Than You Realize* (Grand Rapids: Zondervan, 2002), 50 (emphasis McLaren's).

15. Burke and Taylor, *Heretic's Guide*, 126 – 27.

16. Some sympathetic friends have begun to criticize postmodern Christians for their unwillingness to make doctrinal commitments. See James K. A. Smith, *Who's Afraid of Postmodernism?* (Grand Rapids: Brazos, 2006), 25 – 26, 116 – 26; and Scot McKnight, "The Future or Fad?" *Covenant Companion*, February 2006, 7 – 10.

17. First John 3:23.

18. Nicodemus, a Pharisee and "a member of the Jewish ruling council" (John 3:1), rebuked the other council members for condemning Jesus without a trial (7:50 – 51) and brought a large "mixture of myrrh and aloes, about seventy-five pounds," to bury Jesus (19:39).

19. John 3:3. It is interesting that McLaren did not address this important story about the kingdom of God in his book on that subject. Perhaps he did not include it in *The Secret Message of Jesus* because its call for regeneration does not fit his understanding of the kingdom.

20. John 3:5. I take water in this verse not as a reference to baptism but to "the cleansing and purifying work of God's Spirit." See W. L. Kynes, "New Birth," in *Dictionary of Jesus and the Gospels*, ed. Joel B. Green and Scot McKnight

(Downers Grove, Ill.: InterVarsity, 1992), 575. Cf. Titus 3:5, where Paul says that we are saved "through the washing of rebirth and renewal by the Holy Spirit."

21. John 3:9.
22. John 3:16, 18, 36 (emphasis mine). Cf. John 1:12 – 13: "Yet to all who received him [Jesus], to those who believed in his name, he gave the right to become children of God — children born not of natural descent, nor of human decision or a husband's will, but born of God." I wonder how postmodern innovators would interpret these rather straightforward passages in John. The lack of comment in their writings seems significant.
23. Second Thessalonians 2:13 (emphasis mine).
24. Romans 10:13 – 15.
25. *D. Martin Luthers Werke: Kritische Gesamtausgabe* (Weimar, 1883 –), 38:136 (hereafter WA). I thank Richard Muller for the "unmediated bolt from the blue" comment.
26. John Calvin, *The Institutes of the Christian Religion* 1.9.3, ed. John T. McNeill and trans. Ford Lewis Battles (Philadelphia: Westminster, 1960), 1:95.
27. Calvin, *Institutes* 1.9.1. Also see John Calvin, "Reply to Sadolet," in *Calvin: Theological Treatises*, ed. J. K. S. Reid (Philadelphia: Westminster, 1954), 229 – 31.
28. Augustine also says as much in "Rebuke and Grace," chap. 11 (7), in *The Works of Saint Augustine: A Translation for the 21st Century*, trans. Roland J. Teske and ed. John E. Rotelle (Hyde Park, N.Y.: New City, 1999), 1/26:116. Most Christians make hopeful exceptions for infants and the mentally impaired, for it seems that a just and loving God would not condemn those whose minds are unable either to receive or reject the gospel. We do not have slam-dunk scriptural support for this view — and for good reason. Imagine if God had promised that all babies go to heaven: wouldn't some well-meaning Christians slaughter Muslim children and think they were doing them a favor? So while we understandably do not have a divine promise, we may still rely on the character of God to do right by our children and not condemn them to hell because they did not respond to a message they could not comprehend. But note that children and the mentally handicapped people are the exception, not God's revealed rule for judging the human race.
29. Acts 16:29 – 31 (emphasis mine).
30. James 2:19.
31. John 2:23 – 24 (the Greek word translated "entrust" is *pisteuō*, the same Greek word translated "believe" in "many … believed in his name").
32. The Reformers used three Latin words to explain the necessary components of faith. First, people must possess *notitia*, or knowledge of something (they "notice" it). Then they move on to *assensus*, where they agree or give approval to what they know (they "assent" to it). Finally, they move beyond mere knowledge to genuine faith when they express *fiducia*, a hearty trust that boldly relies on the object of knowledge.
33. Acts 10:43.
34. Mark 1:15.

35. Acts 20:21.
36. Colossians 1:15 – 20 and John 1:1 – 14 explain Jesus' dual role as Creator and Redeemer. Romans 5:10 and Colossians 1:21 – 22 state that before our salvation we were the enemies of God.
37. "The Athanasian Creed," in *The Book of Concord*, trans. and ed. Theodore G. Tappert (Philadelphia: Fortress, 1959), 19 – 21.

Chapter 3. Do Right Beliefs Get in the Way of Good Works?

1. Hebrews 10:25.
2. Brian McLaren, *More Ready Than You Realize* (Grand Rapids: Zondervan, 2002), 41.
3. Brian McLaren, *The Last Word and the Word after That* (San Francisco: Jossey-Bass, 2005), 197 (emphasis mine).
4. Brian McLaren, *The Secret Message of Jesus* (Nashville: Word, 2006), 163.
5. Brian McLaren, *A Generous Orthodoxy* (Grand Rapids: Zondervan, 2004), 247 (emphasis McLaren's). See also Tony Jones, *The New Christians* (San Francisco: Jossey-Bass, 2008), 71.
6. McLaren, *Secret Message of Jesus*, 167 (emphasis McLaren's).
7. Ibid., 169 (emphasis mine).
8. McLaren, *Generous Orthodoxy*, 109 – 10 (emphasis McLaren's).
9. Quoted in Peter J. Walker and Tyler Clark, "Missing the Point: The Absolute Truth Behind Postmodernism, Emergent and the Emerging Church," *Relevant Magazine*, July – August 2006, 72. Cf. Jones, *New Christians*, 79: "The concentration on correct doctrine is also the reflection of an earlier time. Beginning with the Enlightenment in the eighteenth century, the modern era vaunted reason and the life of the mind above all other aspects of human existence.... as often happens, the pendulum swung too far in one direction, and the human intellect was overvalued.

   "... concentration on one aspect of Christianity — a doctrine that is ultimately accepted or rejected by the human intellect — is an articulation of modern Christianity, and it's one that is clearly helpful to a lot of people. But many faithful followers of Christ are becoming more reticent to place so much reliance on the human intellect. It's just failed us too many times."
10. LeRon Shults, "Doctrinal Statement," email from *Emergent*, May 4, 2006, in Jones, *New Christians*, 233 – 35. More examples of valuing behavior over belief are found in Doug Pagitt and Tony Jones, eds., *An Emergent Manifesto of Hope* (Grand Rapids: Baker, 2007), 43 – 44, 56, 101 – 6, 191 – 96.
11. Peter Rollins, *How (Not) to Speak of God* (Brewster, Mass.: Paraclete, 2006), 7 – 8, 17.
12. Ibid., 131.
13. Ibid., 3, 66.
14. Ibid., 56.
15. Ibid., 133.
16. See Matthew 18:15 – 18; 1 Corinthians 5:1 – 13.
17. Eddie Gibbs and Ryan K. Bolger, *Emerging Churches* (Grand Rapids: Baker, 2005), 131.

18. Rollins, *How (Not) to Speak of God*, 53 – 54.
19. Peter Rollins, as quoted in Gibbs and Bolger, *Emerging Churches*, 132.
20. Rollins, *How (Not) to Speak of God*, 42.
21. I owe this phrase to Cornelius Plantinga Jr. See also Arthur C. McGill, *Suffering: A Test of Theological Method* (Philadelphia: Westminster, 1982), 53 – 82.
22. Matthew 3:17.
23. John 14:31.
24. Luke 22:42.
25. John 14:26; 15:26; 16:7, 13 – 15.
26. John 8:50, 54; 14:13; 16:14; 17:1 – 5, 24.
27. Matthew 12:31 – 32.
28. Philippians 2:6 – 11 (emphasis mine).
29. Gerald F. Hawthorne, *Philippians*, Word Biblical Commentary 43 (Dallas: Word, 1983): 85. Hawthorne explains that the Greek term *hyparchōn* is best translated here as "because" rather than "being" and that the New American Standard Bible's translation of "although," as if being God is an obstacle to being humble, couldn't be more wrong. I thank Cornelius Plantinga Jr. for calling this to my attention.
30. Augustine, "The Confessions," 11.14, ed. John E. Rotelle, trans. Maria Boulding, *The Works of Saint Augustine, A Translation for the 21st Century* (Hyde Park, N.Y.: New City, 1997), 294.
31. First John 4:8.
32. Matthew 16:24 – 25.
33. This is true of Protestant Christianity. Roman Catholicism teaches that our acceptance with God is accomplished by grace alone but not faith alone. Grace enables us to become righteous, which then merits our acceptance with God (contra Luther, who argued that we are declared righteous for Christ's sake even though we are not).
34. Titus 2:11 – 14.
35. Luke 7:36 – 47.
36. Martin Luther, as quoted in Roland Bainton, *Here I Stand* (New York: Abingdon-Cokesbury, 1950), 45. For the original German quote, see WA 38:143.25.
37. Martin Luther, as quoted in E. Gordon Rupp, *The Righteousness of God: Luther Studies* (London: Hodder and Stoughton, 1953), 104. The original quote appears in Luther's "Lectures on Galatians (1535)," in *Luther's Works* 27, ed. Lewis W. Spitz and Helmut T. Lehmann (Philadelphia: Muhlenberg, 1960), 13; and WA 40, 2:15.15.
38. Martin Luther, as quoted in Bainton, *Here I Stand*, 59.
39. Martin Luther, "Preface to the Complete Edition of Luther's Latin Writings (Wittenberg, 1545)," in *Luther's Works* 34:337.
40. Martin Luther, as quoted in Bainton, *Here I Stand*, 65. The source of this quote is Luther's preface to the 1545 edition of his writings and can be read in *Luther's Works* 34:337.
41. Martin Luther, "The Freedom of a Christian," in *Martin Luther's Basic Theological Writings*, 2nd ed., ed. Timothy F. Lull (Minneapolis: Fortress, 2005), 392.

42. Luther, "The Freedom of a Christian," 406 (emphasis mine).

43. See Herbert Simon, "A Mechanism for Social Selection and Successful Altruism," *Science* 250 (December, 1990): 1665–68, as cited in Alvin Plantinga's lecture "Science and Christian Belief: Conflict or Concord?" at the January Series of Calvin College (Grand Rapids), January 18, 2005.

44. First John 4:19.

45. James 2:26; 1 Corinthians 13:2.

Chapter 4. Are People Generally Good or Basically Bad?

1. Abraham Kuyper, *Principles of Sacred Theology*, trans. J. Hendrik De Vries (Scribner, 1898; repr., Grand Rapids: Baker, 1980), 150–76. Kuyper explains how this antithesis appears in science in his 1898 *Lectures on Calvinism* (1931; repr., Grand Rapids: Eerdmans, 1999), 130–41. It is worth noting that Kuyper did not say much about how a Christian interpretation of science differs from other monotheistic religions, but limited his comments to the pressing issue in the Netherlands in his day, the difference between Christianity and secular humanism.

2. First Corinthians 6:9–11.

3. Isaac Watts, "At the Cross" (1707; refrain by Ralph E. Hudson, 1885; public domain; emphasis mine).

4. Karl Barth describes the impotence of sin, saying that it is "what God has not willed and does not will and will not will, of that which absolutely is not, or is only as God does not will it, of that which lives only as that which God has rejected and condemned and excluded." See Karl Barth, *Church Dogmatics* 4.1, trans. G. W. Bromiley, ed. G. W. Bromiley and T. F. Torrance (Edinburgh: T. & T. Clark, 1956), 409.

5. F. Bente, *Historical Introductions to the Book of Concord* (St. Louis: Concordia, 1965), 144.

6. Spencer Burke and Barry Taylor, *A Heretic's Guide to Eternity* (San Francisco: Jossey-Bass, 2006), 63, 69 (emphasis mine).

7. Ibid., 64.

8. Tony Jones, *The New Christians* (San Francisco: Jossey-Bass, 2008), 78.

9. Ibid., 78. Jones's interpretation of this metaphor is surprisingly literal. He misses that the chasm between two cliffs is a physical picture illustrating a spiritual truth rather than a literal statement depicting sin as a matter of distance.

10. Matthew 15:18–20.

11. Jones, *New Christians*, 78. Jones's comments occur within a story in which he denies the necessity of penal substitution (pp. 76–79) and adds, "What happened, economically speaking—what was the cosmic transaction on Good Friday—is a subject to be bandied about in theological circles until the end of time." Regardless of how the cross saves, Jones insists that "the crucifixion of Jesus Christ is the impetus for healed and healing relationships in a world that desperately needs them" (pp. 78–79). I wonder how Jones can be sure that the cross will heal our social relationships if he does not know how it cleanses us from personal sin.

12. Doug Pagitt, "The Emerging Church and Embodied Theology," in *Listening to the Beliefs of Emerging Churches* (Grand Rapids: Zondervan, 2007), 128–29. In a new book, *A Christianity Worth Believing* (San Francisco: Jossey-Bass, 2008), Pagitt goes beyond considering Pelagius's position and embraces it (pp. 120–70).

13. Lewis B. Smedes, *Mere Morality: What God Expects from Ordinary People* (Grand Rapids: Eerdmans, 1983).

14. See http://www.worldpress.org/Americas/2408.cfm. Accessed April 21, 2008.

15. John Calvin, *Institutes of the Christian Religion* 2.2.15–16, ed. John T. McNeill, trans. Ford Lewis Battles (Philadelphia: Westminster, 1960).

16. Genesis 4:20–22.

17. See Augustine, "The Perfection of Human Righteousness," chap. 14 (32), *The Works of Saint Augustine: A Translation for the 21st Century* 1/23, trans. Roland J. Teske and ed. John E. Rotelle (Hyde Park, N.Y.: New City, 1997), 306; and Calvin, *Institutes* 1.1.1–3; 3.14.9.

18. Augustine, "Nature and Grace," chap. 57 (49), in *Works of Saint Augustine* 1/23, p. 254.

19. A notable exception are the churches that arose from the Campbellite movement, an eighteenth- and nineteenth-century American attempt to restore what they considered biblical purity to the church. An example is the Churches of Christ, which, though they deny the doctrine of original sin, still assume that sin is universal, and so require baptism for its forgiveness.

20. This is a paraphrase from Henri Blocher, *Original Sin* (Grand Rapids: Eerdmans, 1999), 91.

21. Augustine, "Nature and Grace," chap. 62 (53), in *Works of Saint Augustine* 1/23, p. 256. Cf. "Grace and Free Choice," chap. 9 (4), 10 (5), 32 (16), 33 (17), 41 (20); and "Rebuke and Grace," chap. 32 (11), in *Works of Saint Augustine* 1/26, pp. 77–78, 93–94, 99–100, and 131.

22. Augustine, "Rebuke and Grace," chaps. 3 (2) and 38 (12), in *Works of Saint Augustine* 1/26, pp. 110, 136. The term "invincibly" comes from *Saint Augustine: Anti-Pelagian Writings*, in *A Select Library of the Nicene and Post-Nicene Fathers of the Christian Church*, vol. 5, ed. Philip Schaff, trans. Peter Holmes, Robert Ernest Wallis, and Benjamin Warfield (Edinburgh: T. & T. Clark; repr., Grand Rapids: Eerdmans, 1991), 487.

23. Augustine, "Grace and Free Choice," chap. 15 (6), in *Works of Saint Augustine* 1/26, p. 81.

24. Augustine left open the possibility that Christians could become perfect in this life. See "Nature and Grace," chap. 49 (42); "The Perfection of Human Righteousness," chap. 13 (6); and "Grace and Free Choice," chap. 31 (15), in *Works of Saint Augustine* 1/23, pp. 249–50, 294 and 1/26, pp. 91–92.

25. "Epitome of the Formula of Concord," pt. 4, sec. 8, in *The Book of Concord*, trans. Theodore G. Tappert (Philadelphia: Fortress, 1959), 552. Martin Luther taught that "works are acceptable not for their own sake, but because of the faith" and that "faith alone makes all other works good, acceptable and worthy, in that it trusts God and does not doubt that for it all things that a man does are well done" (WA 6:206, 190. Cf. WA 6:202, 208; and 10/3:289.7–10 ("On Good Works").

26. Calvin, *Institutes* 3.17.4.
27. John Calvin, *The Sermons of M. John Calvin upon the Fifth Booke of Moses Called Deuteronomie*, trans. Arthur Golding (London: 1583; repr., Carlisle, Pa.: Banner of Truth Trust, 1987), 944 (emphasis mine). Cf. Calvin, *Institutes* 3.14.9; 3.17.3, 8. Cf. Anthony A. Hoekema, "Taking Them for Good," *Reformed Journal* 38 (1988): 8 – 10. See also the *Westminster Confession*, chap. 16, art. 6: "Notwithstanding (the fact that we cannot by our best works merit anything from God), the persons of believers being accepted through Christ, their good works also are accepted in him; not as though they were in this life wholly unblameable and unreprovable in God's sight; but that he, looking upon them in his Son, is pleased to accept and reward that which is sincere, although accompanied with many weaknesses and imperfections."
28. John Wesley, *A Plain Account of Christian Perfection* (Kansas City: Beacon Hill, 1966), 72 – 77; J. A. Wood, *Christian Perfection, as Taught by John Wesley* (Salem, Ohio: Schmul, 1981).
29. Isaiah 64:6; cf. Romans 4:1 – 8.
30. Jeremiah 17:9. Martin Luther concurs with my experience: "Our flesh is so evil that it often deceives us in the very midst of tribulation and humility, so that we are pleased by our humility and disregard of ourselves, and by our own confession of sins; we become proud of accusing ourselves of being proud" (WA 5:564), as quoted in Paul Althaus, *The Theology of Martin Luther*, trans. Robert T. Schultz (Philadelphia: Fortress, 1966), 149.
31. John Newton in the film *Amazing Grace* (Los Angeles: Bristol Bay Productions, 2007), directed by Michael Apted, written by Steve Knight.
32. This complaint is raised by John Wesley, *Plain Account of Christian Perfection*, 70, 119; and Johannes Dietenberger, *Whether the Christians Are Able to Merit Heaven through Their Good Works* (Strassburg, 1523), 27.
33. I thank Richard Muller for this illustration.
34. Matthew 25:23.
35. Psalm 103:12 – 14.
36. Romans 3:23.
37. Genesis 3:5.
38. Acts 16:31 and Romans 10:9. Other passages that emphasize the lordship of Jesus include 1 Corinthians 8:6; 12:3; 2 Corinthians 4:5; Philippians 2:11; Colossians 2:6; 1 Timothy 6:15; 1 Peter 3:15; Revelation 11:15; 17:14; and 19:16.
39. First Corinthians 12:3.

Chapter 5. Which Is Worse: Homosexuals or the Bigots Who Persecute Them?

1. Learn more about Soulforce by visiting their website at www.soulforce.org.
2. Space does not permit an in-depth discussion of the biblical viewpoint, so I will focus on the main arguments and recommend books for further study. Books opposed to homosexual practice include Robert A. J. Gagnon, *The Bible and Homosexual Practice: Texts and Hermeneutics* (Nashville: Abingdon, 2001); Stanley J. Grenz, *Welcoming but Not Affirming* (Louisville:

Westminster John Knox, 1998); Marion L. Soards, *Scripture and Homosexuality* (Louisville: Westminster John Knox, 1995); Donald J. Wold, *Out of Order* (Grand Rapids: Baker, 1998); James B. DeYoung, *Homosexuality* (Grand Rapids: Kregel, 2000); and William J. Webb, *Slaves, Women, and Homosexuals* (Downers Grove, Ill.: InterVarsity, 2001). Books that support homosexual activity include Jack Rogers, *Jesus, the Bible, and Homosexuality* (Louisville: John Knox, 2006); Robin Scroggs, *The New Testament and Homosexuality* (Philadelphia: Fortress, 1983); Pim Pronk, *Against Nature?* trans. John Vriend (Grand Rapids: Eerdmans, 1993); and David G. Myers and Letha Dawson Scanzoni, *What God Has Joined Together: The Christian Case for Gay Marriage* (San Francisco: HarperSanFrancisco, 2005). For a dialogue between views, see Dan O. Via and Robert A. J. Gagnon, *Homosexuality and the Bible: Two Views* (Minneapolis: Fortress, 2003); Jeffrey S. Siker, ed., *Homosexuality in the Church: Both Sides of the Debate* (Louisville: Westminster John Knox, 1994); and Timothy Bradshaw, ed., *The Way Forward?* 2nd ed. (Cambridge: Hodder and Stoughton, 1997; Grand Rapids: Eerdmans, 2004).

3. Genesis 2:24.

4. Jon Stewart, *The Daily Show*, June 6, 2006.

5. Leviticus 18:6 – 23; cf. 20:10 – 21.

6. Myers and Scanzoni, *What God Has Joined Together*, 90.

7. Alert readers may notice that Leviticus 18:19 warns against having sex with a menstruating woman. Isn't this one example of sexual activity that we would tolerate today? And if this is now morally permissible, then why not also homosexual relations? I respond that (1) though we may no longer consider it a violation of God's law, we can understand why God would consider sex with a menstruating woman to be an act that defiles (Lev. 18:24; 15:24). Its inclusion in a list of other sexual acts — including homosexual ones — indicates God's low view of all of them. (2) Unlike the other sexual acts in the list, this alone refers to the *timing* rather than the *partner* of sex. Thus, even though I concede that sex during menstruation is not a sin, my point still stands that it would be morally wrong to have sex with any *partner* in this list.

8. Leviticus 18:24 – 25.

9. Grenz, *Welcoming but Not Affirming*, 56 – 59; Soards, *Scripture and Homosexuality*, 18 – 20; Gagnon, "The Bible and Homosexual Practice: Key Issues," in *Homosexuality and the Bible: Two Views*, 67, 82 – 84; and Wold, *Out of Order*, 189 – 96.

10. Scroggs, *The New Testament and Homsexuality*, 128 – 29; Myers and Scanzoni, *What God Has Joined Together*, 84, 94; and Via, "The Bible, the Church, and Homosexuality," in *Homosexuality and the Bible: Two Views*, 11.

11. Grenz, *Welcoming but Not Affirming*, 137; Soards, *Scripture and Homosexuality*, 47 – 50; and Gagnon, *The Bible and Homosexual Practice*, 350 – 61, claim that homosexual activity did take place among consenting adults in ancient Greece and Rome, so Paul would not have been oblivious to the concept of homosexual marriage.

12. Romans 1:18, 25.

13. Romans 1:24, 26–27.

14. Myers and Scanzoni, *What God Has Joined Together*, 98; and Lewis B. Smedes, "Like the Wideness of the Sea?" 6 (accessed August 7, 2006), www.soulforce. org/article/638.

15. Myers and Scanzoni, *What God Has Joined Together*, 99–100; Allen Verhey, *Remembering Jesus: Christian Community, Scripture, and the Moral Life* (Grand Rapids: Eerdmans, 2002), 237; Lewis B. Smedes, "Like the Wideness of the Sea?" 5–6 (accessed April 28, 2007), www.soulforce.org/article/638; and Mel White, "What the Bible Says — and Doesn't Say — about Homosexuality," 15–16 (accessed April 28, 2007), www.soulforce.org/article/homosexuality-bible.

16. Via, "The Bible, the Church, and Homosexuality," 14.

17. Grenz, *Welcoming but Not Affirming*, 49, observes that the Greek text of Romans 1:26 literally reads, "*the* natural sexual functioning" rather than "*their* natural" sexual preference.

18. Soards, *Scripture and Homosexuality*, 23–24.

19. Stanley Grenz surveys the church's historical position against homosexuality in *Welcoming but Not Affirming*, 63–80.

20. Smedes, "Like the Wideness of the Sea?" 5, 7.

21. While Romans 1:24–32 may not describe a downward spiral, it seems significant that the third time God's wrath is revealed — after heterosexual and homosexual sin — God is giving people over to such sins of the spirit as "greed ... envy, murder, strife, deceit and malice. They are gossips, slanderers, God-haters, insolent, arrogant and boastful; they invent ways of doing evil; they disobey their parents; they are senseless, faithless, heartless, ruthless." Sins of the spirit may be worse, or at least equally bad, as sexual sins.

22. Brian McLaren, *The Last Word and the Word after That* (San Francisco: Jossey-Bass, 2005), 23.

23. Ibid., 21: "One in two thousand live births requires attention from a specialist in sexuality." This represents only .05 percent of the population, which certainly is too small to change the rule for everyone else.

24. I thank Becky Hammond for this insight.

25. I thank Ben Irwin for this helpful way of putting it.

26. Walter Rauschenbusch, *A Theology for the Social Gospel* (1945; repr., Nashville: Abingdon, 1978), 36.

27. Isaiah 3:15; 10:1–2.

28. Isaiah 6:5.

29. Matthew 5:21–22, 27–28; 6:5–6, 16–18.

30. Matthew 23:4; 25:31–46; Luke 10:25–37.

31. Romans 13:8–14. Scripture does not seem to neatly distinguish between private and public sin but intersperses them together. Jesus groups sins that one commits alone with those that directly hurt others in his list of sins that arise from an individual's heart: "evil thoughts, sexual immorality, theft, murder, adultery, greed, malice, deceit, lewdness, envy, slander, arrogance and folly"

(Mark 7:21 – 22). Paul does the same when he describes the sins of the flesh as "sexual immorality, impurity and debauchery; idolatry and witchcraft; hatred, discord, jealousy, fits of rage, selfish ambition, dissensions, factions and envy; drunkenness, orgies, and the like" (Gal. 5:19 – 21).

32. Tim Stafford, "Ed Dobson Loves Homosexuals," *Christianity Today*, July 19, 1993, 22. See also Dean Merrill, "The Education of Ed Dobson: How a Lieutenant in the Moral Majority Rediscovered the Power of the Local Church," *Christianity Today*, August 11, 1997, 26 – 30.

Chapter 6. Is the Cross Divine Child Abuse?

1. Robert Lowry, "Nothing but the Blood" (1876; public domain).
2. Charitie Less Bancroft, "Before the Throne" (1863; public domain).
3. John Goldingay challenges the traditional view that Old Testament sacrifices vicariously bore the punishment in place of the worshipers who offered them. He writes: "Sacrifice does not involve penal substitution in the sense that one entity bears another's punishment. By laying hands on the offering, the offerers identify with it and pass on to it not their guilt but their stain. The offering is then not vicariously punished but vicariously cleansed" (John Goldingay, "Old Testament Sacrifice and the Death of Christ," in *Atonement Today*, ed. John Goldingay [London: SPCK, 1995], 10). Goldingay does not supply an argument for his view, so I see no reason to take his side against the traditional view that Old Testament sacrifices bore both the stain and guilt of sin (they were not merely "cleansed" but killed for the worshiper's sin). Henri Blocher wonders, "When J. Goldingay claims that offerers 'pass on to [the victim] not their guilt but their stain,' we ask: what *is* the spiritual stain of sin if not their guilt before God?" See Henri Blocher, "The Sacrifice of Jesus Christ: The Current Theological Situation," *European Journal of Theology* 8 (1999): 31.
4. Romans 3:25; Galatians 3:13; 2 Corinthians 5:21.
5. Anselm, "Why God Became Man," in *Anselm of Canterbury: The Major Works*, ed. Brian Davies and G. R. Evans (New York: Oxford University Press, 1998), 260 – 356.
6. John Calvin, *Institutes of the Christian Religion* 2.16.5, ed. John T. McNeill, trans. Ford Lewis Battles (Philadelphia: Westminster, 1960), 1:509: "To take away our condemnation, it was not enough for him to suffer any kind of death: to make satisfaction for our redemption a form of death had to be chosen in which he might free us both by transferring our condemnation to himself and by taking our guilt upon himself. If he had been murdered by thieves or slain in an insurrection by a raging mob, in such a death there would have been no evidence of satisfaction. But when he was arraigned before the judgment seat as a criminal, accused and pressed by testimony, and condemned by the mouth of the judge to die — we know by these proofs that he took the role of a guilty man and evildoer."
7. One chapter is not sufficient space to demonstrate the truthfulness of the penal substitution view, so I will limit my focus to contemporary objections to it. Readers who wish to delve more deeply into the arguments for and against

penal substitution should begin with the four views presented in James Beilby and Paul R. Eddy, eds., *The Nature of the Atonement* (Downers Grove, Ill.: InterVarsity, 2006). Penal substitution is defended in Charles E. Hill and Frank A. James III, eds., *The Glory of the Atonement* (Downers Grove, Ill.: InterVarsity, 2004); David Peterson, ed., *Where Wrath and Mercy Meet* (Waynesboro, Ga.: Paternoster, 2001); Leon Morris, *The Apostolic Preaching of the Cross* (London: Tyndale, 1955); and John R. W. Stott, *The Cross of Christ* (Downers Grove, Ill.: InterVarsity, 1986). Its alleged shortcomings are examined in Joel B. Green and Mark D. Baker, *Recovering the Scandal of the Cross* (Downers Grove, Ill.: InterVarsity, 2000).

8. Joel B. Green, "Kaleidoscopic View," in Beilby and Eddy, *Nature of the Atonement*, 165 – 71, and Green and Baker, *Recovering the Scandal of the Cross*, 116 – 52.

9. Gustaf Aulén, *Christus Victor*, trans. A. G. Herbert (New York: Macmillan, 1969), 16 – 60.

10. C. S. Lewis, *The Lion, the Witch, and the Wardrobe* (1950; repr., New York: Harper Trophy, 2000), 163. Greg Boyd, who advocates the Christus Victor view, concedes that this position leaves unanswered "precisely how did Calvary and the resurrection defeat the powers." See Gregory A. Boyd, "Christus Victor View," in Beilby and Eddy, *Nature of the Atonement*, 37.

11. Hebrews 2:14 – 15: "Since the children have flesh and blood, he too shared in their humanity so that by his death he might destroy him who holds the power of death — that is, the devil — and free those who all their lives were held in slavery by their fear of death."

12. Peter Abailard, "Exposition of the Epistle to the Romans (An Excerpt from the Second Book)," in *A Scholastic Miscellany: Anselm to Ockham*, Library of Christian Classics, vol. 10, ed. and trans. Eugene R. Fairweather (London: SCM Press; Philadelphia: Westminster, 1956), 283 – 84.

13. First John 3:16; 4:9 – 12; 1 Peter 2:21.

14. I thank my friend Zachary Bartels for this illustration. See http://www.imdb.com/title/tt0199232.

15. First John 4:19.

16. Alert readers may wonder why I have left out other theories of the atonement, such as the governmental and recapitulation views (I regard the latter as a method — how penal substitution and Christus Victor were accomplished — rather than a stand-alone theory). I reply that while all the theories contribute something important, I have chosen to focus on the key theories that directly address our main problems. Just as a football team needs eleven players to field an offense and yet most of the attention falls on the quarterback, running back, and wide receiver, so I agree that we need every theory of the atonement even while I focus on the Big Three. A recent book that argues persuasively for incorporating all of the atonement theories is Scot McKnight, *A Community Called Atonement* (Nashville: Abingdon, 2007).

17. Boyd, "Christus Victor View," 48; Green and Baker, *Recovering the Scandal of the Cross*, 25; and Scot McKnight, "What Is the Gospel?" Talking Points

seminar at Grand Rapids Theological Seminary, September 25, 2006, http://grts.cornerstone.edu/resources/tpoints/fa06.

18. Boyd, "Christus Victor View," 47 – 49; Green, "Kaleidoscopic Response," in Beilby and Eddy, *Nature of the Atonement*, 114; and Green and Baker, *Recovering the Scandal of the Cross*, 149.

19. Martin Brecht, *Martin Luther: Shaping and Defining the Reformation, 1521 – 1532*, trans. James L. Schaaf (Minneapolis: Fortress, 1990), 288 – 89.

20. Martin Brecht, *Martin Luther: The Preservation of the Church, 1532 – 1546*, trans. James L. Schaaf (Minneapolis: Fortress, 1993), 262 – 64.

21. Feminist accounts are found in Joanne Carlson Brown and Carole R. Bohn, eds., *Christianity, Patriarchy, and Abuse: A Feminist Critique* (New York: Pilgrim, 1989). See especially the following chapters: Joanne Carlson Brown and Rebecca Parker, "For God So Loved the World?" 1 – 30; Rita Nakashima Brock, "And a Little Child Will Lead Us: Christology and Child Abuse," 42 – 61; and Beverly W. Harrison and Carter Heyward, "Pain and Pleasure: Avoiding the Confusions of Christian Tradition in Feminist Theory," 148 – 73.

Other objections include that penal substitution is (1) too modern (first expressed in the sixteenth-century Reformation and peaking in nineteenth- and twentieth-century evangelicalism), (2) culturally irrelevant to Eastern cultures that worry about eliminating shame rather than guilt, and (3) impersonal, for it implies that God cannot forgive without obliging some higher, abstract standard of justice.

(1) Against the modern objection, I reply with C. S. Lewis that we cannot tell truth by a clock. The origin of a belief has no bearing on whether it is true or false. Not all modern ideas are wrong, just as not all postmodern notions are right. The truth of any belief must be determined on other grounds than its timing.

(2) Joel Green and Mark Baker argue that because penal substitution was developed by Western Christians who sought a way to eliminate their guilt, this understanding of the atonement does not transfer to Eastern cultures in which people are more troubled by shame. Eastern cultures are seeking a solution to a different problem, and so they will not understand our penal perspective on the gospel. To communicate effectively with them, we must discover how salvation heals our shame. And since the Bible is an Eastern book, this recasting of the cross into Eastern categories actually draws us closer to its original meaning (Green and Baker, *Recovering the Scandal of the Cross*, 153 – 70).

Green and Baker make a good point: Eastern cultures are concerned with shame and saving face. My Western mind could not understand the two Chinese adults screaming at each other over a bicycle fender bender, neither one able to back down before the large crowd that had gathered. So I suspect there is something important here. Yet I believe that Green and Baker oversell their case. In my years in China, I never met a person who complained that they could not understand my explanation of the gospel because it focused too much on guilt and not enough on shame. Perhaps this is because shame and guilt are intertwined. Genuine shame arises from genuine guilt. We are rightly ashamed only when we are truly guilty.

Thus, penal substitution seems foundational even to a shame-based culture. Jesus did not die on the cross merely so people could save face. He did bear our shame, but only because he bore our underlying guilt. Jesus removed both our guilt and shame, and we cannot have one without the other.

(3) This objection forgets that the law of God is grounded in the nature of God. Thus, God is obliging himself rather than some abstract principle when he responds to sin with wrath and justice. His personal affront to sin runs so deep that he compares our sin to adultery. See Thomas R. Schreiner, "Penal Substitution View," in Beilby and Eddy, *Nature of the Atonement*, 77–78.

22. Steve Chalke and Alan Mann, *The Lost Message of Jesus* (Grand Rapids: Zondervan, 2003), 182–83. Cf. Brian D. McLaren, *The Story We Find Ourselves In* (San Francisco: Jossey-Bass, 2003), 102. Elsewhere Chalke states, "The theological problem with penal substitution is that it presents us with a God who is first and foremost concerned with retribution flowing from his wrath against sinners." He adds, "On the cross Jesus does not placate God's anger in taking the punishment for sin, but rather absorbs its consequences and, in his resurrection, defeats death." See Steve Chalke, "Cross Purposes," *Christianity* (September 2004), www.christianitymagazine.co.uk/engine. cfm?i=92&id=22&arch=1.

N. T. Wright suggests that Chalke did not mean to disparage all forms of penal substitution but only the models that depict God as a vengeful Father who vents his wrath on his innocent Son. However, since penal substitution historically insists that God has wrath that needs satisfied (though this does not necessarily make him vengeful), it seems that Chalke does have issues with penal substitution as traditionally understood. See N. T. Wright, "The Cross and the Caricatures" (Eastertide 2007), 9, www.fulcrum-anglican.org. uk/page.cfm?ID=205.

23. Brian McLaren, *The Last Word and the Word after That* (San Francisco: Jossey-Bass, 2005), 40. Neil asks, "Daniel, do you really think God is like a petty human being, full of anger and revenge? Do you think God wants to inflict torture on people to retaliate for their wrongs? Do you think God would require us to forgive and then be unwilling to do the same?"

24. F. LeRon Shults and Steven Sandage, *The Faces of Forgiveness* (Grand Rapids: Baker, 2003), 148–49. Cf. Gregory A. Boyd, "Christus Victor Response," in Beilby and Eddy, *Nature of the Atonement*, 103: "Satan, not God, holds that no one can be forgiven truly for free: someone or other must pay!"

25. Brian D. McLaren, *More Ready Than You Realize* (Grand Rapids: Zondervan, 2002), 80.

26. John 10:17–18.

27. Matthew 12:1–14; 22:36–40; Romans 13:8–10.

28. James 1:13–15. My argument that God is obliging his own nature when he metes out justice defeats the view that God is hamstrung by some higher, abstract property. Brian McLaren, *Last Word*, 40, has Neil explain this mis-

guided objection: "You have to say that God doesn't want people to go to hell, but he's forced to do so against his will by the mechanisms of the court or the requirements of some higher abstraction called justice or something like that. He's a nice guy caught in a tough fix. He wants to forgive us, but he has to play by the rules of the court."

29. Matthew 26:42.

30. First John 4:8; Isaiah 13:13; 51:17; John 3:36; Romans 1:18.

31. Philippians 2:5 – 11; Revelation 11:15.

32. Romans 6:4. Cf. 2 Corinthians 5:17: "Therefore, if anyone is in Christ, he is a new creation; the old has gone, the new has come!" In philosophical terms, we must die ethically (to sin) in order to rise to new life (both ontologically and ethically).

33. Karl Barth, *Church Dogmatics* 4/1, trans. G. W. Bromiley, ed. G. W. Bromiley and T. F. Torrance (Edinburgh: T. & T. Clark, 1956), 294 – 95.

34. Some conservatives argue that penal substitution is an end in itself rather than a means to another end, such as Christus Victor. While I am sympathetic to this argument, I am simply asking here why God's wrath needs to be satisfied. I believe the answer is not merely for its own sake — for God could have chosen to leave his wrath unsatisfied and save no one (and the existence of hell indicates that God's wrath is never entirely spent) — but for the sake of delivering us from sin, death, and the Devil. Either way, I firmly believe that Jesus bore the penalty of sin in our place when he endured the Father's wrath on the cross.

Likewise, I recognize that my telling of the battle between God and Satan may not stress God's sovereignty enough for some. I reply that I believe that God decrees whatever comes to pass and that from his perspective the final outcome of this cosmic struggle was never in doubt. But just as our choices do not jeopardize God's sovereignty, so his sovereignty does not eliminate the significance of what happens in human history. My story follows the Bible's lead and focuses on the latter — the real though never precarious battle between God and Satan for control of the world.

35. Genesis 3:15.

36. Matthew 4:8 – 10. I owe this "tip of the hat" idea to Karl Barth, *Church Dogmatics* 4/1, p. 262: "He had only to lift His hat to the usurper."

37. Luke 10:18; John 12:31. For Satan's authority over the world, see John 14:30; 16:11; 2 Corinthians 4:4; Ephesians 2:2; 1 John 5:19. For Christ's ministry defeating Satan, see Matthew 4:23 – 24; 8:16 – 17, 28 – 34; 9:32 – 33; 10:1; 12:22 – 29; Luke 10:17 – 20; 11:14 – 22; Acts 2:32 – 36; 10:38; Colossians 2:15; Hebrews 2:14; 1 John 3:8; Revelation 11:15.

38. Colossians 2:15.

39. Colossians 1:20. See Boyd, "Christus Victor View," 33 – 35.

40. Boyd, "Christus Victor View," 46 – 49.

Chapter 7. Can You Belong before You Believe?

1. Brian McLaren, *More Ready Than You Realize* (Grand Rapids: Zondervan, 2002), 83 – 87. Cf. Brian McLaren, *A New Kind of Christian* (San Francisco:

Jossey-Bass, 2001), 108, where Neo says that he might invite a seeking non-Christian to come on his church's "short-term mission trip" so she could discover more about his Christian community and their faith.

2. Nanette Sawyer, "What Would Huckleberry Do?" in Doug Pagitt and Tony Jones, eds., *An Emergent Manifesto of Hope* (Grand Rapids: Baker, 2007), 44; and Eddie Gibbs and Ryan K. Bolger, *Emerging Churches* (Grand Rapids: Baker, 2005), 119–20. This use of the Lord's Supper seems similar to an earlier American innovation, when in 1700 Solomon Stoddard, the grandfather of Jonathan Edwards, opened the Eucharist to non-Christians in the hopes that its grace might convert them. Fifty years later Edwards was dismissed by the church in Northampton, Massachusetts, when he attempted to repeal his predecessor's policy.

3. Doug Pagitt raised this question in his lecture entitled "Church" at the *Emergent YS Convention* (Nashville, May 20, 2005).

4. Michael Frost and Alan Hirsch, *The Shaping of Things to Come* (Peabody, Mass.: Hendrickson, 2003), 47.

5. Steve Chalke and Alan Mann, *The Lost Message of Jesus* (Grand Rapids: Zondervan, 2003), 141–44.

6. Holly Rankin and Sue Wallace, as quoted in Gibbs and Bolger, *Emerging Churches*, 120, 129–30.

7. Brian D. McLaren, *The Secret Message of Jesus* (Nashville: Nelson, 2006), 168–69.

8. Frost and Hirsch, *Shaping of Things to Come*, 49.

9. Ibid., 48.

10. For example, see Nanette Sawyer, "What Would Huckleberry Do?" 43–44, who complains that her childhood pastor "was defining Christian identity as assent to a list of certain beliefs, and he was defining Christian community as those people who concur with those beliefs. This didn't leave any room for questions, doubts, or growth in faith. It made community acceptance of each other completely conditional on having already arrived at a particular intellectual destination. In asking me if I was a Christian, and accepting my preteen answer, he essentially told me that I wasn't part of the community. I wasn't *in*; I was *out*. And so I found myself spiritually homeless" (emphasis hers). See also Pagitt and Jones, *An Emergent Manifesto of Hope*, 101–6, 191–96.

11. Spencer Burke and Barry Taylor, *A Heretic's Guide to Eternity* (San Francisco: Jossey-Bass, 2006), 217–18.

12. Frost and Hirsch, *Shaping of Things to Come*, 49–50.

13. Pip Piper, as quoted in Gibbs and Bolger, *Emerging Churches*, 131.

14. Dave Tomlinson, *The Post Evangelical* (Grand Rapids: Zondervan, 2003), 138.

15. Chalke, *Lost Message of Jesus*, 147–52.

16. Gibbs and Bolger, *Emerging Churches*, 196–203.

17. Doug Pagitt, *Preaching Re-imagined* (Grand Rapids: Zondervan, 2005). Other churches conduct meetings that consist "of an open mic, where anyone can

share at any time. The service does not come to a final resolution, nor is there any expectation that it should" (Gibbs and Bolger, *Emerging Churches*, 69).

18. Gibbs and Bolger, *Emerging Churches*, 103: "Mark Scandrette (ReIMAGINE! San Francisco) feels that to call his 'urban swarm' a church is to formalize their function and deaden the experience. 'There is so much baggage from the idea of church, so I hesitate to call it that.' There is no official gathering, but the community gets together quite often as people participate in kingdom life together. 'It didn't make sense to be intentional about spiritual things anymore. For some reason, we just needed to be real and be friends and to let something develop naturally.'" See more anecdotes on pp. 89, 100, and 103, with helpful correctives on pp. 104 ("church cannot be confused with simply hanging out with friends") and 106.

19. Friedrich Schleiermacher, *On Religion: Speeches to Its Cultured Despisers* (New York: Cambridge University Press, 1988). Helpful studies on Schleiermacher's theology include James C. Livingston, *Modern Christian Thought*, 2nd ed. (1997; repr., Minneapolis: Fortress, 2006), 1:93–105; B. A. Gerrish, *A Prince of the Church* (Philadelphia: Fortress, 1984); Robert R. Williams, *Schleiermacher the Theologian* (Philadelphia: Fortress, 1978); and Keith W. Clements, ed., *Friedrich Schleiermacher: Pioneer of Modern Theology* (Minneapolis: Fortress, 1987, 1991).

20. Brian D. McLaren, *More Ready Than You Realize*, 84–85. McLaren says that he does not use the term "belong" to mean being "an official member" but merely being "accepted into the community without reservation" (86).

21. Cyprian, *Epistle* 72, sec. 21, in *The Ante-Nicene Fathers*, ed. Alexander Roberts and James Donaldson (Grand Rapids: Eerdmans, 1995), 5:384.

22. John Calvin, *Institutes of the Christian Religion* 4.1.4, ed. John T. McNeill, trans. Ford Lewis Battles (Philadelphia: Westminster, 1960).

23. McLaren, *New Kind of Christian*, 130.

Chapter 8. Does the Kingdom of God Include Non-Christians?

1. Jon Meacham, "Pilgrim's Progress," *Newsweek*, August 14, 2006, 43. Graham's spokesman, A. Larry Ross, elaborated on Graham's comment: "As an evangelist for more than six decades, Mr. Graham has faithfully proclaimed the Bible's Gospel message that Jesus is the only way to Heaven. However, salvation is the work of Almighty God, and only he knows what is in each human heart."

   Brian McLaren shares Graham's reluctance to comment on the fate of non-Christians. He responds to the question of their destiny by declaring, "Why do you consider me qualified to make this pronouncement? Isn't this God's business? Isn't it clear that I do not believe this is the right question for a missional Christian to ask?" (Brian McLaren, *A Generous Orthodoxy* [Grand Rapids: Zondervan, 2004], 112).

2. Brian D. McLaren, *The Secret Message of Jesus* (Nashville: Nelson, 2006), 216–17 (italics McLaren's, boldface mine).

3. Cf. McLaren, *Generous Orthodoxy*, 264. Here McLaren appeals to the "C1–C6 Spectrum" controversy in missions, in which missiologists debate

whether and to what extent people must forsake their non-Christian religions to follow Jesus. As is his custom, McLaren avoids giving a direct answer to this question, but he seems to favor the "not very much" side. He provocatively writes: "In this light, although I don't hope all Buddhists will become (cultural) Christians, I do hope all who feel so called will become Buddhist followers of Jesus; I believe they should be given that opportunity and invitation. I don't hope all Jews or Hindus will become members of the Christian religion. But I do hope all who feel so called will become Jewish or Hindu followers of Jesus. Ultimately, I hope that Jesus will save Buddhism, Islam, and every other religion, including the Christian religion, which often seems to need saving about as much as any other religion does."

4. Dave Sutton, as quoted in Eddie Gibbs and Ryan K. Bolger, *Emerging Churches* (Grand Rapids: Baker, 2005), 133. Gibbs and Bolger elaborate: "Their attitude of service reflects a true openness regarding other religions. Rachelle Mee-Chapman explains, 'We try to make as much space for people as possible. We breathe on what God is doing in people's lives, see if we can fan the flame. We are not concerned with differences but whether we can dance in the overlap. Maybe the rest of who God is will be worked out through relationship'" (130).

5. Holly Rankin Zaher, as quoted in Gibbs and Bolger, *Emerging Churches*, 53.

6. Using the word *saved* does not address each religion on its own terms but slants our question in a Christian direction. However, it seems appropriate in this case since I am asking the question from a Christian perspective and not attempting to produce an objective, full-scale comparison of religions.

The best place to begin a study on the status of non-Christians is with books that contain a dialogue between multiple views. The best of these are Dennis Okholm and Timothy R. Phillips, eds., *More Than One Way?* (Grand Rapids: Zondervan, 1995); John Sanders, ed., *What about Those Who Have Never Heard?* (Downers Grove, Ill.: InterVarsity, 1995); and William V. Crockett and James G. Sigountos, eds., *Through No Fault of Their Own?* (Grand Rapids: Baker, 1991). A balanced presentation of the issues is also found in Millard Erickson, *How Shall They Be Saved?* (Grand Rapids: Baker, 1996).

The clearest arguments for pluralism are found in John Hick, *A Christian Theology of Religions* (Louisville: Westminster John Knox, 1995) and *God Has Many Names* (Philadelphia: Westminster, 1980). Individual books that argue for inclusivism include Clark Pinnock, *A Wideness in God's Mercy* (Grand Rapids: Zondervan, 1992); John Sanders, *No Other Name* (Grand Rapids: Eerdmans, 1992); and Terrance L. Tiessen, *Who Can Be Saved?* (Downers Grove, Ill.: InterVarsity, 2004).

Books that defend various degrees of exclusivism include James R. Edwards, *Is Jesus the Only Savior?* (Grand Rapids: Eerdmans, 2005); Daniel Strange, *The Possibility of Salvation among the Unevangelised* (Carlisle, U.K., and Waynesboro, Ga.: Paternoster, 2001); Ronald H. Nash, *Is Jesus the Only Savior?* (Grand Rapids: Zondervan, 1994); John Piper, *Let the Nations Be Glad!* (Grand Rapids: Baker, 1993); Ramesh Richard, *The Population of Heaven* (Chicago: Moody, 1994); and Harold Netland, *Encountering Religious Pluralism* (Downers Grove, Ill.: InterVarsity; Leicester: Apollos, 2001).

7. Karl Barth is the most able defender of this position. He argued from his Calvinist perspective that an omnipotent and omnibenevolent God may likely exert his power to lovingly sweep aside our sinful rejection of him and save us anyway. However, Barth refused to say for sure, for to guarantee what God must do would compromise God's freedom. See Karl Barth, *Church Dogmatics*, 2/2, ed. G. W. Bromiley and T. F. Torrance, trans. G. W. Bromiley, J. C. Campbell, Iain Wilson, J. Strathearn McNab, Harold Knight, and R. A. Stewart (Edinburgh: T. & T. Clark, 1957), 27, 51, 101, 177, 186–87, 195, 218–20, 316, 317, 325, 333, 352, 416–19, 422–23, 453; *Church Dogmatics* 4/3, ed. G. W. Bromiley and T. F. Torrance, trans. G. W. Bromiley (Edinburgh: T. & T. Clark, 1961), 463–65, 468, 476; and "The Humanity of God," in *God, Grace, and Gospel*, trans. James Strathearn McNab, *Scottish Journal of Theology Occasional Papers*, no. 8 (Edinburgh: Oliver and Boyd, 1959): 43–50.

   Postmodern innovators who value human freedom could look to Origen, who used our never-ending ability to choose as a reason to be a universalist. Unfortunately, Origen believed that it would take a series of reincarnations in new worlds until everyone used their freedom to become perfect, and even then we might use our freedom to fall back into sin, which in turn would cause us to be recreated in evil bodies. Thus, despite Origen's emphasis on human freedom, his Platonic view of our bodies and his notion that we will continually be reborn until we get it right discredits his view for most Christians. See Origen, *On First Principles*, 1.6.3; 2.1.1–2; 2.8.3; 3.5.3; 3.6.3, in *The Ante-Nicene Fathers*, ed. Alexander Roberts and James Donaldson (Grand Rapids: Eerdmans, 1994), 4:261, 268, 287–88, 341–42, 345.

   Learn more about universalism in Robin A. Parry and Christopher H. Partridge, eds., *Universal Salvation? The Current Debate* (Grand Rapids: Eerdmans, 2003); and Jan Bonda, *The One Purpose of God*, trans. Reinder Bruinsma (Uitgeverij Ten Have, 1993; Grand Rapids: Eerdmans, 1998).

8. Brian McLaren, *The Last Word and the Word after That* (San Francisco: Jossey-Bass, 2005), 138. Cf. McLaren, *Generous Orthodoxy*, 109, where he observes that universalism "can too easily lead to complacency about injustice here and now and can create a kind of nice, relaxed, magnanimous apathy."

9. Spencer Burke and Barry Taylor, *A Heretic's Guide to Eternity* (San Francisco: Jossey-Bass, 2006), 196–202.

10. Cf. Gregory MacDonald, *The Evangelical Universalist* (Eugene, Ore.: Cascade, 2006), 6–7, 28–32, 130–31. Under the pseudonym Gregory MacDonald, this evangelical theologian argues along similar lines that all creatures, including Lucifer, will repent of their sin and submit to Christ once they experience the torment of hell. Thus, no one goes to hell for very long, but all will eventually be redeemed.

11. Eddie Gibbs and Ryan K. Bolger, *Emerging Churches* (Grand Rapids: Baker, 2005), 132.

12. Burke and Taylor, *Heretic's Guide to Eternity*, 196–97.

13. For instance, see Brian McLaren's dismissive attitude toward pluralism in *A Generous Orthodoxy*, 249: "When I say we are linked and bound through Christ's incarnation to all people, I am not saying *all religions are the same, it*

doesn't matter what you believe, truth is relative, blah, blah, blah" (emphasis McLaren's). Cf. McLaren, *Last Word*, 183.

However, while postmodern innovators tend to deny that other religions may provide salvation, they do emphasize that other religions get a lot right. Samir Selmanovic, "The Sweet Problem of Inclusiveness," in Doug Pagitt and Tony Jones, eds., *An Emergent Manifesto of Hope* (Grand Rapids: Baker, 2007), 194–95, says: "Is our religion the only one that understands the true meaning of life? Or does God place his truth in others too? Well, God decides, and not us. The gospel is not *our* gospel, but the gospel of the kingdom of God, and what belongs to the kingdom of God cannot be hijacked by Christianity. God is sovereign, like the wind. He blows wherever he chooses" (emphasis Selmanovic's).

Selmanovic adds that "emerging Christians" celebrate the truth found in other religions. He writes: "We don't want to just tolerate the godliness of 'the other' as if we regret the possibility. The godliness of non-Christians is not an anomaly in our theology. Instead of adding it as an appendix to our statement of beliefs, we want to move it closer to the center and celebrate it as the heavens certainly celebrate it. The gospel has taught us to rejoice in goodness we can find in others."

14. Inclusivism is increasingly popular among all varieties of evangelical Christians. John Sanders, *No Other Name*, 21, cites surveys that show that more than twenty years ago one-third of evangelical college and seminary students held "to some kind of hope for the possible salvation of the unevangelized. Among college professors at evangelical liberal arts colleges, only 56 percent ruled out all hope for the unevangelized." That number has likely risen with the onset of postmodern influence in evangelical circles. Read the survey data in James Davidson Hunter, *Evangelicalism: The Coming Generation* (Chicago: University of Chicago Press, 1987), 34–40.

    Indeed, recent news supports my suspicion. According to a just-released 2007 survey conducted by the Pew Forum on Religion and Public Life, 57 percent of evangelical churchgoers said they believe that many religions may lead to everlasting life. Thus, the majority of self-described evangelical Christians are not merely comfortable with inclusivism, but have moved beyond it to embrace religious pluralism. Read the full report at http://religions.pewforum.org.

15. John Sanders, *No Other Name*, 215: inclusivists believe "that the work of Jesus is ontologically necessary for salvation (no one would be saved without it) but not epistemologically necessary (one need not be aware of the work in order to benefit from it)." Inclusivists find support for their view in biblical passages that emphasize God's love for the world (John 12:32; Rom. 5:18; 2 Cor. 5:15; 1 Tim. 2:4; 2 Peter 3:9; and 1 John 2:2) and God's acceptance of believers who were not yet Christians (e.g., Cornelius in Acts 10).

16. Clark Pinnock, "An Inclusivist View," in Okholm and Phillips, *More Than One Way?* 101; and John Sanders, "Inclusivism," in *What about Those Who Have Never Heard?* 54.

17. Tiessen, *Who Can Be Saved?* 125–37; Pinnock, *Wideness in God's Mercy*, 157–58; and Clark Pinnock, "Toward an Evangelical Theology of Religions," *Journal of the Evangelical Theological Society* 33 (1990): 367. See also John Wesley, "On Faith," in *The Works of John Wesley*, 3rd ed., 14 vols. (Peabody, Mass.: Hendrickson, 1986), 7:197. Wesley argued that the unevangelized cannot be blamed for not believing in Jesus. He wrote: "Inasmuch as to them little is given, of them little will be required.... No more therefore will be expected of them, than the living up to the light they had. But many of them ... we have great reason to hope, although they lived among the Heathens, yet were quite of another spirit; being taught by God, by his inward voice, all the essentials of true religion."

18. Sanders, *No Other Name*, 233–36; Sanders, "Inclusivism," 36; and Pinnock, "Inclusivist View," 117–18.

19. "Dogmatic Constitution on the Church" (*Lumen Gentium*), 16, in Austin P. Flannery, ed., *Documents of Vatican II* (Grand Rapids: Eerdmans, 1975), 351. See also the discussion of other religions in the *Catechism of the Catholic Church* §836–48 (Liguori, Mo.: Liguori, 1994), 222–25.

20. Pinnock, *Wideness in God's Mercy*, 157–58. See also Sanders, "Inclusivism," 36–37: "People are acceptable to God if they respond in faith, however limited their knowledge is. God judges people on the basis of the light they have and how they respond to that light."

21. C. S. Lewis, *The Last Battle* (1956; repr. New York: HarperTrophy, 2000), 188–89.

22. W. H. Lewis and Walter Hooper, eds., *Letters of C. S. Lewis* (New York: Harcourt Brace Jovanovich, 1966; rev. and enlarged, 1993), 428.

23. Karl Rahner coined the phrase "anonymous Christians," which unfairly biases the religion question in favor of Christians (why not call Christians "anonymous Buddhists"?). See Harvie M. Conn, "Do Other Religions Save?" in Crockett and Sigountos, *Through No Fault of Their Own?* 201.

    See Karl Rahner, *Theological Investigations*, vol. 5 (New York: Seabury, 1966), 131: "Christianity does not simply confront the member of an extra-Christian religion as a mere non-Christian but as someone who can and must already be regarded in this or that respect as an anonymous Christian. It would be wrong to regard the pagan as someone who has not yet been touched in any way by God's grace and truth."

    Cf. Pinnock, "Inclusivist View," 119–20; Nash, *Is Jesus the Only Savior?* 111–12; and Sanders, *No Other Name*, 224–32.

24. Romans 3:23. Paul's intent to include every Jew and Gentile is explained in Douglas Moo, *The Epistle to the Romans* (Grand Rapids: Eerdmans, 1996), 93–98, 201. Romans 1:18–32 explains the sin of every Gentile; 2:17–29 records the sin of every Jew; 3:9 clarifies that Paul is speaking about everyone rather than merely some ("We have already made the charge that Jews and Gentiles alike are all under sin"); and 3:10–23 repeatedly states Paul's conclusion that everyone is a sinner who needs Christ's redemption.

25. Romans 1:20, 32.

26. The religions that come closest to teaching grace are Amida Buddhism and the Ramanuja and Madhva forms of Hinduism. The former grants escape into the "pure land" to anyone who trusts in the Buddha, while the latter sometimes suggests that believers are saved by God just as kittens are passively carried in the mouth of their mother. However, since neither of these religions teaches our need for atonement — a substitute to die in our place — they seem to lack a full appreciation for the severity of sin. This shallow understanding of sin, or our need for deliverance, must also produce a corresponding superficial appreciation for the grace that saves us. Thus, although these religions may speak of grace, it is not the robust Christian view of the God who endured our punishment for sin.

    Furthermore, neither Buddhism nor Hinduism offers salvation. Instead, they hope for the termination of personal existence, where individuals are dissolved into the oneness of the universe. Their free offer of personal extinction sounds more like death than anything that might count as grace.

27. Romans 1:18.

28. Helpful introductions to Islam include Peter G. Riddell and Peter Cotterell, *Islam in Context* (Grand Rapids: Baker, 2003); Anees Zaka and Diane Coleman, *The Truth about Islam* (Phillipsburg, N.J.: Presbyterian & Reformed, 2004); George Braswell, *Islam* (Nashville: Broadman & Holman, 1996); George Braswell, *What You Need to Know about Islam and Muslims* (Nashville: Broadman & Holman, 2000).

29. Exclusivists also argue that their position is necessary to encourage missionary work. If the unevangelized may already be accepted by God, then why should we sacrifice to tell them the gospel, especially given the possibility that they may reject our further light and end up damned? It would seem wise to leave well enough alone.

    Inclusivists reply that their motivation for missions is higher than saving individuals from hell. They want people to prosper now by advancing in their knowledge of God and joining his kingdom. This good news is worth sharing, regardless of the risk of rejection and ultimate damnation. See Pinnock, "Inclusivist View," 120, and Sanders, "Inclusivism," 53 – 54.

30. Romans 10:17. Exclusivists cite the following Scriptures for their position: John 3:16 – 18; 14:6; Acts 4:12; Romans 10:9 – 15.

31. The differing degrees of exclusivism are discussed in Okholm and Phillips, eds., *More Than One Way?* 19 – 24.

32. Some exclusivists reportedly believe that God may also accept an individual's pre-Christian faith as sufficient for salvation. This seems indistinguishable from inclusivism, the only difference being that while inclusivists suggest this is a routine, widespread occurrence, exclusivists limit God's acceptance of faith in general revelation to a few "very special circumstances." See Geivett and Phillips, "A Particularist View," in *More Than One Way?* 214.

33. Cf. the dialogue among Alistair McGrath, Clark Pinnock, R. Douglas Geivett, and W. Gary Phillips in Okholm and Phillips, eds., *More Than One Way?* 178 – 80, 187 – 88, 197.

34. David VanDrunen, "The Two Kingdoms," *Calvin Theological Journal* 40 (2005): 248–66; Michael Horton, "How the Kingdom Comes," *Christianity Today*, January 2006, 42–46; and "How to Discover Your Calling," *Modern Reformation*, May–June 1999: 8–13. These authors prefer to use the term "kingdom of God" to refer to God's reign over his church and the terms "providence" and "common grace" to refer to his rule over our work in the world.

35. Stanley J. Grenz and Roger E. Olson, *Twentieth-Century Theology* (Downers Grove, Ill.: InterVarsity, 1997), 51–62; James C. Livingston, *Modern Christian Thought*, 2nd ed. (1997; repr., Minneapolis: Fortress, 2006), 1:270–98; and Walter Rauschenbusch, *A Theology for the Social Gospel* (1945; repr., Nashville: Abingdon, 1978), 95–109.

36. George Eldon Ladd, *The Presence of the Future* (New York: Harper & Row, 1964; Grand Rapids: Eerdmans, 1974, repr. 1996), 144: the kingdom is "the reign or rule of God."

37. Colossians 1:15–20; Acts 3:21; and Ephesians 1:10. See Michael E. Wittmer, *Heaven Is a Place on Earth* (Grand Rapids: Zondervan, 2004).

38. At Jesus' first coming: "The kingdom of God is near. Repent and believe the good news!" (Mark 1:15; cf. Matt. 3:2; 4:17; 12:28; Luke 11:20; 17:21). At Jesus' second coming: "The kingdom of the world has become the kingdom of our Lord and of his Christ, and he will reign for ever and ever" (Rev. 11:15). Now through the church: "And I tell you that you are Peter, and on this rock I will build my church, and the gates of Hades will not overcome it" (Matt. 16:18; cf. Acts 1:6–8).

39. Matthew 16:18.

40. Matthew 4:23–25; 8:28–34; 9:1–8; 10:1–8; 11:2–6; 12:28. See Cornelius Plantinga, *Engaging God's World* (Grand Rapids: Eerdmans, 2002), 108–10, 113–14; and Albert Wolters, *Creation Regained*, 2nd ed. (Grand Rapids: Eerdmans, 2005), 71, 73–74, 76.

41. To my knowledge none of these claim to be followers of Jesus in the traditional, evangelical sense. Please accept this premise for argument's sake, or feel free to replace with other examples of non-Christians doing good things.

42. Plantinga, *Engaging God's World*, 111–12.

43. Harry S. Stout, *The Divine Dramatist* (Grand Rapids: Eerdmans, 1991), 228.

44. Augustine, *Confessions*, 7.15, trans. Henry Chadwick (New York: Oxford University Press, 1991), 123, and "On Christian Doctrine," bk. 2, chap. 40, in *The Nicene and Post-Nicene Fathers*, first series, vol. 2, ed. Philip Schaff (Edinburgh: T. & T. Clark; repr., Grand Rapids: Eerdmans, 1993), 554. Cf. Exodus 3:21–22; 11:2–3; 12:35–36; 35:20–29.

Chapter 9. Is Hell for Real and Forever?

1. Rick Warren, *The Purpose-Driven Life* (Grand Rapids: Zondervan, 2002), 36 (emphasis Warren's). An alternative to this Platonic view of life is offered in Michael E. Wittmer, *Heaven Is a Place on Earth* (Grand Rapids: Zondervan, 2004).

2. Brian McLaren, *A Generous Orthodoxy* (Grand Rapids: Zondervan, 2004), 100.

3. Brian McLaren, *The Last Word and the Word after That* (San Francisco: Jossey-Bass, 2005), 166 (emphasis McLaren's). Cf. pp. 83–84, 94, 149–50, 165, 169, 191–92.

4. McLaren, *Last Word*, xii. Learn more about the current controversies surrounding the issue of hell in Edward Fudge and Robert Peterson, *Two Views of Hell: A Biblical and Theological Dialogue* (Downers Grove, Ill.: InterVarsity, 2000); and William Crockett, ed., *Four Views on Hell* (Grand Rapids: Zondervan, 1992). The discussion among evangelicals in Great Britain is found in their official report, *The Nature of Hell* (London: Evangelical Alliance Commission on Unity and Truth among Evangelicals [ACUTE], 2000).

   Defenses of the traditional view of endless torment include Christopher W. Morgan and Robert A. Peterson, eds., *Hell under Fire* (Grand Rapids: Zondervan, 2004); Robert A. Peterson, *Hell on Trial: The Case for Eternal Punishment* (Phillipsburg, N.J.: Presbyterian & Reformed, 1995); Peter Toon, *Heaven and Hell* (Nashville: Nelson, 1986); and Anthony A. Hoekema, *The Bible and the Future* (Grand Rapids: Eerdmans, 1979), 265–73. The best explanation of what Old Testament saints believed about the afterlife is Philip S. Johnston, *Shades of Sheol: Death and Afterlife in the Old Testament* (Downers Grove, Ill.: InterVarsity, 2002). For a philosophical examination of hell, see Jonathan L. Kvanvig, *The Problem of Hell* (New York: Oxford University Press, 1993).

5. McLaren, *Last Word*, xii (emphasis McLaren's). Cf. Neil's comments (the protagonist in McLaren's story): the traditional view of hell makes God into "a petty human being, full of anger and revenge," who commands us to forgive our enemies but is "unwilling to do the same" (40); and "... our way of talking about hell sounds absolutely wacky. 'God loves you and has a wonderful plan for your life,' we say, 'and he'll fry your butt in hell forever unless you do or believe the right thing.' 'God is a loving father,' we say, 'but he'll treat you with a cruelty that no human father has ever been guilty of—eternal conscious torture'" (75).

6. Ibid., 45–47.

7. Ibid., 59–60. In his endnotes McLaren concedes that a physical resurrection is not entirely missing from the Old Testament, so that "the idea of an afterlife in the ancient Jewish world ... is a bit more complex than Dan and Neil realize" (189). He cites Isaiah 26:19 and Daniel 12:2, each of which suggests a resurrection of individuals, and the latter even hints at heaven and hell (190). Readers who skip McLaren's endnotes and only read his story may come away with the false belief that the idea of hell came entirely from pagan religions and has no foundation in the Hebrew Scriptures.

8. Ibid., 61–62.

9. Ibid., 63. Cf. pp. 62, 71–74, 121, 136.

10. Ibid., 74.

11. Ibid., 163. Cf. pp. 64, 74.

12. Ibid., 71: Neil exclaims, "The point isn't hell: the point is justice! The point is God's will! Just as we've been saying, over and over—Jesus doesn't invent the idea of hell. It evolves ... over time; it's constructed, as all human ideas are, through the interaction of religions and cultures as we were talking about

earlier. The point is not whether there is a hell: the point is God's justice! The point isn't whether Jesus — by using the language of the construction — confirms it. The point is, for what purpose does he use the language?"

Cf. pp. 80 – 81: "My point is that hell itself isn't the point. The point is the purpose for which Jesus uses the language of hell, or whatever other imagery he uses to convey the negative consequences of rejecting God's way."

13. Luke 16:24. See also Matthew 3:12; 5:22, 29 – 30; 8:12; 10:28; 13:40 – 42, 47 – 50; 18:6 – 9; 22:13; 23:33; 24:51; 25:30, 41, 46; Mark 9:42 – 48; Luke 3:17; 12:5; 13:28; 17:1 – 2. Stephen Travis offers a different view. He says that the story of the rich man and Lazarus was "a popular Jewish tale, and so we would be rash to press the details of the story." Stephen Travis, *I Believe in the Second Coming of Christ* (Grand Rapids: Eerdmans, 1982), 197.

14. Matthew 7:13 – 14. McLaren, *Last Word*, 77. McLaren should be more critical of Neil's idiosyncratic interpretation of this verse. Although Neil's interpretation is theoretically possible, anyone who proposes to overturn two thousand years of exegesis on a particular passage should offer some reason to support his view.

15. Revelation 20:15.

16. Second Kings 16:3; 23:10; 2 Chronicles 28:3; 33:6; Jeremiah 7:31 – 33.

17. Isaiah 66:24; cf. 30:33; Jeremiah 7:31 – 32. See Timothy R. Phillips, "Hell," in *Evangelical Dictionary of Biblical Theology*, ed. Walter A. Elwell (Grand Rapids: Baker, 1996), 338.

18. Matthew 5:29 – 30; 8:11 – 12; 18:6 – 9; Mark 9:42 – 48; Luke 13:27 – 28.

19. McLaren, *Last Word*, 78.

20. Ibid., 79.

21. Ibid., 80.

22. John Calvin, *Institutes of the Christian Religion* 3.25.12, ed. John T. McNeill, trans. Ford Lewis Battles (Philadelphia: Westminster, 1960): "Now, because no description can deal adequately with the gravity of God's vengeance against the wicked, their torments and tortures are figuratively expressed to us by physical things, that is, by darkness, weeping, and gnashing of teeth, unquenchable fire, and undying worm gnawing at the heart." Cf. Sinclair B. Ferguson, "Pastoral Theology: The Preacher and Hell," in *God under Fire*, ed. Douglas S. Huffman and Eric L. Johnson (Grand Rapids: Zondervan, 2002), 226 – 27.

23. Matthew 5:29 – 30; 18:8 – 9.

24. Clark Pinnock, "The Conditional View," in Crockett, *Four Views on Hell*, 135 – 66; John R. W. Stott, in the book he wrote with David Edwards, *Essentials: A Liberal-Evangelical Dialogue* (London: Hodder & Stoughton, 1988), 313 – 20; Edward Fudge, *The Fire That Consumes* (Houston: Providential, 1982); David J. Powys, *Hell: A Hard Look at a Hard Question* (Carlisle, Cumbria: Paternoster, 1998); Philip E. Hughes, *The True Image: The Origin and Destiny of Man in Christ* (Grand Rapids: Eerdmans, 1989), 389 – 407; Travis, *I Believe in the Second Coming*, 196 – 99; Michael Green, *Evangelism through the Local Church* (London: Hodder & Stoughton, 1990), 70.

Brian McLaren implies as much when he has Markus say, "You know, if God judges, forgives, and eliminates all the bad stuff, there might not be much left of you — maybe not enough to enjoy heaven, maybe not enough to feel too much in hell either" (McLaren, *Last Word*, 137).

25. Pinnock, "Conditional View," 140, 149, 151 – 52.

26. Isaiah 66:24; Mark 9:48. Pinnock, "Conditional View," 155 – 56.

27. Pinnock, "Conditional View," 157. Fudge, *Fire That Consumes*, 44 – 50, 195; and Travis, *I Believe in the Second Coming*, 199, say that eternal fire, judgment, destruction, and punishment do not mean that there is a continuous burning, judging, destroying, and punishing, but that the effects of these actions last forever.

28. Pinnock, "Conditional View," 147 – 49; Fudge, *Fire That Consumes*, 65 – 76.

29. Fudge, *Fire That Consumes*, 51 – 76. Fudge's treatment of the tradition's belief in the soul's immortality is fairer and more accurate than Pinnock's (see "Conditional View," 147 – 49). For the early church's view on the length of suffering in hell, compare William Crockett, "The Metaphorical View," in Crockett, *Four Views on Hell*, 65 – 68, and Fudge, *Fire That Consumes*, 313 – 42.

30. Crockett, "Metaphorical View," 69, 71; and "Response to Clark H. Pinnock," in Crockett, *Four Views on Hell*, 172. Fudge, *Fire That Consumes*, 304, tellingly concedes that "there is no easy solution" for reconciling his annihilationist view with Satan's everlasting torment. He gamely says that Satan is still different from a human, and Revelation 20:10 does not "say that any of Adam's race are tormented for ever and ever."

31. Stanley J. Grenz, *Theology for the Community of God* (Nashville: Broadman & Holman, 1994; Grand Rapids: Eerdmans, 2000), 639 – 40, adds other objections to annihilationism. (1) Scripture uses the term "eternal" to describe both the destiny of the righteous and the unrighteous. If eternal life means that the righteous will live forever, then shouldn't eternal death mean that the unrighteous will suffer forever? (2) Annihilationism eliminates the possibility of degrees of punishment in hell. If everyone is simply annihilated, then everyone, from Satan and Hitler to half-decent pagans, has the same end. (3) Annihilationism does not seem to take our sin seriously enough. Can sinners escape their punishment so easily? (4) Annihilationism does not completely solve the problem of God's love, for annihilating sinners is still worse than saving them.

32. Romans 9:20; 11:33. The Fall and the ontological gap between God and creation are two reasons why our theological questions will always end in mystery. Paul combines both in Romans 9 – 11, declaring that God's reason for not choosing Esau (Fall) lies in his unfathomable divine transcendence (ontological gap).

33. Dallas Willard, *Renovation of the Heart* (Colorado Springs: NavPress, 2002), 57: "Thus no one chooses in the abstract to go to hell or even to be the kind of person who belongs there. But their orientation toward self leads them to become the kind of person for whom away-from-God is the only place for which they are suited. It is a place they would, in the end, choose for themselves, rather than come to humble themselves before God and accept who he is. Whether or not God's will is infinitely flexible, the human will is not.

There are limits beyond which it cannot bend back, cannot turn or repent.... They have become people so locked into their own self-worship and denial of God that *they cannot want God*" (emphasis Willard's).

34. C. S. Lewis, *The Great Divorce* (New York: Macmillan, 1946, 1978), 72. Cf. C. S. Lewis, *The Problem of Pain* (New York: Macmillan, 1962), 127. If love respects the other, then God shows love when he respects his image bearers enough to allow their ill-advised rejection of him to stand. In this way allowing people to choose hell is a loving thing for God to do.

35. Matthew 27:46.

36. Revelation 6:10; 11:15–18; 14:14–15:4; and 19:1–8 say that the saints will praise God for his sovereign justice when he returns to right the wrongs of our fallen world. These passages do not say that the saved will delight in the torments of hell.

37. Martin Luther, "The Freedom of a Christian," in *Martin Luther's Basic Theological Writings*, 2nd ed., ed. Timothy F. Lull (Minneapolis: Fortress, 2005), 406.

38. Ephesians 1:3.

Chapter 10. Is It Possible to Know Anything?

1. For the record, I believe that there is a right way to interpret God's Word on these controversial issues and that my interpretation is better than alternate views. Still, it is a naive cheap shot to say that those who read the Bible differently simply don't believe the Bible.

2. Kristen Bell, as quoted in Andy Crouch, "The Emergent Mystique," *Christianity Today*, November 2004, 38.

3. To learn more about how Christians are processing the postmodern impact on knowledge, start with the illuminating dialogue between six professors in Myron B. Penner, ed., *Christianity and the Postmodern Turn* (Grand Rapids: Brazos, 2005). Books that defend a more traditional approach to knowledge include Douglas Groothuis, *Truth Decay: Defending Christianity against the Challenges of Postmodernism* (Downers Grove, Ill.: InterVarsity, 2000); R. Scott Smith, *Truth and the New Kind of Christian* (Wheaton: Crossway, 2005); Andreas Köstenberger, *Whatever Happened to Truth?* (Wheaton: Crossway, 2005); D. A. Carson, *The Gagging of God* (Grand Rapids: Zondervan, 1996); and D. A. Carson, *Becoming Conversant with the Emerging Church* (Grand Rapids: Zondervan, 2005). Important books that adopt insights from postmodernism into their Christian faith are James K. A. Smith, *Who's Afraid of Postmodernism?* (Grand Rapids: Brazos, 2006); Stanley J. Grenz and John R. Franke, *Beyond Foundationalism* (Louisville: John Knox, 2001); and John R. Franke, *The Character of Theology* (Grand Rapids: Baker, 2005).

4. A great introduction to modern epistemology, where it went wrong, and how to fix things is Kelly James Clark, *Return to Reason* (Grand Rapids: Eerdmans, 1990).

5. Friedrich Schleiermacher, *The Christian Faith*, ed. H. R. Mackintosh and J. S. Stewart (2nd German ed., 1830; New York: Harper & Row, 1963), 1:12–18;

and idem, *On Religion: Speeches to Its Cultured Despisers*, trans. John Oman (New York: Harper & Row, 1958), 218 – 19, 224 – 27, 239 – 44.

6. Charles Hodge, *Systematic Theology* (New York: Scribner, 1871; repr., Grand Rapids: Eerdmans, 1946), 1:10 – 11, 50 – 60, 129; Benjamin B. Warfield, "Apologetics," in *The Works of Benjamin B. Warfield* (New York: Oxford University Press, 1932; repr., Grand Rapids: Baker, 1981), 9:3 – 15; and Benjamin B. Warfield, "Introductory Note," in Francis Beattie, *Apologetics* (Richmond, Va.: The Presbyterian Committee of Publication, 1903), 1:19 – 32. Hodge and Warfield did not write consistently on this issue. They said that reason and evidence must establish the authority of Scripture, but they also wrote that Scripture contains an inherent authority that verifies itself. See Mark A. Noll, ed., *The Princeton Theology 1812 – 1921* (1983; repr., Grand Rapids: Baker, 2001), 26 – 27, 132 – 34, 302 – 7.

   Hodge and Warfield's rational and empirical method remains the way that most evangelicals defend their faith. Examples of this approach to apologetics are Josh McDowell, *The New Evidence That Demands a Verdict: Fully Updated to Answer the Questions Challenging Christians Today* (Nashville: Nelson, 1999); and R. C. Sproul, John Gerstner, and Arthur Lindsley, *Classical Apologetics* (Grand Rapids: Zondervan, 1984).

7. Some postmodern innovators also object to modernity's notion that logical inference only moves in one direction, from foundational to less certain beliefs. They prefer to think of beliefs as an interrelated web rather than an orderly structure in which one belief builds upon another. See Grenz and Franke, *Beyond Foundationalism*, 38 – 54; and John R. Franke, "Christian Faith and Postmodern Theory: Theology and the Nonfoundationalist Turn," in Penner, *Christianity and the Postmodern Turn*, 105 – 21.

8. Smith, *Who's Afraid of Postmodernism?* 34 – 42; Franke, "Christian Faith and Postmodern Theology," 108; Dave Tomlinson, *The Post-Evangelical* (Grand Rapids: Zondervan, 2003), 102 – 4; and Brian McLaren and Duane Litfin, "Emergent Evangelism," *Christianity Today*, November 2004, 42 – 43.

9. The postmodern point runs deeper than my example, for it declares that even the act of observing the melting ice cap, inasmuch as it is viewed from the unique perspective of the knowing subject, is an act that requires interpretation. Any two people observing the same act may disagree to some extent on the facts. For a counterargument that some acts of knowing do not require interpretation, see Smith, *Truth and the New Kind of Christian*, 95 – 104; and R. Scott Smith, "Christian Postmodernism and the Linguistic Turn," in Penner, *Christianity and the Postmodern Turn*, 53 – 69.

10. Kevin Vanhoozer, "Pilgrim's Digress: Christian Thinking on and about the Post/Modern Way," in Penner, *Christianity and the Postmodern Turn*, 83 – 85, and Smith, *Who's Afraid of Postmodernism?* 81 – 107.

11. Smith, *Who's Afraid of Postmodernism?* 117 – 21; Merold Westphal, "Onto-theology, Metanarrative, Perspectivism, and the Gospel," in Penner, *Christianity and the Postmodern Turn*, 152; Esther Lightcap Meek, *Longing to Know* (Grand Rapids: Brazos, 2003), 30 – 35; D. A. Carson, *Becoming Conversant with the Emerging Church*, 105 – 15; and D. A. Carson, "Domesticating the

Gospel: A Review of Grenz's Renewing the Center," in *Reclaiming the Center*, ed. Millard J. Erickson, Paul Kjoss Helseth, and Justin Taylor (Wheaton: Crossway, 2004), 46.

12. John D. Caputo, *On Religion* (New York: Routledge, 2001), 22: "That means that the believers in that Book should temper their claims about The Revelation they (believe they) have received, since it is their interpretation that they have received a revelation, while not everyone else agrees. A revelation is an interpretation that the believers believe is a revelation, which means that it is one more competing entry in the conflict of interpretations. Believers should accordingly resist becoming triumphalistic about what they believe, either personally or in their particular community."

   Whether or not John Caputo himself fits the definition of a postmodern innovator, he and his ideas are enthusiastically embraced by the leaders of this movement. Note how Brian McLaren, Tony Jones, and John Franke praise his latest book written for an evangelical publisher, a book in which Caputo declares that the Bible is wrong about homosexuality, slavery, and the treatment of women. See John D. Caputo, *What Would Jesus Deconstruct?* (Grand Rapids: Baker, 2007), 108–11.

13. John Franke, "The Nature of Theology: Culture, Language, and Truth," in Penner, *Christianity and the Postmodern Turn*, 209. Cf. Franke, *Character of Theology*, 75.

14. Merold Westphal, "Of Stories and Languages," in Penner, *Christianity and the Postmodern Turn*, 235 (emphasis mine). While Westphal himself is not a postmodern innovator, his illustration was used by Franke in his lecture entitled "Truth" at the Emergent YS Convention in Nashville on May 19, 2005. Cf. Caputo, *On Religion*, 99–100.

   Franke's view is unclear. While he rightly declares that "God is truly revealed through the appointed creaturely media" ("The Nature of Theology," 209, and *The Character of Theology*, 75), he also approvingly cited Westphal's illustration that revelation amounts to misinformation. Furthermore, Franke's self-described "transition from a realist to a constructionist view of truth and the world," so that "no simple, one-to-one relationship exists between language and the world, and thus no single linguistic description can serve to provide an objective conception of the 'real' world,'" implies as much (Franke, "Christian Faith and Postmodern Theory," in *Christianity and the Postmodern Turn,* 108). Kevin Vanhoozer, "Disputing About Words," in *Christianity and the Postmodern Turn,* 198, states that "The implications of Franke's constructionism for the project of biblical interpretation, if pursued consistently, are in my view devastating to biblical authority."

   Franke's statement and Westphal's illustration remind me of the view expressed by Cornelius Van Til, who wrote in his introduction to *The Inspiration and Authority of the Bible* by Benjamin B. Warfield (Philadelphia: Presbyterian and Reformed, 1948), 33: "Protestants also claim that Scripture is perspicuous. This does not mean that it is exhaustively penetrable to men. When the Christian restates the content of scriptural revelation in the form of a 'system,' such a system is based upon and therefore analogous to the 'existential system' that God himself possesses. Being based upon God's revelation, it is, on the one hand, fully true and, on the other hand, at no point identical with the content of God's mind."

Gordon H. Clark rightly responded in "Apologetics," in *Contemporary Evangelical Thought*, ed. Carl F. H. Henry (New York: Harper Channel, 1957), 159: "Now if God knows all truths and knows the correct meaning of every proposition, and if no proposition means to man what it means to God, so that God's knowledge and man's knowledge do not coincide at any single point, it follows by rigorous necessity that man can have no truth at all. This conclusion … undermines all Christianity."

15. Peter Rollins, *How (Not) to Speak of God* (Brewster, Mass.: Paraclete, 2006), 32, 26 (emphasis his).

16. Ibid., 44.

17. Samir Selmanovic, "The Sweet Problem of Inclusiveness," in Doug Pagitt and Tony Jones, eds., *An Emergent Manifesto of Hope* (Grand Rapids: Baker, 2007), 194. Cf. Caputo, *On Religion*, 110 – 14.

18. For more detail than I have space to develop here, see my two bonus chapters to *Heaven Is a Place on Earth* at www.heavenisaplaceonearth.com.

19. Smith, *Who's Afraid of Postmodernism?* 117 – 21.

20. C. S. Lewis, *Miracles: A Preliminary Study* (New York: Macmillan, 1978), 12 – 24; C. S. Lewis, *Christian Reflections*, ed. Walter Hooper (1967; repr., Grand Rapids: Eerdmans, 1989), 63 – 71; Victor Reppert, *C. S. Lewis's Dangerous Idea* (Downers Grove, Ill.: InterVarsity, 2003); and the themed edition of *Philosophia Christi* 5, no. 1 (2003): 8 – 184.

21. Alvin Plantinga, "Justification and Theism," *Faith and Philosophy* 4 (1987): 403 – 26; *Warrant and Proper Function* (New York: Oxford University Press, 1993), 216 – 37; and *Warranted Christian Belief* (New York: Oxford, 2000), 227 – 40. In "Justification and Theism," 408 – 9, Plantinga elaborates on what he means by a "suitable environment." He explains that if we are in an environment unsuited for our cognitive faculties, say a planet near Alpha Centauri, then perhaps what in that world is an elephant may be interpreted by us as a trumpet sounding. In that case we misinterpret what is actually occurring, not because our minds are malfunctioning, but simply because we are not operating in our proper environment.

22. This approach will not work every time. Some people may become angry when told that they already believe in God. This is to be expected, for Romans 1:18 says that people "suppress the truth" about God, and calling them on this suppression may make them uncomfortable. This is why it is better to ask rather than tell others that they believe in God. Ask the question and see if the Holy Spirit doesn't empower them to overcome their blindness and embrace what they already know.

23. John Calvin, *Institutes of the Christian Religion* 1.7.5, ed. John T. McNeill, trans. Ford Lewis Battles (Philadelphia: Westminster, 1960). Calvin inserted this definition of self-authentication into his French translation of the *Institutes*. It does not appear in English editions, which were translated from the Latin *Institutes*. The French version can be found in *Corpus Reformatorum*,

in *Opera Quae Supersunt Omnia*, 59 vols., ed. Guilielmus Baum, Eduardus Cunitz [et] Eduardus Reuss (Brunsvigae: C. A. Schwetschke et Filium, 1863 – 1900; repr., New York: Johnson Reprint Corporation, 1964): 3:96.

24. Calvin, *Institutes* 1.7.2. Cf. Plantinga, *Warranted Christian Belief*, 258 – 66; and James M. Grier, "The Apologetical Value of the Self-Witness of Scripture," *Grace Theological Journal* 1 (Spring 1980): 71 – 76.

25. Calvin, *Institutes* 1.7.4.

26. The failure of modernity's quest for an objective *method* of knowledge does not eliminate my belief in Scripture as an objective *source* and *content* of knowledge. In other words, I subjectively yet truly know that Scripture is an objective revelation from God (i.e., it originates from beyond me and any finite community).

    The fact that I do not need to prove that the Bible is God's Word does not mean that I lack evidence in its favor. Immediately after declaring that only the Holy Spirit's witness can authenticate Scripture, Calvin cites a list of reasons why the Bible is a unique book. While no amount of evidence can prove that the Bible is from God, Calvin says that human arguments are "very useful aids" to confirm Scripture's special status (Calvin, *Institutes* 1.8.1 – 13).

    Other religions may also claim to hear the voice of God in their Scriptures. But just as meeting someone with a different ethical code does not force me to discard my own moral standard, so the fact that others claim to possess a different scripture does not invalidate my belief in the Bible.

27. Calvin, *Institutes*, 1.13.1: "For who even of slight intelligence does not understand that, as nurses commonly do with infants, God is wont in a measure to 'lisp' in speaking to us? Thus such forms of speaking do not so much express clearly what God is like as accommodate the knowledge of him to our slight capacity. To do this he must descend far beneath his loftiness."

28. Vanhoozer, "Pilgrim's Digress," 88: "*The world is there, mind-independent and differentiated, yet indescribable apart from human constructions and only partially accessible to any single theory.* The moderate realist insists that though our knowledge of the world is partial it can still be true" (emphasis Vanhoozer's).

Chapter 11. Is the Bible God's True Word?

1. This statement is similar to the argument in Nicholas Wolterstorff, *Divine Discourse* (Cambridge, U.K.: Cambridge University Press, 1995), 51 – 54. In this important and otherwise helpful book, Wolterstorff argues that much of Scripture may amount to "divinely appropriated human discourse." Rather than initiate revelation, God may have merely approved of what human authors already wrote. He recognized that their words expressed what was in his heart, and saying in effect, "This speaks for me," he chose to include their work in his canon. While this supplies a useful way to think about canonicity (why some books rather than others made the cut as Scripture), it does not do justice to the act of inspiration. Paul declares that Scripture is not merely God-approved but is "God-breathed" (2 Tim. 3:16). Thus, conservative Chris-

tians believe that God wrote letters and documents with and through human authors (something Wolterstorff allows but does not think is necessary), many of which he later collected and preserved for us in the canon of Scripture.

2. Karl Barth denied that Scripture "in itself and as such" was revelation because he feared that people would then control the speech of God, opening the Bible when they wanted to hear God speak and closing it when they had heard enough. So to protect the sovereign freedom of God, Barth insisted that the Bible only becomes revelation to us when God chooses to meet us there in a subjective, personal encounter. See Karl Barth, *Church Dogmatics* 1/1, chap. 1, §4.2 – 3, pp. 109 – 20. While I appreciate Barth's emphasis on divine transcendence, he confuses revelation with illumination. The Bible remains God's revelation whether or not we understand it and find God there. We need the Holy Spirit's illumination to rightly respond to Scripture, but it remains God's revelation even if this does not happen.

3. Conservative Christians believe that Scripture's original autographs were composed without error and that our present copies, though not quite perfect, are the best-preserved manuscripts in the history of the world.

4. John R. Franke, "Christian Faith and Postmodern Theory: Theology and the Nonfoundationalist Turn," in Myron B. Penner, ed., *Christianity and the Postmodern Turn* (Grand Rapids: Brazos, 2005), 108 – 12; Stanley J. Grenz and John R. Franke, *Beyond Foundationalism* (Louisville: John Knox, 2001), 23 – 25, 29 – 54.

5. Grenz and Franke, *Beyond Foundationalism*, 65; cf. 24 – 25, 69, 114 – 15.

6. Ibid., 74 – 75 (emphasis theirs).

7. Ibid., 65, 68. Cf. John Perry, "Dissolving the Inerrancy Debate: How Modern Philosophy Shaped the Evangelical View of Scripture," *Journal for Christian Theological Research* 6, no. 3 (2001): §47 — "In most postmodern philosophy the Bible's authority rests in the church's recognition that the Bible is inspired, and therefore authoritative." §48 — "In short, how does one ensure (without an indubitable foundation) that the Bible is interpreted faithfully? ... The evangelical church must be willing to recognize that its reading of Scripture is a community-based activity that embodies the ongoing history of a church's tradition." Online: http://apu.edu/~CTRF/articles/2001_articles/perry.html.

8. Grenz and Franke, *Beyond Foundationalism*, 53 – 54.

9. John R. Franke, *The Character of Theology* (Grand Rapids: Baker, 2005), 78 (emphasis mine).

10. Grenz and Franke, *Beyond Foundationalism*, 114 – 15. Cf. Brian McLaren, *A New Kind of Christian* (San Francisco: Jossey-Bass, 2001), 50 – 51.

11. Carl Raschke, *The Next Reformation: Why Evangelicals Must Embrace Postmodernity* (Grand Rapids: Baker, 2004), 135. Cf. John Caputo, *What Would Jesus Deconstruct?* (Grand Rapids: Baker, 2007), 110: "I am not an idolater. In deconstruction, the Scriptures are an archive, not the arche (which means they are not God). I take the second commandment very seriously and I do not put false gods — like books (biblical inerrancy) or the Vatican (papal infallibility) — before God, who is the 'wholly other.'"

12. Raschke, *Next Reformation*, 121–43.

13. John Franke, "Generous Orthodoxy and a Changing World," in Brian McLaren, *A Generous Orthodoxy* (Grand Rapids: Zondervan, 2004), 11; McLaren, *Generous Orthodoxy*, 139, 164; Grenz and Franke, *Beyond Foundationalism*, 32–35; Raschke, *Next Reformation*, 140–41; Nancey Murphy, *Beyond Liberalism and Fundamentalism: How Modern and Postmodern Philosophy Set the Theological Agenda* (Valley Forge, Pa.: Trinity, 1996), 1–35; and Perry, "Dissolving the Inerrancy Debate," §10–12.

14. McLaren, *New Kind of Christian*, 53.

15. McLaren, *Generous Orthodoxy*, 164 (emphasis McLaren's).

16. Dave Tomlinson, *The Post-Evangelical* (Grand Rapids: Zondervan, 2003), 110.

17. Ibid., 77.

18. Perry, "Dissolving the Inerrancy Debate," §10.

19. Luke 6:17; Matthew 5:1.

20. Luke 18:35–43; Matthew 20:29–34; Mark 10:46–52.

21. Mark 14:30, 72; Matthew 26:34, 74–75; Luke 22:34, 60–62.

22. Norman L. Geisler and Thomas Howe, *When Critics Ask: A Popular Handbook on Bible Difficulties* (Grand Rapids: Baker, 1999), 388; Harold Lindsell, *The Battle for the Bible* (Grand Rapids: Zondervan, 1976), 175.

23. R. Albert Mohler Jr., "Truth and Contemporary Culture," in Andreas Köstenberger, *Whatever Happened to Truth?* (Wheaton: Crossway, 2005), 71; Kevin J. Vanhoozer, "Lost in Interpretation? Truth, Scripture, and Hermeneutics," in Köstenberger, *Whatever Happened to Truth?* 111–12, 119, 122–24.

24. Conservative historians persuasively argue that, while earlier Christians did not use the same words as modern conservatives (because they were not wrestling with modern issues), yet they did believe that the Bible is without error. For example, see Carl F. H. Henry, *God, Revelation and Authority* (Waco, Tex.: Word, 1979), 4:368–84; and the essays in John D. Hannah, ed., *Inerrancy and the Church* (Chicago: Moody, 1984).

25. Second London Baptist Confession (1677, 1689), chap. 1.1. See William L. Lumpkin, *Baptist Confessions of Faith* (Chicago: Judson, 1959), 248.

26. "A Short Statement of the Chicago Statement on Biblical Inerrancy," 4, in Norman L. Geisler, ed., *Inerrancy* (Grand Rapids: Zondervan, 1979), 494.

27. Alvin Plantinga, "Reason and Belief in God," in *Faith and Rationality*, ed. Alvin Plantinga and Nicholas Woltersdorff (Notre Dame: University of Notre Dame Press, 1983), 16–93; and Alvin Plantinga, *Warranted Christian Belief* (New York: Oxford University Press, 2000), 81–85, 93–99, 167–98, 241–323; Kelly James Clark, *Return to Reason* (Grand Rapids: Eerdmans, 1990), 132–58; Grenz and Franke, *Beyond Foundationalism*, 47–49; and R. Scott Smith, "Postmodernism and the Priority of the Language-World Relation," in Penner, *Christianity and the Postmodern Turn*, 175.

28. Weak foundationalism is the position held by Reformed Epistemology, a popular method of apologetics among postmodern Christians. See Plantinga and Wolterstorff, eds., *Faith and Rationality*; Plantinga, *Warranted Christian Belief*; and Clark, *Return to Reason*.

29. David Wells, *Above All Earthly Powers* (Grand Rapids: Eerdmans, 2005), 83, discusses Grenz and Franke's proposal: "Authority, then, lies with the Spirit who speaks rather than the biblical Word he inspired; this is the old pietism whose Achilles' heel made it vulnerable to the old Liberalism. On hermeneutics, this is Protestantism leaning toward Catholicism. However, given its postmodern framing, with its more local reference than the universal truths of traditional Catholicism, this hermeneutical work may be vulnerable to the relativism of local communities as they define truth for themselves.... Whether this direction can be sustained without cost to historical orthodoxy is doubtful." Cf. Kevin J. Vanhoozer, *The Drama of Doctrine* (Louisville: Westminster John Knox, 2005), 182, 294; and Kevin J. Vanhoozer, "Disputing about Words? Of Fallible Foundations and Modest Metanarratives," in Penner, *Christianity and the Postmodern Turn*, 197–99.

30. Grenz and Franke, *Beyond Foundationalism*, 162. Cf. Franke, "Christian Faith and Postmodern Theory," 114–15.

31. Kevin Vanhoozer objects that besides lacking biblical warrant, the idea that the Spirit speaks authoritatively through human culture causes theological confusion. The Spirit's work of revelation is inextricably tied to Jesus and Scripture (John 14:26; 16:13). He writes, "The Spirit ministers the Word (who is Truth and Life), nothing else. As such, the Spirit is the executor of the living Word and the word written." See Vanhoozer, "Disputing about Words?" 198–99.

    Roger Olson, *Reformed and Always Reforming* (Grand Rapids: Baker, 2007), 113–14, agrees that Franke's belief that the Spirit speaks authoritatively through culture opens the door "to a kind of relativism." However, Olson says that Franke "does not walk through that door" because of his emphasis on the church's continuity with tradition.

32. Contra McLaren, *Generous Orthodoxy*, 133–34, which implies that our fallible interpretations undermine the authority of Scripture. I reply that the Scriptures remain the authoritative Word of God whether or not I correctly understand them.

33. Ephesians 2:20.

34. John Perry, "Dissolving the Inerrancy Debate," §26–28; Robert C. Greer, *Mapping Postmodernism* (Downers Grove, Ill.: InterVarsity: 2003), 38, 81–85.

35. McLaren, *The Last Word and the Word after That* (San Francisco: Jossey-Bass, 2005), 111: Pastor Dan says, "I believe that the Word of God is inerrant, but I do not believe that the Bible is absolutely equivalent to the phrase 'the Word of God' as used in the Bible.... I would prefer to use the term *inherency* to describe my view of Scripture: God's *inerrant* Word is *inherent* in the Bible." Karl Barth said that Scripture is part of the threefold Word of God (Jesus, Scripture, and Proclamation), but only insofar as it testifies to God's primary Word in Jesus Christ. He argued that Scripture in itself and as such is not the Word of God, but only becomes so when God meets us there in a subjective encounter of revelation. Barth wrote: "The Bible is God's Word to the extent that God caused it to be His Word, to the extent that He speaks through it"

and "The Bible, then, becomes God's Word in this event, and in the statement that the Bible is God's Word the little word 'is' refers to its being in this becoming. It does not become God's Word because we accord it faith but in the fact that it becomes revelation to us" (*Church Dogmatics,* 1/1, §2, p. 109, 110).

36. Van A. Harvey, *The Historian and the Believer* (New York: Macmillan, 1966), 4, 169. These modern standards still apply in our postmodern world, as evidenced by the scandal that erupts when purported histories turn out to include falsehood (e.g., note the controversies surrounding Jayson Blair's fabricated reporting for the *New York Times* and James Frey's revisionist biography, *A Million Little Pieces*).

37. Luke 5:27 – 32; Matthew 9:9 – 13.

38. Luke 4:9 – 13; Matthew 4:8 – 11.

39. Matthew 28:18.

40. The heart of Luke (chaps. 10 – 19) records Jesus' journey to Jerusalem. The trip begins when "Jesus resolutely set out for Jerusalem" (Luke 9:51), and it ends with his death and resurrection.

41. "Of God" and its partners appear elsewhere in Luke's writings (Luke 2:26; 23:35; Acts 3:18; 4:26), and "Son of God" is found often in Matthew's gospel (Matt. 3:17; 4:3; 14:33; 27:54).

42. Daniel P. Fuller, "The Nature of Biblical Inerrancy," *Journal of the American Scientific Affiliation* (June 1972): 47 – 51; and "Benjamin B. Warfield's View of Faith and History," *Bulletin of the Evangelical Theological Society* 11, no. 2 (Spring 1968): 75 – 83. Cf. George Marsden, *Reforming Fundamentalism* (Grand Rapids: Eerdmans, 1987), 211 – 19.

43. Joshua 10:12 – 14. Modern people still speak in such phenomenological terms, for meteorologists refer to sunrise and sunset even though no one believes that the sun actually rises and sets.

44. Matthew 13:31 – 32; Mark 4:31 – 32.

45. Matthew 24:2. Biblical prophecy often uses hyperbole and stereotypical denunciations to warn of impending judgment. Prophecies that promise complete famine, barrenness, and desolation do not mean that absolutely no crops, children, or wealth will survive. When checking the accuracy of a biblical prophecy, we should ask what the prophet meant to say. If he did not intend to be taken literally to the last detail, then his prophecy is not false should some of its details not come true. See D. Brent Sandy, *Plowshares and Pruning Hooks* (Downers Grove, Ill.: InterVarsity, 2002), and D. Brent Sandy, "The Inerrancy of Illocution," presented at the Evangelical Theological Society's annual meeting (San Antonio, November 2004).

46. That Genesis 1 – 2:3 is not necessarily a scientific report is apparent in its literary structure. Genesis 1:2 provides the topic sentence when it declares that "the earth was formless and empty." The rest of the chapter explains how God solves this problem, creating forms on the first three days and then filling these spaces on the final three days. This explains why light precedes the sun, for the light of Day 1 is the space that is filled by the sun, moon, and stars on Day 4.

47. I owe this insight to my colleague David Kennedy.

48. Second Timothy 3:16; 2 Peter 1:21.
49. Benjamin B. Warfield, "The Biblical Idea of Revelation," in *The Inspiration and Authority of the Bible*, ed. Samuel G. Craig (Phillipsburg, N.J.: Presbyterian & Reformed, 1948), 155–56. Cf. p. 91: "What the prophets are solicitous that their readers shall understand is that they are in no sense co-authors with God of their messages. Their messages are given them, given them entire, and given them precisely as they are given out by them. God speaks through them: they are not merely His messengers, but 'His mouth.' "
50. Luke 1:3; Romans 16:3–16.
51. First Corinthians 10:31; Matthew 22:36; 14:30; Psalm 106:2.
52. David K. Clark, "Beyond Inerrancy: Speech Acts and an Evangelical View of Scripture," in *For Faith and Clarity: Philosophical Contributions to Christian Theology*, ed. James K. Beilby (Grand Rapids: Baker, 2006), 113–31; Nicholas Wolterstorff, "True Words," and Stephen T. Davis, "What Do We Mean When We Say, 'The Bible Is True,' " in *But Is It All True?* ed. Alan G. Padgett and Patrick R. Keifert (Grand Rapids: Eerdmans, 2006), 34–43, 86–103.
53. Lesslie Newbigin, *Proper Confidence* (Grand Rapids: Eerdmans, 1995), 54–55, 71–78, 98–100; Greer, *Mapping Postmodernism*, 82–85.
54. Many Christians do manage to have faith in God without holding to inerrancy. They suggest that any book written by fallen humans is bound to contain errors and that mistakes in one area does not prevent another part from being true. Fair enough. But they too easily dismiss the argument that even one error in Scripture would indicate that the Bible was not written by God, which then casts doubt upon its status as revelation and the reliability of its promises.

Chapter 12. The Future Runs through the Past

1. Diana Butler Bass, "Believing the Resurrection," on God's Politics: A Blog by Jim Wallis and Friends, April 4, 2007 [emphasis mine], www.beliefnet.com/blogs/godspolitics/2007/04/diana-butler-bass-believing.html.
2. Alfred H. Ackley, *He Lives*. © Homer A. Rodeheaver, 1933; renewed by The Rodeheaver Co., 1961.
3. Brian McLaren, *A Generous Orthodoxy* (Grand Rapids: Zondervan, 2004), 131. Cf. p. 140; and Brian McLaren, *A New Kind of Christian* (San Francisco: Jossey-Bass, 2001), ix–x; Stanley J. Grenz, *Renewing the Center* (Grand Rapids: Baker, 2000), 325–31; John R. Franke, *The Character of Theology* (Grand Rapids: Baker, 2005), 38–40; and "Generous Orthodoxy and a Changing World," in McLaren, *Generous Orthodoxy*, 10–11; and Nancey Murphy, *Beyond Liberalism and Fundamentalism* (Philadelphia: Trinity Press International, 1996), 1.
4. This view was held by H. Richard Niebuhr. See Michael Wittmer, "Analysis and Critique of 'Christ the Transformer of Culture' in the Thought of H. Richard Niebuhr" (Ph.D. diss., Calvin Theological Seminary, 2000), 158–69.
5. Immanuel Kant, *Religion within the Limits of Reason Alone*, trans. Theodore M. Greene and Hoyt H. Hudson (New York: Harper Torchbooks, 1960), 54–57, 66–68, 97–107, 182–88.

6. James C. Livingston, *Modern Christian Thought*, 2nd ed. (1997; repr., Minneapolis: Fortress, 2006), 1:270–98.

7. Walter Rauschenbusch, *A Theology for the Social Gospel* (1945; repr., Nashville: Abingdon, 1978), 1–5, 34–36, 96–108, 119, 131, 220–38, 245–74.

8. J. Gresham Machen, *Christianity and Liberalism* (1923; repr., Grand Rapids: Eerdmans, 1994), 7.

9. Ibid., 160.

10. Ibid., 1: "There are many who prefer to fight their intellectual battles in what Dr. Francis L. Patton has aptly called a 'condition of low visibility.' Clear-cut definition of terms in religious matters, bold facing of the logical implications of religious views, is by many persons regarded as an impious proceeding."

11. Martin Gardner, *The Flight of Peter Fromm* (1973; repr., Amherst, N.Y.: Prometheus, 1994), 208. Cf. Machen, *Christianity and Liberalism*, 111–12, 165.

12. Edward Dobson, *In Search of Unity* (Nashville: Nelson, 1985), 37–40. See *The Fundamentals*, 12 volumes, ed. R. A. Torrey, A. C. Dixon, et al. (1910–15; repr., Grand Rapids: Baker, 1970).

13. George W. Dollar, *A History of Fundamentalism in America* (Greenville, S.C.: Bob Jones University Press, 1973; 2nd ed., published by the author, 1983), vi (emphasis mine).

14. Joel A. Carpenter, *Revive Us Again* (New York: Oxford University Press, 1997), 66; George Marsden, *Understanding Fundamentalism and Evangelicalism* (Grand Rapids: Eerdmans, 1991), 1.

15. Carpenter, *Revive Us Again*; Marsden, *Understanding Fundamentalism and Evangelicalism, Reforming Fundamentalism*, and *Fundamentalism and American Culture* (New York: Oxford University Press, 1980).

16. Cal Thomas and Ed Dobson, *Blinded by Might: Can the Religious Right Save America?* (Grand Rapids: Zondervan, 1999); and Jim Wallis, *God's Politics: Why the Right Gets It Wrong and the Left Doesn't Get It* (San Francisco: HarperSanFrancisco, 2005).

17. Learn more about postliberalism in George Hunsinger, "Postliberal Theology," in *The Cambridge Companion to Postmodern Theology*, ed. Kevin J. Vanhoozer (New York: Cambridge University Press, 2003), 42–57; Timothy R. Phillips and Dennis L. Okholm, ed., *The Nature of Confession* (Downers Grove, Ill.: InterVarsity, 1996); George A. Lindbeck, *The Nature of Doctrine* (Philadelphia: Westminster, 1984); Franke, *Character of Theology*, 28–40.

18. Lindbeck, *Nature of Doctrine*, 33, 80. Lindbeck's principal analogy is language, the rules of which are intuitively recognized by native speakers. I prefer their lesser-used sports analogy because it more easily communicates their point.

19. Ibid., 47–52: Lindbeck argues that the best religions are those whose doctrines or rules for the game are the most adequate in making sense of the world.

20. Ibid., 54; cf. 40–42, 46–69.

21. Hans Frei, "Response to 'Narrative Theology: An Evangelical Proposal,'" in *Theology and Narrative: Selected Essays*, ed. George Hunsinger and William C. Placher (New York: Oxford University Press, 1993), 207–8. Frei wrote that

"we need a kind of generous orthodoxy which would have in it an element of liberalism — a voice like the *Christian Century* — and an element of evangelicalism — the voice of *Christianity Today.*" Cf. Franke, *Character of Theology*, 9 and McLaren, *Generous Orthodoxy*, 131 – 43, for examples of postconservatives finding common ground with postliberals.

The question of relativism in postliberalism is discussed in Phillips and Okholm, *Nature of Confession*, 35 – 44, 71 – 80, 110 – 14. Lindbeck does not want to commit either way on this subject. He writes in *Nature of Doctrine*, 68 – 69, that "There is nothing in the cultural-linguistic approach [his view] that requires the rejection (or the acceptance) of the epistemological realism and correspondence theory of truth...." However, he adds that doctrines are "second-order rather than first-order propositions and affirm nothing about extra-linguistic or extra-human reality. For a rule theory, in short, doctrines qua doctrines are not first-order propositions, but are to to [*sic*] be construed as second-order ones: they make ... intrasystematic rather than ontological truth claims" (80).

22. The most comprehensive description of postconservative theology is Roger Olson, *Reformed and Always Reforming* (Grand Rapids: Baker, 2007). Olsen declares that postconservativism includes Brian McLaren, John Franke, Stanley Grenz, and Leron Shults (pp. 17, 28, 155). Cf. Franke, *Character of Theology*, 28 – 40.

23. My critique fulfills John Franke's prediction, "Ironically, one of the general critiques of postliberals by liberals will be that they have become too conservative, while conservatives will accuse postconservatives of being too liberal" (Franke, *Character of Theology*, 39).

24. Matthew 10:37; cf. Luke 14:26.

25. Samir Selmanovic, "The Sweet Problem of Inclusiveness," in Doug Pagitt and Tony Jones, eds., *An Emergent Manifesto of Hope* (Grand Rapids: Baker, 2007), 190 – 92 (emphasis mine). For other authors who suggest, to a lesser degree, that it matters more that we live like Jesus than that we believe in him, see pp. 43 – 45, 56, 100 – 102.

26. I say "most" postmodern innovators because, in addition to private conversations with other postmodern innovators that I will not divulge, John Caputo has issues with revelation and Scripture and Spencer Burke is a self-professed panentheist, which would logically diminish the deity of Jesus and his power to work miracles. See John D. Caputo, *On Religion* (New York: Routledge, 2001), 22, and John D. Caputo, *What Would Jesus Deconstruct?* (Grand Rapids: Baker, 2007), 104 – 12; Spencer Burke and Barry Taylor, *A Heretic's Guide to Eternity* (San Francisco: Jossey-Bass, 2006), 195.

27. Machen, *Christianity and Liberalism*, 19, 160.

28. Ibid., 160, 81 (first emphasis is mine, second is Machen's).

29. Ibid., 64, 66, 68 (emphasis mine).

30. Ibid., 125, 129 – 32.

31. Ibid., 129, 131, 132 (emphasis Machen's).

32. Ibid., 157 – 58.

33. Ibid., 122 – 23.

34. Ibid., 147–48, 149.
35. Ibid., 151, 152 (emphasis Machen's).
36. Ibid., 155.
37. Olson, *Reformed and Always Reforming*, 12: "Postconservatives emphatically do not consider themselves part of an 'evangelical left.' To them, 'left' and 'right' in theology are both defined by the Enlightenment and modernity, which are increasingly being challenged and marginalized by postmodernity." See also John Franke, "Generous Orthodoxy and a Changing World," in McLaren, *Generous Orthodoxy*, 11; and Tony Jones, *The New Christians* (San Francisco: Jossey-Bass, 2008), 18–22.
38. First Corinthians 15:32.
39. Gardner, *Flight of Peter Fromm*, 18–27, 36–41, 96–104, 208, 225, 243–53, 273, and 278. The author says in the afterword that this book is semiautobiographical and that many initial readers believed it was a true story. Thus, far from being a conservative slur, this is a realistic story written from a sympathetic, liberal perspective.
40. See pp. 56–58.
41. Jonathan Edwards, *The Religious Affections* (1746; repr., Carlisle, Pa.: Banner of Truth Trust, 1997), 332.
42. James 2:17–26.
43. Romans 4:2.
44. First John 3:23.

Epilogue

1. Joshua 24:14.
2. Second Corinthians 10:5.
3. Acts 17:23, 30–31.

DISCUSSION QUESTIONS

Chapter 1: A New Kind of Christian

1. How have recent changes in society and the world enhanced your understanding of God and the gospel?
2. What recent changes in society and the world present challenges to the gospel? Where are Christians tempted to compromise their faith to fit in with others?
3. Would you describe yourself as mostly modern or postmodern? What about our culture? Are some parts of your life and our world more postmodern than others?

Chapter 2: Must You Believe Something to Be Saved?

1. What do you think a person must believe to be saved? Must not reject? What else should every Christian believe?
2. What is the relationship between beliefs and ethics? Do our beliefs determine how we live or does how we live determine what we believe?
3. Explain the significance of John 6:28 – 29 for the role of beliefs and ethics: "Then they asked him, 'What must we do to do the works God requires?' Jesus answered, 'The work of God is this: to believe in the one he has sent.'"
4. Explain the significance of James 2:14 – 26 for the role of beliefs and ethics: "As the body without the spirit is dead, so faith without deeds is dead" (v. 26).

Chapter 3: Do Right Beliefs Get in the Way of Good Works?

1. How would you explain that Jesus is the only way to God without sounding arrogant or judgmental?
2. Everyone draws a boundary somewhere. Despite their desire to be inclusive, what boundaries do postmodern innovators draw?

3. Why might marriage (Gen. 1:27) and church (John 17:20 – 23) provide the best opportunities to imitate the self-giving love of the Trinity?

Chapter 4: Are People Generally Good or Basically Bad?

1. Where would you place yourself on a scale of one to ten, with one being pure evil and ten meaning completely good? Is a single number able to convey your status as a fallen creature? Why or why not?
2. Do you believe that it is possible to do an entirely good act? If so, what are some of yours? If not, when did you come closest?
3. This chapter describes morality in negative terms — we are merely moral when we do not hurt others. But does morality sometimes require us also to do something for others? Hint: think of the role of parents, presidents, and other leaders. Note that these positive actions can also be expressed in negative terms. For example, parents are morally obligated to do — — — because if they do not do so, they are violating their child's right to — — —.

Chapter 5: Which Is Worse: Homosexuals or the Bigots Who Persecute Them?

1. Are some sins worse than others? By what criteria would you make such judgments?
2. How can you love people without approving of what they do? What practical steps can the church take to reach out to homosexuals?
3. Should homosexuals be allowed to marry? To unite in civil unions? Why or why not?

Chapter 6: Is the Cross Divine Child Abuse?

1. Can someone be saved without a basic understanding that Jesus suffered the penalty of their sin on the cross?
2. Which is the most important aspect of Christ's atonement — that he satisfied his Father's wrath; that he defeated sin, death, and the Devil; or that he left us an example of love? What do we lose if we forget any of these?
3. What do Jesus' earthly life and bodily resurrection contribute to our atonement? How essential is it that he is both God and man?

Chapter 7: Can You Belong before You Believe?

1. How might a church maintain a distinction between Christians and non-Christians while still welcoming the latter?
2. Should we baptize new converts immediately upon their profession of faith or wait until after they have learned more about the religion they wish to join?
3. Are non-Christians headed in the right direction, or do they need to convert? Are they seeking God or suppressing their knowledge of him (Romans 1:18 – 23)? To what extent does the answer vary from person to person?

Chapter 8: Does the Kingdom of God Include Non-Christians?

1. Where would you place yourself on a scale of one to ten, with one being hard exclusivism, five meaning inclusivism, and ten representing universalism? Defend your position.
2. Do Muslims, Jews, and Christians worship the same God?
3. What practical impact — for good or bad — might belief in an inclusive gospel have on evangelism and missions?

Chapter 9: Is Hell for Real and Forever?

1. Does your church speak a lot or a little about hell? Why do you think that is?
2. Do you believe that there are degrees of punishment in hell? Why or why not?
3. Would the existence of hell — and our knowledge that our loved ones are suffering there — spoil the pleasures of heaven?

Chapter 10: Is It Possible to Know Anything?

1. What is your foundational belief, or beliefs? How do you justify starting with them?
2. What if someone tells you that she does not believe in God or the Bible. Is common ground possible to continue a conversation, or must we simply agree to disagree?
3. Would you argue that the modern attempt to ground knowledge on reason and experience is actually a larger leap of faith than grounding our beliefs on the existence of God and his revelation in Scripture? If so, how?

Chapter 11: Is the Bible God's True Word?

1. Is it important to assign equal authority to the Word and Spirit? Why or why not? What problems arise if we elevate one over the other?
2. Does God also speak to us outside of Scripture (e.g., by dreams, the counsel of others, or strong promptings and impressions)? What are the benefits and dangers of claiming that he does?
3. Although it seems necessary to insist on the Bible's inerrancy, how might our concern to protect its truthfulness distract us from its larger goal of spiritual transformation? How can we defend the foundational doctrines that need protecting without losing sight of the bigger picture?

Chapter 12: The Future Runs through the Past

1. Rather than sing that "he lives within my heart," how might we better support our claim that Jesus is alive?
2. While we wouldn't want to be either extreme, is it worse to be a fighting fundamentalist or a loving liberal?
3. How might we best transcend the liberal-conservative controversy of the modern world and achieve an authentically Christian postmodern faith?

CASE STUDIES

Chapter 1: A New Kind of Christian

1. You strike up a conversation with your seatmate on a transatlantic flight. When your dialogue turns to world events, your new friend states that religion is the root cause of most of the world's wars. If we would only recognize that no religion is necessarily better than another, then we could agree to disagree and live in peace. How would you respond?

2. During a meeting of your church's outreach committee, one of its more conservative members enthusiastically declares that since the meaning of the Bible never changes, our only job is to find the best method to communicate that unchanging message to our contemporary culture. After reading chapter 1, how might you nuance that statement?

Chapter 2: Must You Believe Something to Be Saved?

1. You meet Charlene at a party, and after ten minutes of small talk, you ask if she is wearing a cross necklace because she is a Christian. Charlene replies that she isn't one for labels, but she does believe that Jesus died for the sins of the world and that if she does her best to obey him, she will go to heaven. What follow-up questions would you ask to discern whether Charlene is a Christian?

2. Rick is a leader in your church who owns his own business. Recently some of his employees have complained that Rick broke his promise to raise their wages to the industry standard. When you asked Rick whether this was true, he swore at you and told you to mind your own business. What follow-up actions would you take to discern whether Rick is a Christian?

3. Which person — Rick or Charlene — is least likely to be a genuine Christian? Which person would receive the sharpest rebuke from Jesus?

Chapter 3: Do Right Beliefs Get in the Way of Good Works?

1. Ann Coulter created a national uproar when she told a television host that Christians believe that they are "perfected Jews." Is this the best way to publicly express the Christian attitude toward another religion? How might we lovingly yet accurately explain the difference between Judaism and Christianity?
2. You have been asked to lead a small-group Bible study that includes a large number of modern conservatives and a few younger, postmodern innovators. What issues or themes would you emphasize to this mixed group on the opening night? What two or three points would you make as you begin your study?

Chapter 4: Are People Generally Good or Basically Bad?

1. One side says that a man who molested and then murdered a child should die for his crime. Another declares that he is a human being whose valuable life should be protected. How does the content of this chapter help to sort out these views? Is there a way to argue for or against capital punishment that honors the truth that we are both created and fallen?
2. Your close friend is a Buddhist immigrant from Thailand. When you ask whether she is interested in learning more about your Christian faith, she replies that she already has a loving family and a good life. She does not think that you or her other Christian friends have anything that she does not already possess, so why should she become a Christian? What would you say to her?

Chapter 5: Which Is Worse: Homosexuals or the Bigots Who Persecute Them?

1. An old friend from your church youth group sends a general email announcing that he is gay. How would you respond?
2. A person knocks on your door and asks your support for a ballot proposal to ban discrimination against homosexuals. When you ask what discrimination he has in mind, he says "the usual — housing, employment, health care, marriage, and so on." Do you sign?

Chapter 6: Is the Cross Divine Child Abuse?

1. One of the junior high kids in your after-school program says that she thinks she is a Christian and would like to be baptized. When you inquire about her faith, you find that she is unable to clearly explain how Jesus bore the penalty for her sin, but she is excited to join Jesus' fight to defeat sin and Satan. Would you baptize her?

2. The Muslim you are interviewing for your world religions class informs you that since God cannot die, it is impossible to believe that Jesus — if he is God like you say — actually died on the cross. He concludes that the Muslim view that the Jews crucified Judas by mistake is more honoring to Jesus than what Christians believe. What would you say?

Chapter 7: Can You Belong before You Believe?

1. A group of your church friends have decided to skip the traditional Sunday worship service throughout the summer so they can befriend the unchurched guys who play in Sunday morning soccer leagues. Would you join them?

2. Because you are a pastor, non-Christian couples who want a church wedding sometimes ask if they can get married in your building. They also wonder whether you would be willing to perform the ceremony. What is your policy and why?

Chapter 8: Does the Kingdom of God Include Non-Christians?

1. At the funeral of your Muslim friend's father, your friend asks where you believe his father is now. What would you say?

2. Your university professor compares conservative Christians to Muslim extremists, for both groups insist that they possess the only path to God. He says that such Christians have more in common with the Taliban than with their fellow Americans. He knows that you are a Christian, and with his eyes locked on you, asks whether you have anything to say. How would you respond?

Chapter 9: Is Hell for Real and Forever?

1. A German guard kills a religious Jew in a Nazi gas chamber. If the guard repents and seeks the forgiveness of Christ, is it true that he will go to heaven while his non-Christian victim will go to hell? If so, how is this just?
2. You meet a relief worker whose Christian agency is using a natural disaster as an opportunity to do mission work in a previously closed country. When you inquire about their intentions, the aid worker proudly tells you that they spend 80 percent of their resources on evangelism and only 20 percent on relief efforts. After all, it's more important that people avoid hell than that they have clean water and a roof over their heads. What would you say to him?

Chapter 10: Is It Possible to Know Anything?

1. *The Matrix* movie asked whether we and our world may exist merely as a software program inside of someone else's computer. This notion seems preposterous, but how could you prove that it is not true? How do you know that we and our world are real?
2. Your scientific friend declares that there is not enough evidence to believe in God. He has never seen or heard God, and the amount of evil in the world makes it unlikely that an all-good and all-powerful being exists. What could you say that might cause him to rethink some of his assumptions?

Chapter 11: Is the Bible God's True Word?

1. Your friend is a philosophy major who is not impressed with your knowledge of the Bible. "God is bigger than any book can explain," she says. "Talking about God is like trying to paint a bird in flight. God is always on the move, and so our words and concepts never completely capture him." What is true and what is potentially misleading about your friend's view?
2. Your classmate laughs when he sees a Bible in your pile of books. He says that he cannot believe that there are still people around who believe that the Bible is the Word of God. He asks, "How can an intelligent person like yourself believe that the Bible's fantastic miracle stories are true?" What would you tell him?

Chapter 12: The Future Runs through the Past

1. A fellow at church thinks that all good people go to heaven. When you inform him that this is a liberal view, he declares that liberalism is a modern label that does not apply to his postmodern faith (because he is postmodern he is able to transcend the liberal and conservative labels of modernity). Is he right? Why or why not?

2. Your more inclusive friends suggest that your conservative views are divisive. "Why can't you live and let live?" they ask. "You are allowed to believe that Christianity is the only true religion and that people must believe in Jesus to be saved, but why must you try to force this view on others?" What would you say?

I value your thoughts about what you've just read.
Please share them with me. You'll find contact information
in the back of this book.

Share Your Thoughts

With the Author: Your comments will be forwarded to the author when you send them to *zauthor@zondervan.com*.

With Zondervan: Submit your review of this book by writing to *zreview@zondervan.com*.

Free Online Resources at
www.zondervan.com/hello

Zondervan AuthorTracker: Be notified whenever your favorite authors publish new books, go on tour, or post an update about what's happening in their lives.

Daily Bible Verses and Devotions: Enrich your life with daily Bible verses or devotions that help you start every morning focused on God.

Free Email Publications: Sign up for newsletters on fiction, Christian living, church ministry, parenting, and more.

Zondervan Bible Search: Find and compare Bible passages in a variety of translations at www.zondervanbiblesearch.com.

Other Benefits: Register yourself to receive online benefits like coupons and special offers, or to participate in research.